ATL COM
Programmer's Reference

Richard Grimes

Wrox Press Ltd. ®

ATL COM Programmer's Reference

Published by Wrox Press Ltd. 30 Lincoln Road, Olton, Birmingham, B27 6PA
Printed in USA
ISBN 1-861002-4-91

Trademark Acknowledgements

Wrox has endeavored to provide trademark information about all the companies and products mentioned in this book by the appropriate use of capitals. However, Wrox cannot guarantee the accuracy of this information.

Credits

Author
Richard Grimes

Development Editor
John Franklin

Editors
Chris Hindley
Karli Watson

Technical Reviewers
Richard Anderson
Tom Armstrong
Davide Marcato
Christian Nagel
Gavin Smyth
Byron Vargas
Sing Li
Jon Pinnock
M. G. Ravichandran
Jason Whittington
Gary Howard
Alex Stockton

Cover
Andrew Guillaume
Image by Rita Ruban

Design/Layout
Tony Berry

Index
Andrew Criddle

About the Author

Richard started programming in the days when an 8-bit computer with 32K of memory was considered a powerful machine. His professional career started as a post Doctorate research scientist studying semiconductor physics. Rejecting academia in favor of industry, Richard went on to become a trainer, teaching people how to program. Consequently, he found himself at the start of the distributed objects revolution and joined a vanguard European company in that arena as a COM and DCOM specialist.

After many years as a developer and architect, Richard started his real authoring career with the book: *Professional DCOM Programming*. Since then he has added his name to the books: *Beginning ATL COM Programming* and *Professional ATL COM Programming* as well as countless articles for all the major programming journals, magazines and web sites. He lives in England with his young family and has been known to partake of a glass of ale.

Acknowlegements

Both major and minor characters on the ATL and Visual C++ teams. I've enjoyed the open discussions and instruction that's flowed over the past two years. The technology keeps inspiring me to write and, by doing so, I hope I put a little back into the coding community's understanding of the potential of COM.

Table of Contents

Introduction

This book provides a concise yet comprehensive guide to the different ways ATL 3.0 can be utilized to create COM components. The book is divided into two parts, starting with a guide to how ATL operates, followed by an extensive reference section to augment the learning experience. We see you using this book as a reference to 'techniques' as well as syntax.

The Active Template Library is the future of COM development and this book will help you realize that in code. ATL takes the word Active, implying that it is part of the Microsoft family of Active technologies: ActiveX Controls, Active Server Pages, the Active Desktop. These technologies are built upon the Component Object Model (COM) which is Microsoft's (now open) standard. Writing a COM component in C++ requires code to create the component, handle its lifetime and expose its functionality. In addition to this, components must be registered on the system where they will be used and the component itself should be capable of carrying out this registration. Much of this code is common to all components and is tedious to write. ATL is a template library that provides all these facilities for you and more. ATL is, therefore, the development library of choice for C++ COM development.

What Is ATL?

ATL has been growing exponentially since its first trial as a downloadable version (1.0) in the heady days of Visual C++ 4.x. Back then it was just a CPP file and some headers! Visual C++ 5.0 came soon after, and this had ATL 2.1 and support within the IDE for ATL through an AppWizard, Object Wizard and ClassView. Creating ATL classes became incredibly easy — all you had to worry about was implementing the functionality specific to your component, with all the COM plumbing code taken care of for you. The advantage of ATL was clear — it acted as an entry to COM, without the steep learning curve that was involved in straight C++ COM development. With version 3.0, it's now a maturing set of Wizards and Libraries that enable the Visual C++ programmer to develop very efficient COM objects and, especially, data access controls.

Why ATL?

With Visual C++ you can write a COM object or control directly in C++, via MFC or with ATL. If you decide to write a COM object directly in C++ you will need to write all the code yourself; the module initialization, server registration, class factory and object code. Much of the code required here is boilerplate, so it makes sense, therefore, to use a class or template library that will do this work for you.

This leads to MFC and ATL. MFC is a class library, with a few templates for collection classes. MFC is really designed for visual objects: witness the support for doc objects, inplace objects, drag and drop and compound documents. MFC is therefore well suited for creating UI based Windows projects. However, while it has been adapted for COM development, it is far from ideal in this arena, leading to bloated code and COM components with an unnecessarily large overhead.

ATL, on the other hand, is specifically designed for COM development. Firstly, it is a finely tuned template library, resulting in efficient COM components with a small footprint. Secondly, there is extensive wizard support for ATL in Visual C++ 6. AppWizard simply allows you to determine the type of module to create — DLL, EXE or NT service. The ATL Object wizard, however, allows you to create a wide range of COM objects, from simple objects to a variety of ActiveX controls, dialog boxes and data access controls. This is integrated with the Visual Studio Component Gallery, so you can add your own object types to those provided by Microsoft.

Who Is This Book For?

This book is a reference guide for the ATL programmer. It demonstrates and explains the features of ATL 3.0 and the ways that these features can be applied. This book addresses the novice ATL programmer upwards, though it isn't a beginner's guide — if you've programmed using C++ and you have an in-depth understanding of template usage plus exposure to basic COM, then you can work your way through the ATL landscape using this book as a guide. We advise reading *Beginning ATL COM Programming* if you're a complete ATL virgin. This will give sufficient grounding for you to get the most from this Programmer's Reference.

What Does It Cover?

Just about everything that you need to write powerful ATL code!

Although the book is comprehensive, some things must be left to thicker and more in-depth tutorials. Few ATL topics aren't covered, but for some we suggest you study specialist texts, for example on COM security and optimization techniques. Compiler COM support is not covered and we leave the details of IDL and MIDL to the Microsoft documentation. Indeed, when the ATL documentation is clear and complete, we tell you so and don't try to re-package that knowledge.

What Do I Need To Use This Book?

You need one of the versions of Visual C++ 6.0: Standard, Professional, Enterprise etc. ATL 3.0 is included with the product.

You should be running Visual C++ on at least a 486 PC, but in reality, a high powered Pentium 200 or better, running Windows NT 4 Workstation is preferable.

A copy of the COM specification, or at least a good COM tutorial would be a suitable companion for a detailed code planning session.

Knowledge of IDL is a good idea, but so much of the book accepts and uses ATL generated IDL that the core actions of ATL are perfectly clear without IDL smarts.

Conventions Used

We use a number of different styles of text and layout in the book to help differentiate between the different kinds of information. Here are examples of the styles we use, and an explanation of what they mean:

> These boxes hold important, not-to-be-forgotten, mission critical details that are directly relevant to the surrounding text.

Background information, asides and references to information located elsewhere appear in text like this.

❑ **Important words** are in a bold font

❑ Words that appear on the screen, such as menu options, are in a similar font to the one used on the screen — the File menu, for example

❑ Keys that you press on the keyboard, like *Ctrl* and *Delete*, are in italics

❑ All filenames are in this style: ATL.dll

❑ Function names look like this: CoCreateInstance()

❑ Templates look like this: CComPtr<>

❑ Code that's new, important, or relevant to the current discussion will be presented like this:

```
int main()
{
    cout << "Professional ATL COM Programming";
    return 0;
}
```

Code that you've seen before, or that isn't directly relevant to the matter at hand, looks like this:

```
int main()
{
    cout << "Professional ATL COM Programming";
    return 0;
}
```

Enjoy the book !

ATL and COM

COM is our Future

COM is **the future of Windows development**. You only have to look at all the new products from Microsoft that use COM to realize that, in the future, it will be the de facto method of accessing and managing libraries and services. OLE DB and DirectDraw are two examples of services that can only be accessed through COM.

COM enforces **interface programming**. The only way to access a COM object is through its interface. A client talks to an object using only the methods of the interface and the parameters that are defined for those methods. Interface programming is a good thing, because it means that there is a fixed contract between the client and the object about how they communicate. Once a client knows that an object supports a particular interface, it knows *exactly* how to talk to the object. Once published, an interface never changes, thus providing some stability in a software developer's life! If the object needs to extend its functionality, it merely needs to add a new interface and hence will support new as well as older clients.

Interfaces also allow you to group together related functionality. Once you have defined an interface you can make other objects support it too, indicating that they offer the same functionality. Thus, one client will be able to use many objects as long as those objects have interfaces that the client is aware of. Interfaces make no assumptions about implementation.

COM is **language neutral**. This means that, once you have written a COM object using your favorite language, you can then create and access that object using any other COM-aware language. If you wanted to, you could write a Scriptlet in VBScript that creates and uses COM objects written in Visual C++, C++, C, Visual Basic, Visual J++, Java or Delphi, as well as other Scriptlets written in VBScript or JScript. The client that uses these COM objects doesn't know which language was used to write them and doesn't care — all it sees are the interfaces that the objects support.

COM is **location independent**. Since all objects are accessed through interfaces, COM can, under certain circumstances, give you access to a proxy object instead of the object you requested. The proxy object has the same interfaces as your object and so it appears to clients to be exactly the same as your object. Proxy objects can be used to manipulate the calls to your object. In particular, they can be used to transmit, or marshal, the interface method calls to another process or machine. Since the client does not know whether it's calling a proxy object or the actual object, it means that a client doesn't need to know about the location of an object in order to use it.

COM is **ubiquitous**. Every Windows 9x machine and every NT machine from version 3.51 onwards has 32-bit COM, and all of these (except NT 3.51) either has, or can have, Distributed COM. With the exception of installing DCOM on Windows 9x machines, you do not have to install any other software on a Windows machine in order to use COM.

The message is clear; if you want to write code that can be used by as many client applications as possible, then the COM route is the way to go.

> For a more comprehensive list of the features of COM, read *Beginning ATL COM Programming* (by Grimes et al, ISBN 1-861000-11-1), Chapter 1 and *Professional COM Applications with ATL* (by Sing Li and Panos Economopoulos, ISBN 1-861001-70-3), Chapters 1 and 2. Both books are published by Wrox Press.

Active Template Library

What is ATL? ATL is a collection of templates and classes that eases the creation of all the boilerplate code that you need to implement COM servers and COM objects. ATL makes good use of C++ templates, enabling you to add support for features to (or remove them from) your class with a minimum of fuss. To make them as flexible as possible, most templates use information that is presented in ATL maps. Maps are macro based and present the data in a clear, concise way. Appendix A explains the common maps that you'll find in ATL.

COM objects are created by COM servers. The ATL AppWizard (covered in Chapter 2 and Appendix D) will generate all the module code that you need to implement a server. When a client requests that an object be created, the COM runtime must be able to locate the server. It does this using information in the system registry. Appendix B lists the facilities that ATL gives you for registering your objects.

Different objects support different interfaces — it's up to you to determine how those objects are implemented. This may require quite a lot of code, so ATL helps by implementing most of the common interfaces. When you add a new object to your project with the Object Wizard (covered in Appendix E), it will make sure that the object implements the correct interfaces.

COM objects are usually created by other objects called class factories. ATL provides four types of class factory (covered in Chapter 3 and Appendix G). These allow your objects to be created on threads in a thread pool, to be licensed, act as singletons, and even to be implemented by you. Threading is an important issue whether you use a thread pool or not — ATL has extensive support to ensure that it is thread safe. You can use these facilities (see Appendix H) to make your own code thread safe.

However, ATL is more than just this. In addition to the templates for COM, ATL also includes templates for implementing windows and OLE DB. The windowing support is provided for implementing ActiveX Controls, but you can also use it to write Windows applications. These templates don't provide you with extensive facilities — you don't get things like MFC's document-view support, or dialog data exchange and validation (DDX and DDV). Instead, you get a lightweight framework. The windowing classes are covered in Chapter 6 and Appendix J.

The OLE DB templates allow you to implement and access data sources. OLE DB uses COM, which means that you will use COM when you use these templates. If you are implementing a data source then the templates will, in turn, be implementing COM objects. However, although the consumer templates use COM, they do not implement objects and so can be used in non-ATL projects. The OLE DB classes are covered in Chapter 5 and Appendix I.

Your COM objects may want to return large amounts of data to a client, or they may contain many other objects and want to give clients access to them. The standard way to give access to large amounts of data in COM is through enumeration objects, which formalize the process of iterating through many items. Collections take this a step further, allowing you to access a single item and to add and remove items. ATL provides templates to implement collections and enumerators. Examples of both can be seen throughout this book. Appendix F lists these templates and explains how to use them.

Since ATL is based on C++ templates, you do need to have a rudimentary understanding of them. I will assume that this is the case, but even so, ATL uses some features of templates that you probably won't have seen or used before. In the next section, I will outline some of the template techniques that are necessary for using the ATL library effectively.

C++ and ATL

ATL makes extensive use of two C++ features: **multiple inheritance** and **templates**. COM objects can implement several interfaces, each allowing access to a different functionality. In C++ an ideal way to realize this is to have each interface implemented in a base class from which you inherit. If you need to inherit from many such classes, you will need to use multiple inheritance.

ATL's use of multiple inheritance is largely trouble free. If you decide that an object should have the functionality described by a particular interface then all you need to do is derive the object class from the appropriate Impl class, which is provided by ATL. You then need to add the interface to the interface map. However, some Impl classes require code from other ATL classes and perhaps additional code or data members in your class.

If you wanted to, you could use multiple inheritance from your own C++ classes to ease the creation of COM components. However, there are two serious problems with this. The first is that, if the implementation class is to be generic, it will need to get access to data and methods in your derived class. If you use a constructor to give access to your class then the code required becomes quite complex. The other problem is that to cater for the multitude of possibilities inherent to COM, you could end up with an unmanageably large library of classes.

Templates solve these problems. They allow you to write boilerplate code, and thus to write a library that is truly generic. The problem of giving access to your derived class is solved by the Impl technique described below. This allows the base classes to access the derived class by casting the this pointer without knowing which class it's being cast to. It also has the advantage of allowing the base classes access to your derived class's members without using a constructor, thus simplifying the code.

There are other features of C++ that ATL uses — a short description of each is given below.

> For a more complete description, refer to Appendix A of my book
> *Professional ATL COM Programming*, ISBN 1-861001-40-1, published by
> Wrox Press.

Templates to Parameterize Code

As I mentioned earlier, the usual purpose of templates is to provide generic, boilerplate code. The idea is that your template code is written using a generic type that is passed as a template parameter. At compile time the compiler reads this parameter and generates the class accordingly. A classic example of this in ATL is a smart pointer template. ATL provides the CComPtr<> smart pointer template to maintain a single reference count on the interface pointer (explained in Appendix K). This is very useful as you don't have to worry about calling reference counting methods, and hence there is no possibility of leaking interfaces. In addition, it provides a type safe QueryInterface() method, ensuring that when an object is initialized from another interface type, QueryInterface() is still called.

To make the code generic, CComPtr<> is written for a generic interface T, and this is passed as a template parameter:

```
void CallDoSomething(IMyInterface* pInterface)
{
    CComPtr<IMyInterface> spInterface(pInterface);
    // note: no explicit call to AddRef()
    spInterface->DoSomething();   // calls spInterface.operator->()
    // note: no explicit call to Release()
}
```

The CComPtr<> code is designed to use a generic interface pointer type. At compile time the compiler will generate a class using the CComPtr<> template, replacing the generic pointer type with the IMyInterface* pointer type. Instances of this class can then only be used with this type. If you do this:

```
void WontCompile(IUnknown* pUnknown)              // note the type
{
    CComPtr<IMyInterface> spInterface(pUnknown); // this will not compile
```

it will not compile. This is because the type of the constructor parameter is defined by the template as `IMyInterface*`, not `IUnknown*`. If you want to convert from one interface pointer type to another (i.e. an implicit `QueryInterface()`) use `CComQIPtr<>` thus:

```
void WillCompile(IUnknown* pUnknown)
{
    CComQIPtr<IMyInterface> spInterface(pUnknown);   // this is OK
```

Notice that in `CallDoSomething()` a copy of the interface pointer is made, but there is no explicit call to `AddRef()` because the smart pointer will do that for you. Similarly, when the interface is no longer needed there is no explicit call to `Release()`. This method is instead called automatically by the smart pointer destructor, executed when `spInterface` goes out of scope.

Using a template parameter to pass the interface type means that `CComPtr<>` can be used on any COM interface pointer. `CComPtr<>` is generic code that only assumes that the data member p has the `IUnknown` methods. It also enforces COM's reference counting rules.

The Impl Technique

Templates like `CComPtr<>` are used to create instances that can be used on their own. This section covers a slightly different situation: adding code to a class. In this case, the template is not designed to be used to create instances, rather it is designed to be added to another class through multiple inheritance. The `Impl` technique adds code which has access to your class. For example, the `IPersist` standard COM interface has a single method that is used to return the CLSID of the object. ATL has an implementation of this interface, which you can find in `atlcom.h`:

```
template <class T>
class ATL_NO_VTABLE IPersistImpl : public IPersist
{
public:
    STDMETHOD(GetClassID)(CLSID *pClassID)
    {
        ATLTRACE2(atlTraceCOM, 0, _T("IPersistImpl::GetClassID\n"));
        if (pClassID == NULL)
            return E_FAIL;
        *pClassID = T::GetObjectCLSID();
        return S_OK;
    }
};
```

You use this template simply by deriving from it and passing your class as the parameter. The code assumes that your class has a `static` member function called `GetObjectCLSID()`, which ATL will provide for you if you derive your class from `CComCoClass<>` (remember that I said earlier that you may need to derive from several ATL classes).

```
class ATL_NO_VTABLE CMyObject :
    public CComObjectRootEx<CComSingleThreadModel>,
    public CComCoClass<CMyObject, &CLSID_MyObject>,
    public IPersistImpl<CMyObject>,
    public IMyObject
```

GetObjectCLSID() merely returns the second parameter of CComCoClass<> (which is CLSID_MyObject). In this case the Impl class calls a static member of your class. If it needs to call a non-static member then it will need to do some casting. For example, IServiceProviderImpl provides an implementation of the IServiceProvider interface, using the services map:

```
template <class T>
class ATL_NO_VTABLE IServiceProviderImpl : public IServiceProvider
{
public:
    STDMETHOD(QueryService)(REFGUID guidService, REFIID riid,
                            void** ppvObject)
    {
        ATLTRACE2(atlTraceCOM, 0, _T("IServiceProviderImpl::QueryService\n"));
        T* pT = static_cast<T*>(this);
        return pT->_InternalQueryService(guidService, riid, ppvObject);
    }
};
```

The services map lists all the services that your object implements. This is declared in your class and implements the _InternalQueryService() method. To get access to this method, the base class must cast its this pointer. For more information on the services map, see Appendix A.

ATL provides classes like CComCoClass<> and CComControl<> that centralize the information and functionality of your object. Many ATL Impl classes get access to this data and functionality using the casting technique shown above.

Making Abstract Classes Concrete

The classes that ATL creates are abstract because they derive from IUnknown but provide no implementation. The reason for this is that, depending on your server, you may decide to use one of several ways to implement these methods. ATL provides classes to do this, the most common being CComObject<>. This template is not designed to be used as a base class for your object. Instead, you should use it like CComPtr<> to create an instance of your ATL class:

```
CComObject<CMyObject>* pObject;
hr = CComObject<CMyObject>::CreateInstance(&pObject);
CComPtr<IMyInterface> pInterface;
pObject->QueryInterface(IID_IMyInterface,
                        reinterpret_cast<void**>(&pInterface));
```

CComObject<> is declared in atlcom.h as:

```
template<class Base>
class CComObject : public Base
{
    ...
    STDMETHOD_(ULONG, AddRef)();
    STDMETHOD_(ULONG, Release)();
    ...
    STDMETHOD(QueryInterface)(REFIID iid, void** ppvObject);
    ...
};
```

So, when you pass your class as a parameter to CComObject<>, the new class will *derive* from the ATL class. Since CComObject<> implements the IUnknown methods, the created class will be concrete. In addition, it has access to any public and protected members of your class.

Initializing Parameters

Typically, if you want to initialize an instance of a class you do it by passing values to the appropriate constructor. However, if ATL used this scheme it would mean that you'd have to derive from the appropriate class and then call the constructor of that class with the initialization parameters. Instead, ATL takes a different root by passing the initialization values as parameters to the template. This means that a class will be generated that specifically uses the constants you declare at compile time. This can make the code smaller and perform better, but only if a single class is generated from the template. If you use the template again, with different parameters, the compiler will generate another class and your code will be larger.

You have already seen an example of using initialization parameters, with `CComCoClass<>`:

```
template <class T, const CLSID* pclsid = &CLSID_NULL>
class CComCoClass
{
public:
    static const CLSID& WINAPI GetObjectCLSID() {return *pclsid;}
    // other members
};
```

Users of this template pass a pointer to their CLSID (typically declared `extern` in an `_i.c` file generated by MIDL or, with later versions of MIDL, declared in the header, using `__declspec(uuid())`) as the second parameter and this is returned by the `static` method `GetObjectCLSID()`.

Templates as Namespaces

This is not limited to templates; you can do the same thing with a C++ class, but templates give you more flexibility. The idea is to create a namespace with `static` members — in other words, to collect together methods that can be referred to by a single name. So, if you want to provide a method to copy, say, VARIANTs you could use this (from `atlcom.h`):

```
template<>
class _Copy<VARIANT>
{
public:
    static HRESULT copy(VARIANT* p1, VARIANT* p2)
    {return VariantCopy(p1, p2);}
    // other methods
};
```

The generic `CComEnumImpl<>` template implements an enumerator (see Appendix F) based on a type you pass as a template parameter. The `CComEnumImpl<>` will need to initialize, copy and destroy these types, and since it's generic it needs to be told the methods that will do this. The appropriate class is passed as the fourth parameter:

```
template <class Base, const IID* piid, class T, class Copy>
class ATL_NO_VTABLE CComEnumImpl : public Base
{
public:
    STDMETHOD(Next)(ULONG celt, T* rgelt, ULONG* pceltFetched);
    // other members
};
```

For our example using VARIANT as the third parameter, you will use
_Copy<VARIANT>, but the same template can be used for LPOLESTRs (use
_Copy<LPOLESTR>), or any other type for which you have declared an appropriate
copy class.

The Next() method uses it like this:

```
HRESULT hr = Copy::copy(pelt, m_iter);
```

The details of this are given in Appendix E, but pelt and m_iter are of type T*, the
templated type. The copy() method is called using the scope resolution operator,
from the Copy parameter, which is why I say that the template creates a namespace.

The beauty of this is that the templated code in Next() can be used for a wide range
of types, so long as the Copy parameter can copy the type given in the parameter T.
This does not necessarily mean that the two parameters of the copy() method are
both of the same type. For example, the enumerator may enumerate BSTRs but the
data could be held in CComBSTRs, so copy() will have BSTR* and CComBSTR*
parameters.

Other Template Features

Templates can have default parameters. As an example, take a look at
CComCoClass<> again. If you use this without specifying the second parameter,
pclsid, then it will point to CLSID_NULL by default. Like default parameters for C++
methods, there cannot be non-default parameters after a default parameter. You'll find
that this is used extensively in ATL and it simplifies your code considerably.

You can also pass templates as parameters to templates. However, make sure that you
separate the closing angled brackets with a space. For example:

```
typedef CComObject<CComEnum<Base, piid, T, Copy> > _class;
```

If you omit the space, the compiler will treat the two angled brackets as the shift
operator >>.

Multiple Inheritance Features

You will find that ATL does not give any problems with multiple inheritance (unlike
MFC, which has ambiguity problems when deriving from two classes that both inherit
from CObject).

> It's true that you may have problems if you have two interfaces that have
> methods with the same name and parameters, but this is fairly easy to
> remedy by using an intermediate class. This technique is demonstrated
> in Chapter 3 of *Professional ATL COM Programming*.

However, there is one small area of which you need to be aware. When you add a dual interface to your `coclass`, ATL will use this to implement `IDispatch`. If you add another dual interface to your ATL class then the map won't know which dual to use. ATL provides a solution, enabling you to nominate one dual as being the `IDispatch` implementation. Unfortunately, this causes a problem with scripting clients, which will then only be able to access one of the dual interfaces. The best solution is, therefore, to avoid this situation completely.

> For more information about this problem and some workarounds, see *Professional ATL COM Programming*, Chapter 3.

If your class inherits from a class that itself inherits from another class, then there's a resulting performance problem. The compiler will generate code that will create the vtable for the base class part of the object and then destroy it when it creates the vtable for the entire object. Your ATL class will *always* be a base class because it's an abstract class (the `CComObject<>` template will derive from the class you pass as a parameter). In an effort to get round this problem, the ATL wizards automatically mark your classes with `_ATL_NO_VTABLE` as an optimization, which prevents the creation of the intermediate vtable.

However, there is a problem with this: it means that you cannot call virtual methods in the constructor. To get round this, ATL class factories use a two-stage construction. The first stage is the creation of the object (with an appropriate template to implement `IUnknown`), and, after this construction is complete, the vtable. In the second stage the class factory will call the `FinalConstruct()` method of your class. You can put any initialization code in this method, safe in the knowledge that the object will have been completely constructed. You can put clean-up code in `FinalRelease()` (which is called immediately before the object is destroyed), but note that you can safely initialize member variables in the constructor.

Because of this two stage construction, you should not create ATL objects with the `new` operator because `FinalConstruct()` will not be called. The `static` method `CreateInstance()` of the various `CComObject<>` templates, will create a new instance and ensure that `FinalConstruct()` is called. In other words:

```
CComObject<CMyObject>* pObject;
hr = CComObject<CMyObject>::CreateInstance(&pObject);   // do this
// pObject = new CComObject<CMyObject>;                 // not this
```

ATL and COM

So, now that you've decided that COM is the best way to write your components and you've seen a little about ATL, why should you use ATL rather than the other possibilities? For example, you could use plain C++, but that would mean you'd need to write the entire framework yourself. Another option is MFC, but MFC is an *application* framework, not a *component* framework, which means that superfluous code will be generated. ATL is a rich, component framework and is clearly the best option for writing components and controls.

I won't go into any further details about how ATL provides its functionality. Instead, I'll give a brief overview of the ATL architecture, to give you a better understanding of the code that's generated for you. ATL can be used as it stands, but most people will use the Visual C++ Wizards to create and manipulate their code. These Wizards will be introduced in the next chapter and are covered in detail in Appendix D.

ATL and Threading

At present, COM has two threading models: single threaded and multithreaded. An object can be run in a **single threaded apartment (STA)**. This means that only one thread will have access to the object, so you need have no concerns about threading issues like synchronization or re-entrance. COM guarantees this by synchronizing all calls to the object using a message queue. COM also allows an object to be run in a **multithreaded apartment (MTA)**. As the name suggests, an MTA can contain more than one thread, and consequently more than one thread can have access to your object. This means that you have to be particularly vigilant to ensure that your objects behave well when accessed by more than one thread at a time.

Usage

Your ATL class should, at the very least, derive from `CComObjectRootEx<>` and the default interface that it will implement. `CComObjectRootEx<>` derives from `CComObjectRootBase`, which contains the code that is used by the various implementations of `IUnknown`. In particular, it has a data member, `m_dwRef`, which is used to hold the reference count on an object. It also has methods to support reference counting for aggregated and non-aggregated objects.

If your object is accessed by more than one thread then more than one of them may attempt to increment or decrement `m_dwRef`. These C++ operators are not atomic — that is, they are composed of more than one CPU operation. Because of this, it's possible that one thread will be half way through incrementing `m_dwRef` when it is preempted by another thread attempting to do the same thing. If this is the case then the data member will be in an invalid state when the second thread is given access to it. Clearly `m_dwRef`, and other instance variables, must be protected from multithreaded access.

You can define code that must only be accessed by one thread as a critical section, but this presents a performance problem if the object is run in an STA where only one thread accesses your object. ATL helps you here, because the `CComObjectRootEx<>` template takes a parameter that represents the threading model under which the object will be run. This parameter will specify whether synchronization is needed or not, and can be one of the two classes given in the following table:

Class	Description
`CComSingleThreadModel`	Used for objects run in an STA
`CComMultiThreadModel`	Used for objects run in an MTA or an STA

When you use the Object Wizard to insert an ATL class into your project, you can select the threading model. This results in the appropriate threading class being used in the generated code. In general, you can use CComMultiThreadModel for objects that will run in either (or both) an STA or an MTA, since it will protect the ATL code from multithreaded access.

Lock() and Unlock()

In addition to protecting the code that ATL provides, you can use methods from CComMultiThreadModel to protect your own code. These methods are Lock() and Unlock(), inherited from CComObjectRootEx<> and implemented in terms of the template's parameter. If you use CComMultiThreadModel as the parameter, these locking methods use a Win32 critical section. Conversely, if you use CComSingleThreadModel then these methods are essentially no-ops, so it is safe to use them even if you don't intend the object to be used in an MTA.

ATL will not call these methods for you. Consequently, if a part of your code should not be preempted, or you change values that might be accessed by other threads, then you should use the locking methods shown in the table below:

Method	Use To
Increment()	Increment a 32-bit integer
Decrement()	Decrement a 32-bit integer
Lock()	Define the start of a block of code that should not be preempted, or accessed by more than one thread
Unlock()	Defines the end of the protected block of code

Increment() and Decrement()

There are two things that you should note about Increment() and Decrement(). Firstly, they only affect 32-bit integers, so if you want to increment a double then you should use Lock() instead:

```
_ThreadModel::Decrement(&m_ulCount);    // declared as ULONG
Lock();
m_dCost++;    // declared as double
Unlock();
```

Notice that CComObjectRootEx<> typedefs the threading class to _ThreadModel, through which you can call Increment() and Decrement(), but it implements Lock() and Unlock() methods based on the methods of the same name in _ThreadModel.

The other thing to note is that you don't need to apply locking in every method. If your object is designed for use in an MTA but the instance is only ever accessed by one client, then you will never have more than one thread accessing the object. However, you cannot always guarantee this. For example, the client that creates the object may pass the object interface pointer to another client (another process or another thread in the same process). If the object is running in an MTA and both clients attempt to access it at the same time, then two server threads will be used.

Regardless of whether your object is designed to be used in an STA or an MTA, you will always need to use locking of some kind if your code uses a resource that is global to your code module. This is because other threads in the process (whether STA or MTA) will have access to that resource. Threading will be covered in more detail in Chapter 3 and the various options and classes used are covered in Appendix H. I explain in Appendix F some of the threading issues involved with enumerator objects that use global resources.

Class Factories

When a client calls CoCreateInstanceEx() to create an instance of a coclass, it is another object, called a class factory, that actually creates the instance. A COM server needs to create an instance of the class factory object and return it to the system. It does this either when the system calls DllGetClassObject() (if the server is a DLL) or when the server starts (if the server is an EXE).

ATL will automatically give you class factory support when you derive the class from CComCoClass<>. ATL will assume that the class factory object will implement IClassFactory and will create a new instance of an object when IClassFactory::CreateInstance() is called. This is reasonable in most cases, but there will still be occasions when you will want to change the behavior of a class factory object.

For example, you may decide that you want to add licensing support to an object, in which case the class factory should support IClassFactory2. Furthermore, you may decide that the class factory should only ever create one instance of an object, and for every call to CreateInstance() it should return a reference to this instance. In this case, you will need a singleton. Finally, you may decide that the class factory should implement an interface other than IClassFactory or IClassFactory2. This would be the case if, for example, you want to be able to pass additional information to the class factory object other than the parameters of CreateInstance(). ATL allows you to do all of these things by using the appropriate ATL macro. More information will be given in Appendix G.

Interface Implementation

An object exposes its functionality through interfaces. For simple objects, you define the interface, its properties and its methods. However, some objects are designed to be used with others, and thus to implement particular 'standard' interfaces. For instance, an ActiveX Control must implement several interfaces to allow the control container (the program that shows the control) to communicate with it. Some of these interfaces are used to set up the communications between the control and container, and others are used to accomplish tasks such as getting the control to draw itself, or to initialize itself to a known state. By their nature, these interfaces are boilerplate, so ATL provides implementations that will work well in almost all situations. If you want to change the implementation, you merely have to override whatever methods are necessary.

You can tell that an ATL template implements an interface by the fact that it has the Impl suffix (for example `IPersistImpl<>` is an implementation of `IPersist`). These templates typically use information that is held in your class (or inherited by your class), so you usually pass your class name to the Impl template — the Impl technique that I explained above.

In most cases, you will allow the ATL Object Wizard to determine the Impl templates that you use. It is possible, however, that you may decide to remove some of this functionality or add support for another interface at a later stage. For example, you may have a **Full Control** created by Object Wizard, but by default, it will not have support for the `IPersistPropertyBag` interface. If you wanted to initialize the control on a web page with `<PARAM>` tags then you would need to add support for this interface by deriving your ATL class from `IPersistPropertyBagImpl<>`. Similarly, a Full Control will be derived from `ISpecifyPropertyPagesImpl<>`, but if the control does not have any property pages then you can remove this base class.

The Impl interfaces work in tandem with the interface map. The Impl templates add functionality to the class, whereas the interface map indicates that this functionality is exposed by the object through an interface. Even if you derive from an Impl template, that functionality can only be used if the interface has been added to the interface map. Conversely, if you remove an Impl base class you will need to remove the entry in the interface map.

In most cases, the Object Wizard can be used to add a new interface to your class. You can use this interface to expose any of your object's functionality that cannot be exposed by a 'standard' interface. The Object Wizard will mark this interface in the IDL file as the default interface for your object. Hence, if you decide to remove it you must edit the IDL by hand to specify another interface to be used as the default.

You can add another, non-standard, interface to your class by using ClassView (as explained in the next chapter). However, note that there are restrictions. The most important is that the appropriate wizard will get the information about the new interface from a type library. This is fine if the interface has already been defined on another object, but if not you will have to edit the IDL and then compile it to generate a type library. Clunky, yes, but this is the only way to use the wizard.

The reliance of the wizard on type libraries presents a further problem. Type libraries cannot be used to describe all interfaces, restricting which interfaces you can add to your class. If your interface cannot be described by a type library, then you must add the interface to the IDL file by hand.

IUnknown

One interface that you do not have to add to your class is IUnknown. Indeed, this interface is not implemented by any of the classes that the Object Wizard adds as base classes to your class (although it will derive from the struct IUnknown, which is an abstract base class). Instead, the interface is implemented in other classes, the most often used being CComObject<>. You use this class by creating an instance with your class as its parameter. CComObject<> derives from your class and adds the IUnknown methods, hence it *implements* this interface. If you look at the definition of this class in atlcom.h, you'll find that it's implemented in terms of methods that your class inherits from CComObjectRootBase and CComObjectRootEx<>.

So, why doesn't the class that the Object Wizard generates just implement the IUnknown methods rather than using a separate class in this way? The reason is that there's more than one way to create an instance of an object (as will be explained in Chapter 3). One possibility is that a client will call CoCreateInstanceEx() through a **class factory** associated with your object. If the instance of your object needs to create other objects at some later point (perhaps for use as return values from interface methods) several techniques are available. The ultimate choice depends on considerations such as what effect these objects would have on the lifetime of your module (DLL or EXE).

For example, you can use CComObjectGlobal<> to create an instance of an ATL class as a global object or as a data member in your class. You can then obtain an interface pointer for this object through QueryInterface(), allowing you to use it. So, whereas CComObject<> is designed to be used to create instances obtained through calls to its static method CreateInstance(), CComObjectGlobal<> is designed to create a single instance and to return multiple references.

The separation of the IUnknown methods from an ATL class by placing them in separate classes is what gives you this flexibility.

Registration

A COM object must be registered somewhere. Registration allows COM to find the code that implements an object. At the very least, an object must be registered on the server machine. If it's accessed through a dispinterface (that is, a known collection of methods available through IDispatch) then there doesn't have to be any interface registration on the client. However, if the object has dual or other oleautomation-compatible interfaces (see Chapter 4), then you need to register the object's type library on both the client and server machines. If the object has an interface that is not oleautomation-compatible then you will need to register a proxy-stub DLL on both the client and server machines.

AppID

NT machines have built-in security, and COM will apply security checking to all objects that are created. COM uses a registry key called `AppID` to control what will be able to launch and access an object. When your object is registered it should add a key to the `AppID` key with the name that is a GUID unique to this code module (hence Application ID). `DCOMCnfg` can be used to add and remove permissions for the accounts that can launch and access objects implemented in this code module. One further complication is that on NT a COM server can be installed as an NT Service. This means that the server has to be registered as a service, which involves adding entries to a separate area of the registry. It also requires the `LocalServer` key to be added to the `AppID` key so that COM knows which service implements requested objects.

Self Registration

All object servers should support **self registration**. The COM specification says that if a server can be self registered, it should have an `OleSelfRegister` string in the `StringFileInfo` section of the server's `VERSIONINFO` resource. In practice it is assumed that all servers do self register, so these entries are not required. Self registration means that a DLL server exports two methods called `DllRegisterServer()` and `DllUnregisterServer()` and that an EXE server supports the command line switches `-RegServer` and `-UnregServer` (as well as `/RegServer` and `/UnregServer`).

As the names suggest, the server must be able to both register *and* unregister itself. Unregistration is important because a server machine's registry can get bloated with a COM object's registration values. It is important to be able to remove a server's entries if you no longer need the server. There are tools to do this (two that come to mind are `RegClean` and `RegMaid`, both available from Microsoft) but if your objects can be (and are) unregistered you should not need to use these.

The Registrar

Anyone who has used the Win32 registry API will agree that it is rather clunky to use. To prevent you from having to use this rather arcane API, ATL supplies a COM object called the registrar. This allows you to provide a registration script as a resource in your server, which you can then pass to the registrar. The registrar can use this to both register and unregister the server, simplifying your code considerably.

I mentioned that the registrar is a COM object, and this means that it too should be registered on the machine where you want to register your server. If your object is likely to be used on machines where you're not sure whether the registrar is registered then you can choose to include the registrar code as a C++ object rather than a COM object. This increases the size of your server, but reduces the dependency on other servers. Details of this so-called 'static registration' and the format of the registration scripts are given in Appendix B.

Type Library Registration

If your ATL object is likely to be used with Visual Basic then type library registration is a good idea, because type libraries are integral to the working of the Visual Basic IDE. Furthermore, if your object uses `dual` interfaces (see Chapter 4) then a type library will be used by ATL as part of the interface implementation. Even if the interface is not `dual`, you may decide to use type library marshaling, in which case the type library must be registered. On the other hand, if your object will not be used with Visual Basic *and* it will not use type library marshaling, then you will not need to register its type library. It is a good idea in this case to remove type library registration, as outlined in Appendix C.

This Book's Example

Throughout this book, I will be using a 'rolling' example to illustrate ATL. This will take the form of a products catalogue with the client side represented by a control that can be placed on a web page, or in any other control container, such as a Visual Basic application.

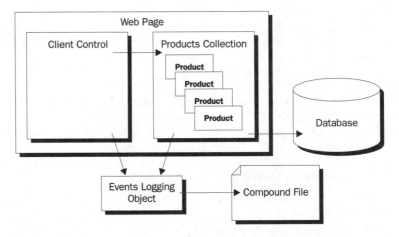

The client control will access the individual `Product` objects through the `Products` collection. The collection determines where the data is held — in the later chapters, a database will be used so the ATL OLE DB classes will be used to access that data. The example uses an Access97 database. This may not be the most suitable database for a high volume application, but I've chosen it because I wanted to make sure that it can be installed on the widest number of machines. Microsoft SQL Server or Oracle would have been better choices in terms of their scalability and robustness, but few people have either of these installed on their personal computers. However, as you'll see, when you use OLE DB, you can change the database implementation very easily anyway.

Relevant events are logged to a logger object. By 'relevant' I mean that if items are added or removed from the database then the details are saved, and if an error occurs then that is logged too. The logging object is a collection called `Events`, which you can query with a separate application to determine what events have been logged. This object saves its data to a compound file using the OLE compound file API. The file is implemented as a singleton object to ensure that only one client at a time has access to it.

This example, and the relevant clients used to test the various objects, will be developed throughout the following chapters and will be used to illustrate the ATL concepts being explained.

Summary

COM is the way forward for distributed application development, and ATL is the ideal framework for C++ development of COM objects. This chapter has introduced the main facilities that ATL offers you. In short, for just about anything that you need to do to create a COM server and write a COM component or control, there will be an ATL class or template.

ATL, as the name suggests, uses C++ templates and although these are gaining popularity with C++ programmers and are fairly widespread, ATL uses some features that you may not be familiar with. I have explained these features and illustrated them with examples from ATL.

Finally, I introduced the example that will be used throughout this book to explain the various ATL concepts. The next chapter will show you how to create the main objects in this example, and we'll look at the code that the Wizards generate for you.

2

ATL Wizards

Introduction

ATL is a class library. To use it you need to include its header files and add the necessary maps to your project. You also need to make sure that the classes you use to implement COM objects derive from certain ATL classes and contain particular maps. If you know all the code that you'll need, then you can create a Win32 Application or DLL project and turn it into an ATL server project. However, most of us can't remember all the code required, so it is far easier to get the various wizards supplied with Visual C++ to add the code for you.

These wizards are not perfect (there is no way that Microsoft can envisage every type of application or object that you might want to create) and hence the code that the wizards generate is fairly generic. Consequently, you'll need to add code to (and, in some cases, remove code from) or modify the code that the wizards have created. This is fine, because the wizards exist simply to give you framework code for your project.

In this chapter, you will create ATL projects and objects using the ATL wizards, which will be developed further in later chapters. I will show you the basics of how to use the wizards. More details about the wizards and their options can be found in Appendices D and E.

The AppWizard

The starting point of every ATL project is the ATL AppWizard. You run this by selecting the New item from the File menu and selecting the ATL COM AppWizard from the Projects tab. You will then be presented with this dialog:

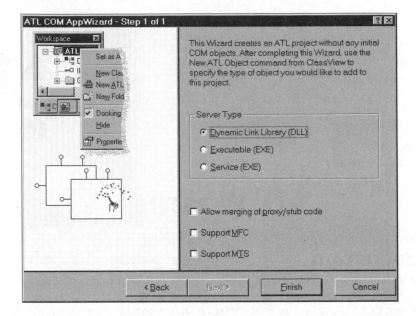

DLL or EXE?

The options in this dialog are explained in full in Appendix D. The two main choices are to implement your objects either in a DLL or an EXE. A DLL has the advantage that the server will be loaded and accessed quickly, but if run on NT it will have no control over the security that will be used. There is also the possibility of objects being able to alter your client's memory. An EXE server will load more slowly, and access to objects will *always* require an intermediate marshaling object. However, objects will be isolated from the client and can manage their own security and threading.

NT Service

If you're targeting NT you can make the server an NT Service EXE, which means that you can make the object class factories long lived. This will mean that the service will not shut down when the last object has been released. You can also configure the service to start when the machine starts. However, you will have to think carefully about using this option because one of the great features of COM is its ability to start servers dynamically and then stop them once all clients have released their object references. A COM service can be dynamically started but after that it will continue to run and hence take up valuable system resources.

Proxy/Stub Code

The three check boxes are only enabled when you have selected the DLL option. The first option will configure the project to have the interface's proxy and stub code incorporated in to the DLL. This is only available for DLLs because proxy and stub objects are `inproc` objects and hence can only be merged into a DLL project.

Why would you want this? Well, if the interfaces of the objects in the DLL are likely to be used across apartment boundaries, then the interface will be marshaled and hence a stub object will be created for the server. A DLL server will load more quickly and use fewer resources if the stub object is implemented in the same DLL as the object. Apartment boundaries are crossed in the following situations:

❑ If the object is created in-process by code in an apartment which is incompatible with the threading model, which is indicated by the object's `ThreadingModel` registry value

❑ If the object is created in a surrogate process such as `DllHost.exe` or in the Microsoft Transaction Server (MTS)

The second situation mentioned above is interesting because this is a way to run an `inproc` object in a separate process from its client. `DllHost.exe` is the system surrogate, and is designed for this purpose. To use this, you must give your DLL an `AppID` key (the ATL Wizards will not do this — Appendix B shows you how to change the server's registration script), and add a value called `DllSurrogate` with no value. If you want to specify a custom surrogate, you should use its path for this value).

The great advantage of this is that it means that the objects in the DLL can be activated on a remote machine. Even on the local machine, it has advantages because the object will be isolated from the client. This means that if it throws an exception it will only kill the surrogate process. You will also be able to configure the security settings of the server, if it's run on NT.

> Do not be tempted to do this by creating an EXE server and using an object implemented in that server to create DLL-based objects, passing references out to external clients. Such a design is asking for trouble, because the DLL objects will not have any control over the lifetime of the EXE. When the last object implemented in the EXE is released, the EXE will unload, which will result in the DLLs being unloaded as well. This will happen even if there are outstanding references on the DLL-served objects. The message is clear, don't pass out references to DLL objects from a server. Either you should use a surrogate (you can write your own) or use the DLL object's functionality by aggregating it into one of the EXE-served objects.

MFC

The MFC option allows you to use MFC code in your project. In Appendix D, I go to great lengths to explain why you should not want to do this. In brief, MFC's threading is primitive compared to ATL's, and its code will add bulk to your object if you statically-link it. In most cases, you will not need to distribute the MFC runtime DLLs because most current Microsoft operating systems have tools that are dependent upon MFC. However, if your ATL component uses an updated version of MFC then you *will* have the responsibility of distributing the MFC DLLs.

MTS

The MTS option needs discussion here. This is only available for DLL servers, because MTS is effectively a super-charged surrogate. It's designed to provide access to objects implemented in DLLs. MTS does more than that, since it allows your object to take part in distributed transactions. It also provides concurrency and state persistence management. If your DLL is run in MTS as part of a package and uses the MTS-provided context object, then you must select the MTS option because MTS DLL servers must be linked to `MTX.lib`.

> *MTS is an important technology and will be part of Microsoft's strategy for Windows 2000 and COM+. This book will not go into details about how to use MTS or write objects for it or COM+. For more information on these topics, I recommend that you look at Microsoft's COM site (http://www.microsoft.com/com) or the MSDN Library.*

Once you have run this wizard, a fully compilable project will be created. However, it will not contain any object code — that is the responsibility of the Object Wizard.

The Object Wizard

The Object Wizard has templates for many different ATL object types. You can run the Object Wizard in either an ATL generated project or an MFC project. In the latter case, other ATL code must be present in order for the ATL objects to be implemented. The first time the wizard is run in such a project, it will add this code for you, warning you first with a dialog.

The Object Wizard is shown in the following screenshot. The object types shown in the right-hand pane belong to the category selected in the left-hand pane:

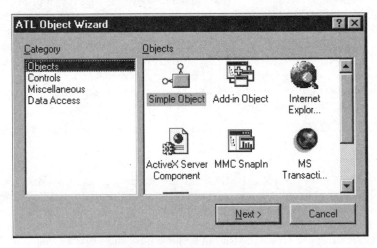

Once you have selected an object type and clicked on the Next▷ button, you will then see a property sheet dialog:

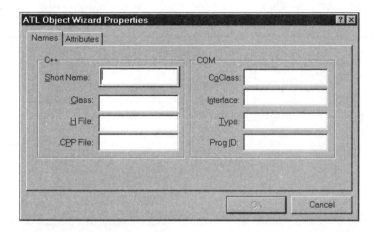

The pages shown will depend on the object type that you select. However, you'll usually get the **Names** page shown here. Appendix E explains the other pages that may be shown.

The Object Wizard will add:

- ❑ A `.h` file with a class defined for the object

- ❑ A `.cpp` file that will be used for the implementations of the methods and properties that you add through the ClassView wizards

- ❑ Various resources, including a registration script and any dialog or bitmap resources needed by the object type

Example: Creating Your First Project

In this example, you'll create a simple object that will be used to get access to data held in a database. The database code will be added later in the book. To start with, we'll create the data access object and initialize it with test data.

The first step is to create a DLL server project called `DataAccess`. You don't need to check **Allow merging of proxy/stub code** because the object will use type library marshaling. You don't need to select the **Support MTS** option either, because the project is used to illustrate ATL concepts and so, in this instance, the facilities provided by MTS are superfluous. In production code, the facilities of MTS would be important.

To add the code for the object to the project, click on the **Insert** menu and select **New ATL Object**. From the **Objects** category select **Simple Object** and give the object a **Short Name** of `Products`. Select the **Attributes** tab and select **Both** for the threading type. This choice is necessary because the object is implemented in a DLL server and you'll want it to be used by as many client apartments as possible. Later chapters will show you how to generate events and use error objects to give rich error information. This object takes an agnostic view about aggregation, so accept the default values for the other options. Generally, if your object will use these facilities then you should select them now.

The idea of this project is to allow a client to access the products in an ordering system. Two ways of doing this should be allowed: products will either be accessed individually (indexed using a product ID) or in groups, using an enumerator object. The `IProducts` interface is an automation collection interface that allows you to do this via the methods and properties shown below. These will be added a little later in this chapter:

Interface Member	Property/Method	Description
_NewEnum	Property	Gives access to an enumerator object
Count	Property	Returns the number of items in the enumerator
Item()	Method	Gets access to a particular item using its product ID
Add()	Method	Adds a new product
Remove()	Method	Removes a particular item using its product ID

If you have used Visual Basic you will recognize these methods and properties as being the items required by a VB collection. Visual Basic programmers are not normally given direct access to the enumerator object, so the first property has an underscore prefixed to its name in order to 'hide' this property from them. This initial version of the object will use the ATL template `ICollectionOnSTLImpl<>` to implement the first three properties. In later chapters, where the data will be held in a database, you will use your own implementation.

Details of this collection implementation class are given in Appendix F, but it's worth pointing out here that there are two problems with it. Firstly, this class does not implement the `Add()` and `Remove()` methods and secondly, the data in **STL** containers is not safe for multi-threaded access. The **Standard Template Library** is an important part of the ANSI C++ standard library. The container templates it provides give a generic mechanism for containing items of a specified type.

These templates are not thread safe. Hence, code needs to be used to ensure that if the object is likely to be used in a situation where more than one thread accesses the enumerator, then the data is not likely to be corrupted. Threading issues are covered in Appendix H and their effects on enumerators are given in Appendix F, but as you'll see in this chapter, the code to ensure that access is thread safe is fairly simple.

For now, the collection object will not implement the `Add()` and `Remove()` methods — they will be added later in this chapter. The `Products` object will be a collection of `Product` (singular) objects, which you should now add to your project with the Object Wizard. Make sure that the object uses the **Both** threading model but retain the default settings for the other options.

> A convention with automation collections is that they are usually named
> as the plural of the objects they contain.

After adding this object, select IProduct from the ClassView and add the following
properties (details of using this wizard are given in Appendix D):

Property	Property Type
ProductID	long
Description	BSTR
UnitCost	CURRENCY

None of these need any property parameters and all should be read/write, so leave the
Get Function and Put Function options selected in the wizard. This will have the effect
of using the [propput] and [propget] attributes in the IDL.

Note that the Item() method of the Products object will be implemented in this
chapter using the index of an item's position in the std::vector<> STL container
rather than the ProductID. This simplifies the code for the initial implementation.

The class needs to have storage for these properties, so add the following to CProduct
in Product.h:

```
private:
    long m_lProdID;
    CComBSTR m_bstrDesc;
    CURRENCY m_cyUnitCost;
};
```

These should be initialized in the constructor with the following code (you do not have
to worry about m_bstrDesc because its constructor will initialize it to an empty
string).

```
CProduct()
{
    m_lProdID = -1;
    VarCyFromI4(0, &m_cyUnitCost);
}
```

Next, you need to implement the get_ and put_ methods for these properties in
Product.cpp:

```
#define CHECK_OUT_PARAM(p) \
    if (p == NULL) return E_POINTER;

STDMETHODIMP CProduct::get_ProductID(long *pVal)
{
    CHECK_OUT_PARAM(pVal);
    *pVal = m_lProdID;
    return S_OK;
}

STDMETHODIMP CProduct::put_ProductID(long newVal)
{
    m_lProdID = newVal;
    return S_OK;
}
```

```
STDMETHODIMP CProduct::get_Description(BSTR *pVal)
{
    CHECK_OUT_PARAM(pVal);
    return m_bstrDesc.CopyTo(pVal);
}

STDMETHODIMP CProduct::put_Description(BSTR newVal)
{
    m_bstrDesc = newVal;
    return S_OK;
}

STDMETHODIMP CProduct::get_UnitCost(CURRENCY *pVal)
{
    CHECK_OUT_PARAM(pVal);
    *pVal = m_cyUnitCost;
    return S_OK;
}

STDMETHODIMP CProduct::put_UnitCost(CURRENCY newVal)
{
    m_cyUnitCost = newVal;
    return S_OK;
}
```

CHECK_OUT_PARAM() is a useful macro to define because it prevents clients calling methods with NULL pointers.

Since the Product object uses the Both threading model, there is a possibility that it could be used in an MTA and so more than one thread will have access to a Product instance. Thus, the get_ and put_ methods should use synchronization around the code that accesses data members. I have not used this code because, in the next chapter, this object will be made read-only and so the code will be deleted anyway.

Although the Product object can be initialized by calling the appropriate property put_ methods, it is useful to have a quick initialization method. This will not be a COM method but merely a C++ method that will be used when the object is first created. So, click on the CProduct class in ClassView and select **Add Member Function**.

> **Make sure that you do not select IProduct. If you do you'll add a new COM method.**

Add the following method:

```
public:
    void Initialize(long lProdID, LPCTSTR strDesc, double dUnitCost);
```

Implement it like this:

```
void CProduct::Initialize(long lProdID, LPCTSTR strDesc, double dUnitCost)
{
    m_lProdID = lProdID;
    m_bstrDesc = strDesc;
    VarCyFromR8(dUnitCost, &m_cyUnitCost);
}
```

Initialize() is public so that external code can create instances of the CProduct C++ object and initialize it with data. To make life easier, the cost of the item is passed as a double and the automation method VarCyFromR8() is used to convert to a CURRENCY value.

Making the Products Object into a Collection

The next task is to implement the collection object. As I mentioned earlier, the
ICollectionOnSTLImpl<> template will do most of the work for you, but there are
still things you need to do. Visual Basic and VBScript clients expect an enumerator
returned from a collection to implement IEnumVARIANT. This is fine because
Product objects have dual interfaces and so they can be placed in a VARIANT.

Adding ICollectionOnSTLImpl<> as a base class is straightforward (full details are
given in Appendix F). It involves deriving the class from ICollectionOnSTLImpl<>
and then adding the appropriate properties to the class. First, add the following
headers to Products.h:

```
#pragma warning(disable : 4530)    // stop warnings about exception handling
#include <vector>
```

The pragma is used to prevent a warning that std::vector<> generates C++
exceptions — by default, ATL turns off exception support to reduce code size. You
have two options. You can either turn on exception support and use guarded blocks
when you access the Products' vector or you can assume (as I do here) that no
exceptions will be thrown and so turn off the compiler warnings.

Now edit your class to derive from ICollectionOnSTLImpl<> using the following
typedefs to make the code more readable:

```
typedef std::vector<CComVariant> VarVector;
typedef CComEnumOnSTL<IEnumVARIANT, &IID_IEnumVARIANT, VARIANT,
                      _Copy<VARIANT>, VarVector> VarEnum;
typedef ICollectionOnSTLImpl<IProducts, VarVector, VARIANT,
                      _Copy<VARIANT>, VarEnum> IProdCollection;

class ATL_NO_VTABLE CProducts :
    public CComObjectRootEx<CComMultiThreadModel>,
    public CComCoClass<CProducts, &CLSID_Products>,
    public IDispatchImpl<IProdCollection, &IID_IProducts,
                      &LIBID_DATAACCESSLib>
```

There is a lot of information here. ICollectionOnSTLImpl<> implements your
collection interface (IProducts). I have typedefed this to IProdCollection.
ICollectionOnSTLImpl<> implements the _NewEnum property with an
enumerator object. This enumerator object has the IEnumVARIANT interface, which is
specified with the VarEnum typedef. This indicates that _NewEnum enumerates
VARIANTs and also specifies that these VARIANTs are held in the class in a
std::vector<VARIANT>. Your class needs to implement the dual interface
IProducts, so you must derive from IDispatchImpl<>.

Note that IProducts is the collection interface of your object and
ICollectionOnSTLImpl<> implements this interface. For this reason, if you want to
add other methods to your class, you should do so by adding a new interface. This is
good interface programming design.

Now use ClassView to add the following read-only properties (i.e. only Get Function
should be checked) to the IProducts interface:

Property	Property Type	Property Parameters
Count	long	
_NewEnum	LPUNKNOWN	
Item	VARIANT	[in] long lIndex

Edit the IDL file to change the value for the id() attributes of _NewEnum and Item to DISPID_NEWENUM and DISPID_VALUE, respectively:

```
interface IProducts : IDispatch
{
    [propget, id(1), helpstring("property Count")]
        HRESULT Count([out, retval] long *pVal);
    [propget, id(DISPID_NEWENUM), helpstring("property _NewEnum")]
        HRESULT _NewEnum([out, retval] LPUNKNOWN *pVal);
    [propget, id(DISPID_VALUE), helpstring("property Item")]
        HRESULT Item([in] long lIndex, [out, retval] VARIANT *pVal);
};
```

These are the standard values for these properties, but ClassView will not allow you to add them through the wizard.

Finally, remove the declarations and definitions of the property methods that the ClassView has added to your Products.h and Products.cpp files. This may seem a little odd, but there is a good reason: the ICollectionOnSTLImpl<> base class will implement these methods so your class should not.

You should be able to compile the entire project now, to confirm that you haven't made any mistakes.

A production implementation of an object like this would use a persistent store to store the products. We haven't got any code like that so, for this initial test, create some data in the Products constructor. To do this you need to create some Product objects, initialize them with some data, put each one into a VARIANT and then add them to the m_coll vector inherited from ICollectionOnSTLImpl<>.

Open Products.h, include Product.h, and then add this code:

```
CProducts()
{
    CComObject<CProduct>* pObj;
    CComVariant var;

    CComObject<CProduct>::CreateInstance(&pObj);
    pObj->Initialize(1, _T("Shoes"), 40.50);
    var = pObj;
    m_coll.push_back(var);

    CComObject<CProduct>::CreateInstance(&pObj);
    pObj->Initialize(2, _T("Shirt"), 20.00);
    var = pObj;
    m_coll.push_back(var);

    CComObject<CProduct>::CreateInstance(&pObj);
    pObj->Initialize(3, _T("Tie"), 12.00);
    var = pObj;
    m_coll.push_back(var);
}
```

There is a lot going on here — I'll say more about it in the next chapter. Basically, `CreateInstance()` is a static member function inherited from `CComObject<>`, and is used to create C++ instances of the class that you pass as a parameter to the template. At this point, the C++ object is not a 'real' COM object because it has a reference count of zero. However, I put the pointer into a `VARIANT`, using the wrapper class `CComVariant` (see Appendix K). The assignment operator of `CComVariant` casts the C++ pointer to `struct IDispatch` (an interface pointer) and then calls `AddRef()`. This function increments the object reference count to one, creating a fully fledged COM object. The `CComVariant` is then put into the `vector` using the `push_back()` method, which calls the copy constructor. This is the reason why `var` can be reused for the other objects.

Once you have compiled this, you can write Visual Basic code like that below:

```
Dim obj As New Products
For Each v In obj         'v contains a VARIANT with an IDispatch pointer
    Dim p As IProduct
    Set p = v            'call QI() to get an IProduct pointer
    Debug.Print p.Description
Next
```

There will be a more complete Visual Basic example at the end of this chapter.

Adding the Add() and Remove() Methods

The code shown above is fine if your collection will only ever have shoes, shirts and ties, with those particular costs, but it's useless for anything else. The `Add()` and `Remove()` methods allow you (or any user of the collection) to add and remove `Product` objects to and from the collection. As I mentioned earlier, `ICollectionOnSTLImpl<>` does not give you these methods, so you have to do it yourself. Use ClassView to add the following to the `IProducts` interface:

```
HRESULT Add([in]VARIANT var);
HRESULT Remove([in]long lIndex);
```

`Add()` is used to add an already created item (wrapped in a `VARIANT`) to the collection. `Remove()` specifies an object to remove using the same index value as would be used in `Item()`.

> Note that the Automation specification is not very clear about the actual parameter of `Add()`. It says it should be a reference to the object type, but using a `VARIANT` works just as well.

Implement the methods as follows:

```
STDMETHODIMP CProducts::Add(VARIANT var)
{
    if (var.vt != VT_DISPATCH)    // check that it is an object
        return E_INVALIDARG;
    m_coll.push_back(var);
    return S_OK;
}
```

```
STDMETHODIMP CProducts::Remove(long lIndex)
{
    if (m_coll.size() < lIndex || lIndex < 1)
        return E_INVALIDARG;
    VarVector::iterator it(&m_coll[lIndex - 1]); // indexed from 1
    m_coll.erase(it);
    return S_OK;
}
```

The `Remove()` method first checks that the index is not too big or too small, and then obtains an iterator for the item to remove. Finally it calls `std::vector<>::erase()` to remove the item.

Now you can write Visual Basic code like this (assuming `obj` is a `Products` object):

```
Dim prod As New Product
prod.ProductID = 4
prod.Description = "Coat"
prod.UnitCost = 50.0
obj.Add prod    'Add new item
obj.Remove 1    'Remove the first item in the collection
```

Tests

I will show you three tests using this example. The first will use VBScript, the second will use Visual Basic 6 and finally I will show you a project that will access the object using C++.

VBScript

Since the `Product` and `Products` objects have dual interfaces and use type library marshaling, they can be accessed from VBScript. This can be done either on a web page or through the Windows Scripting Host (WSH). Here is the script for the WSH:

```
'coll.vbs
Dim coll
Dim prod

Set coll = CreateObject("DataAccess.Products.1")

Set prod = CreateObject("DataAccess.Product.1")
prod.ProductID = 4
prod.Description = "Coat"
prod.UnitCost = 50.0

coll.Add (prod)  'Add new item
coll.Remove 1    'Remove the first item in the collection

Dim output
for each o in coll
    output = output & o.ProductID & " " & o.Description
    output = output & " $" & o.UnitCost & vbCrLf
next

MsgBox output
```

The code first creates a collection object, which contains `Shoes`, `Shirt` and `Tie`. The code adds a new product, `Coat`, and then removes the first item, `Shoes`. The code then iterates through the collection, obtaining details about each item. It then prints out the data in a message box. This script can be run from the command line with:

```
cscript coll.vbs
```

where `cscript` is the WSH command line interpreter. This gives the following results:

The WSH is a standard part of Windows 98. For Windows 95 and NT 4.0, it can be downloaded from the Microsoft scripting site (http://msdn.microsoft.com/scripting). It is also a component of the Windows NT 4.0 Option Pack.

Visual Basic

In this example, I will show you how to add and remove items using a Visual Basic form. Create a VB project that has a list box (called `lstItems`), two text boxes (called `txtItem` and `txtCost`), and two command buttons (`cmdAdd` and `cmdRemove`, both disabled, with the captions **Add** and **Remove**). You will need to use the **Project | References…** menu item to add the type library of the server to the project (**DataAccess 1.0 Type Library**) and then add the code for the project.

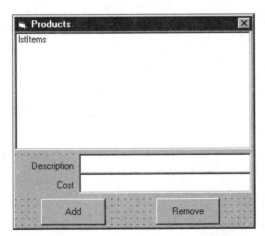

The first thing to add is a global variable for the collection. It needs to be initialized in the `Form_Load` event handler, which also calls `Update`, filling the list box with information about the objects in the collection:

```
Dim coll As Products

Private Sub Update()
    Dim v As Variant
    lstItems.Clear
    For Each v In coll
        Dim p As Product
        Set p = v
        lstItems.AddItem Str$(v.ProductID) + " " + v.Description + _
            " $" + Str$(v.UnitCost)
    Next
End Sub

Private Sub Form_Load()
    Set coll = New Products
    Update
End Sub
```

The next thing to do is add two change event handlers for the text boxes:

```
Private Sub txtCost_Change()
    cmdAdd.Enabled = (Len(txtItem) > 0 And Len(txtCost) > 0)
End Sub

Private Sub txtItem_Change()
    cmdAdd.Enabled = (Len(txtItem) > 0 And Len(txtCost) > 0)
End Sub
```

This ensures that the **Add** button can only be clicked when there is text in both text boxes. You can then implement the **Add** command button as follows:

```
Private Sub cmdAdd_Click()
    Dim prod As New Product
    prod.Description = txtItem.Text
    prod.UnitCost = Val(txtCost.Text)

    If lstItems.ListCount > 0 Then
        Dim lastProd As Product
        Set lastProd = coll.Item(lstItems.ListCount)
        prod.ProductID = lastProd.ProductID + 1
    Else
        prod.ProductID = 1
    End If

    coll.Add prod
    cmdAdd.Enabled = False
    txtItem.Text = ""
    txtCost.Text = ""

    Update
End Sub
```

This creates a new `Product` and initializes it with the data from the text boxes. The product ID is obtained by incrementing the `ProductID` of the last item in the list. Finally, add a click handler for the list box to enable the **Remove** button and implement it like this:

```
Private Sub lstItems_Click()
    cmdRemove.Enabled = True
End Sub

Private Sub cmdRemove_Click()
    coll.Remove lstItems.ListIndex + 1
    cmdRemove.Enabled = False
    Update
End Sub
```

`ListIndex` is the index of the selected item, *starting at* 0. Since Visual Basic collections are indexed from 1, the value is incremented.

With this code you can view and edit the collection.

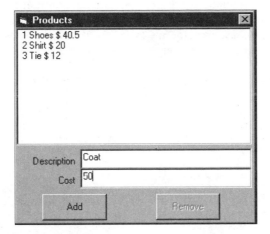

Visual C++

The Visual C++ example will not have quite as many facilities as the Visual Basic example. Instead, I'll mirror the VBScript example given earlier. The example uses a console application and the Visual C++ Compiler support classes, but you could just as easily create an MFC dialog project with a list box and add the items to that.

When you create the project, use the Win32 Console Application from the AppWizard and select A "Hello, World!" application. The AppWizard will just give you basic library support, so open stdafx.h and add a line including windows.h so that you can call the COM API functions.

Add this code to the top of the main source file:

```
#include "stdafx.h"
#import "..\..\DataAccess\DataAccess.tlb" no_namespace

void PrintValues(IEnumVARIANT* pEnum)
{
    _variant_t varArray[5];
    ULONG ulFetched = 1;
    pEnum->Reset();

    while (ulFetched > 0)
    {
        pEnum->Next(5, varArray, &ulFetched);
        for (ULONG ul = 0; ul < ulFetched; ul++)
        {
            IProductPtr pProd;
            pProd = varArray[ul].pdispVal;
            _bstr_t bstrDesc = pProd->Description;
            CURRENCY cyCost = pProd->UnitCost;
            double dCost;
            VarR8FromCy(cyCost, &dCost);
            printf("%ld\t%S\t$%.2lf\n", pProd->ProductID,
                    static_cast<LPWSTR>(bstrDesc), dCost);
            varArray[ul].Clear();
        }
    }
}
```

The #import line accesses the type library generated in the DataAccess project — you should check to see if the relative path is correct for your project. PrintValues() obtains all the Product objects in the collection passed through the interface pointer parameter. I have used the Visual C++ utility classes _bstr_t and _variant_t to manage resources for me, as well as the wrapper classes IProductPtr and IProductsPtr generated by #import.

The code that obtains the enumerator and manipulates the collection is shown here:

```
int main(int argc, char* argv[])
{
    CoInitialize(NULL);

    try
    {
        IProductsPtr pColl(__uuidof(Products));
        IEnumVARIANTPtr pEnum;

        pEnum = pColl->_NewEnum;

        printf("Initial contents\n");
        PrintValues(pEnum);

        IProductPtr pProd(__uuidof(Product));
        _bstr_t bstrDesc(L"Coat");
        pProd->ProductID = 4;
        pProd->Description = bstrDesc;
        CURRENCY cyCost;
        VarCyFromR8(50.00, &cyCost);
        pProd->UnitCost = cyCost;

        IDispatchPtr pDisp = pProd;
        _variant_t var(static_cast<IDispatch*>(pDisp));

        //add new product
        pColl->Add(var);
        //remove first item
        pColl->Remove(1);

        printf("New contents\n");
        PrintValues(pEnum);
    }
    catch(_com_error e)
    {
        printf("Error %s (0x%08x)\n");
    }

    CoUninitialize();
    return 0;
}
```

The first thing to notice here is how complicated the code is compared with Visual Basic or VBScript. This clearly shows that collections were designed for VB rather than C++.

The code creates a Products object and then obtains the enumerator. Notice that pColl->_NewEnum returns an IUnknownPtr object. You need to convert this to an IEnumVARIANTPtr object. This is carried out by the assignment operator in the line:

```
pEnum = pColl->_NewEnum;
```

After printing out the contents of the collection, the code adds a new `Product` and then removes the first one in the collection. Notice all the messing around with `IDispatchPtr` objects. This is because `Add()` needs a `VARIANT`, so we need to create one and initialize it with the `IDispatch` pointer on the `Product` object.

> The cast to `IDispatch*` is required because of a feature of `_variant_t`. This class has two constructors, one has an `IDispatch*` parameter and the other an `IUnknown*` parameter. Since `IDispatch` is derived from `IUnknown`, the compiler does not know which to use when passed an `IDispatchPtr` object. This ambiguity has to be resolved with a cast.

When compiled, this project gives the following results on the command prompt:

```
C:\>vctest
Initial contents
1       Shoes   $40.50
2       Shirt   $20.00
3       Tie     $12.00
New contents
2       Shirt   $20.00
3       Tie     $12.00
4       Coat    $50.00
```

Summary

In this chapter I have shown you how to create a new ATL project and how to implement a simple collection using the ATL 3.0 `ICollectionOnSTLImpl<>` template. This object was then tested using VBScript, Visual Basic and Visual C++ where it became clear that collections were designed for Visual Basic rather than C++.

In the next chapter, I will explain how ATL-implemented objects are created. This leads on to how you can implement class factories and how you can create objects in an ATL object's methods.

3

Creating Objects

Introduction

In the last chapter, you saw how to create a new ATL project. The chapter glossed over how objects are actually created, because that's the very purpose of this chapter! As you'll see, there are several ways to create objects. The most useful involves COM's ability to find and launch the object server before asking it to create the object, requiring object registration. ATL ensures that objects and their interfaces are correctly registered as explained in Appendix B, so to a certain extent you don't have to worry about this. This chapter will concentrate on facilities that ATL provides to ensure your objects are created, both externally, and in your own code.

When a COM object is created by an external client, an object called a **class factory** (sometimes also known as a **class object**) is used. ATL will provide the code necessary to do this for every object that you add to your server. However, there are situations where you will want to create your own class factories. You might want to do this if, for example, you wanted to implement licensing, or maybe some object tracking code. ATL gives you the tools to do this, and in most cases generates the bulk of the required code for you.

Object Creation

So, how are these objects actually created? The most important way involves COM using API calls like `CoCreateInstanceEx()`. This function creates a new instance of an object by resolving the object's CLSID into the name of a server. This can occur locally or via a remote machine. If the server is already running (and marked for multiple use) COM will use it. If this is not the case then the COM runtime will load the server automatically. Whichever is the case, COM will attempt to get a reference to the class factory for the object and ask it to create an instance.

For EXE servers the class factory object is a *static object* in that it's created when the server starts and lives as long as the server does. For DLL servers the class factory object is created when COM calls `DllGetClassObject()` and is created in the apartment that called `CoCreateInstanceEx()`.

COM will keep the class factory alive as long as the DLL server is loaded, so if you call `CoFreeUnusedLibraries()` or `CoUninitialize()` the class factory object will be released. If your client calls `CoCreateInstanceEx()` then COM will query the class factory object for `IClassFactory` or `IClassFactory2` and call either `CreateInstance()` or `CreateInstanceLic()` to create an instance of the object.

Your class factory can have a different interface, but it means that the object cannot be created with `CoCreateInstanceEx()`. Instead you need to call `CoGetClassObject()` to get access to its class factory and then call its interface directly. ATL gives you support for custom class factories as well, allowing you to easily implement the `IClassFactory` interface. However, in both cases COM is involved in the object creation process. There is another way that objects can be created: where one object creates and distributes instances of others.

Creatable and Noncreatable Objects

This title is misleading. All objects are creatable (there would not be much use for an object that you cannot create!), but there are some that should not be *externally* creatable. By this I mean that some objects are designed to be created by external clients through calls to `CoCreateInstanceEx()` (or the object's class factory). Some objects are not designed to be created externally, in which case the client has to request one from another object.

For example, imagine an `AttendenceRegister` object containing information about the students in a class, enabling a class attendance record to be kept. This object could also be made capable of returning information on a specific student via a `Student` object initialized with the student's details. This can be implemented as follows:

```
STDMETHODIMP CAttendenceRegister::GetStudent(BSTR bstrName,
                                             IStudent** pStudent)
{
    HRESULT hr;
    CComObject<CStudent>* pObj;
    hr = CComObject<CStudent>::CreateInstance(&pObj);
    if (FAILED(hr))
        return hr;
    pObj->InternalInitialize(bstrName);
    hr = pObj->QueryInterface(&pStudent);    // uses the type safe QI
    if (FAILED(hr))
        delete pObj;
    return hr;
}
```

Here I create an instance of `CComObject<CStudent>` through the static method `CreateInstance()`. This *does not* use `CoCreateInstanceEx()` and it does not use the COM runtime. It creates an instance of a C++ object that has all the facilities of a COM object, from which, you could get an interface pointer that an external client could use.

`CComObject<>` adds an implementation of `IUnknown` to `CStudent` so that a C++ instance of the class can be created. `CreateInstance()` calls the default constructor of the `CStudent` class, so to initialize the object, I call a C++ method.

> Note that this is a C++ object created on the heap, so you do not have to
> call methods through interface pointers when you access it from within
> the module that creates it.

However, external clients can only access the object through an interface pointer. At this point the object has a zero reference count, so the code calls `QueryInterface()` to get the `IStudent` interface pointer that the client requires, incrementing the reference count in the process. If this call fails, the C++ object is deleted to prevent resource leaks.

Note that `QueryInterface()` has just one parameter in the code above. This is because, in Visual C++ 6, MIDL will add a typesafe version of `QueryInterface()` to all interfaces that it compiles. In addition, it applies `__declspec(uuid())` to the C++ binding classes so that you can determine an interface's ID with `__uuidof()`. The typesafe version of `QueryInterface()` is just a wrapper method (it's not part of the vtable) that uses `__uuidof()` on its parameter and passes this and the out pointer to the actual `QueryInterface()`. This method solves a nasty potential problem where you could query for one interface and put it in an interface pointer of another type. More details are given in Appendix K.

`CComObject<>` implements `Release()` so that when the reference count changes from 1 to 0, the heap object is deleted. Because the object's lifetime is managed by `AddRef()` and `Release()` and it gives access to other interfaces through `QueryInterface()`, it's a fully fledged COM object.

You may decide that a `Student` object is useful and so allow external clients to create instances in the normal way. If this is the case, then you don't have to do anything about the object creation process. ATL ensures that all objects added with the Object Wizard are externally creatable. However, if the external client wants to initialize the object it can do so only through an interface, because an external client cannot call the C++ `InternalInitialize()` method (remember, I said it was not a method on an interface). Instead, the object could implement an interface like `IPersistStreamInit` that is designed to allow you to initialize an object or to add an initialization method to an interface. However, the disadvantage of this is that the object is now a read/write object, which may not have been your intention. You might want the user of a `Student` object to be able to change the student's name, but if not, then you should make the object **noncreatable**.

Noncreatable

To make an object noncreatable, you must edit the object map and the project's IDL (and, optionally, the ATL class). Appendix A gives details of this procedure, but I'll give an overview here. The object map that needs to be edited is contained in the main `.cpp` file. It contains an `OBJECT_ENTRY()` macro for your object, which needs to be replaced with `OBJECT_ENTRY_NON_CREATEABLE()`. This allows the object to be registered (so that it has a registry entry that COM will use for information about the object, like the categories it implements or requires). It also prevents the object from being created externally.

However, it's also prudent to mark the object as noncreatable with the [noncreatable] attribute on the coclass in the project's IDL. This indicates to tools like Visual Basic that you cannot create these objects. In a similar vein, you can remove the CComCoClass<> base class from the ATL object because this class is *mainly* used to provide external creation support. If you do this you also remove the convenience of the Error() method for throwing error objects (explained in the next chapter) You can still throw them, but you will have to call AtlReportError() directly.

Example: Improvements to Add() and Remove()

The example in the last chapter showed how you can give access to a collection of Product objects and then add and remove products from the collection. To add a product you had to externally create a Product object, initialize it and then call Add(). There are problems with this approach. The Automation specification says that the object passed to Add() is added to the collection (rather than a copy being made). Thus, once a new product has been added to the collection, an external client could change its properties without notifying the collection object.

However, the Automation specification also says that the collection object itself can create the object, using information passed by the client, and then add it to the collection. Since the collection object creates a Product object, it should return it to the client. However, this new object can be read-only, preventing the client from making any changes.

To do this you need to edit the IDL file and change IProducts::Add() to the following:

```
[id(2)] HRESULT Add([in] BSTR strDesc, [in] double dCost,
                    [out, retval] VARIANT* pVar);
```

Here, the client passes data that the collection will use to initialize the new object, which it then returns to the client in a VARIANT. You will also need to change the CProducts header:

```
STDMETHOD(Add)(BSTR strDesc, double dCost, VARIANT* pVar);
```

The method is implemented like this:

```
STDMETHODIMP CProducts::Add(BSTR strDesc, double dCost, VARIANT* pVar)
{
    USES_CONVERSION;
    CComObject<CProduct>* pObj;
    CComObject<CProduct>::CreateInstance(&pObj);
    CComVariant var;

    long prodID = 0;
    if (!m_coll.empty())
    {
        VarVector::iterator it;
        it = m_coll.end();
        it--;
        CComPtr<IProduct> pProduct = com_cast<IProduct>((*it).pdispVal);
        pProduct->get_ProductID(&prodID);
    }
```

```
    var = pObj;    // QIs for IDispatch
    pObj->Initialize(++prodID, W2T(strDesc), dCost);
    m_coll.push_back(var);
    var.Detach(pVar);
    return S_OK;
}
```

In this code the object is created by the collection object (without calling
`CoCreateInstance()`), put into a `VARIANT` and initialized. I have made sure that
the `ProductID` is unique by reading the last item in the `vector` and incrementing its
`ProductID`. The collection holds `CComVariants` which contain `IDispatch` pointers
of the objects. To access the properties of the objects you need to extract the
`IDispatch` pointer and then query for the `IProduct` interface.

Utilizing a Smart Pointer

In this code I use the ATL `com_cast<>`. This is defined in `atlbase.h` as:

```
#define com_cast CComQIPtr
```

Hence, the above line is actually:

```
CComPtr<IProduct> pProduct = CComQIPtr<IProduct>((*it).pdispVal);
```

Smart pointers are explained in depth in Appendix K but basically, the parameter to
the template specifies the interface type that the smart pointer will hold. When you
pass an interface pointer of a different type to the constructor of `CComQIPtr<>` it will
call `QueryInterface()` to get the required interface. Thus, the right-hand side of the
assignment will obtain the `IProduct` interface from the `pDispVal` interface pointer.
The assignment then copies the pointer into `pProduct`.

> As you can see, `com_cast<>` behaves like the C++ cast operators
> (`dynamic_cast<>` etc) and makes your code more readable.

Utilizing ProductID

The current version of the `Remove()` method removes items according to their
position in the `vector`. However, it would be far more intuitive to remove items using
their `ProductID`. To do this, I have changed the name of the parameter of `Remove()`
to `lProdID` and implemented the method by searching through the STL container for
the object with the appropriate `ProductID` before removing it:

```
STDMETHODIMP CProducts::Remove(long lProdID)
{
    VarVector::iterator it;
    it = std::find_if(m_coll.begin(), m_coll.end(), FindProd(lProdID));
    if (it == m_coll.end())
        return E_INVALIDARG;
    m_coll.erase(it);
    return S_OK;
}
```

Here I use the STL `std::find_if()` algorithm to find the item in the `vector` that satisfies the predicate `FindProd`. If the item has been found, it is removed from the `vector` with `erase()`.

The predicator is declared in `Products.h` with:

```
#include <algorithm>

class FindProd
{
    long m_lProdID;
public:
    FindProd(long lProdID) : m_lProdID(lProdID)
    {}
    bool operator()(VARIANT var) const
    {
        CComQIPtr<IProduct> pProd = var.pdispVal;
        long prodID;
        pProd->get_ProductID(&prodID);
        return (m_lProdID == prodID);
    }
};
```

`std::find_if()` iterates through the items in the `vector` and passes each one to `FindProd::operator()()`. This checks the item to see if its `ProductID` is the same as the value passed to the constructor. If it is, it will stop `std::find_if()`'s search. This is clearly inefficient for large collections and so it would be better to change the STL container type to, for example, a `std::map<>` that can be searched quicker. For now, I will keep the current type.

Closing all the Doors

The client no longer needs to create `Product` objects, so the next task is to make the object `noncreatable` using the method described in the previous section. The first thing to do is to open `DataAccess.cpp` and edit the object map:

```
BEGIN_OBJECT_MAP(ObjectMap)
OBJECT_ENTRY(CLSID_Products, CProducts)
OBJECT_ENTRY_NON_CREATEABLE(CProduct)
END_OBJECT_MAP()
```

This prevents access to the class factory. The next action is to edit the project's IDL and mark the `coclass` as `noncreatable`. This is a courtesy to tools like Visual Basic to remind them that the object does not have a class factory:

```
[
    uuid(75FB4A43-5E90-11D2-99FC-00104BDC361E),
    noncreatable
]
coclass Product
{
    [default] interface IProduct;
};
```

While you are in the IDL file, edit `IProduct` and remove all the `propput` methods (to make the properties read-only) so that it looks like this:

```
interface IProduct : IDispatch
{
    [propget, id(1)] HRESULT ProductID([out, retval] long *pVal);
    [propget, id(2)] HRESULT Description([out, retval] BSTR *pVal);
    [propget, id(3)] HRESULT UnitCost([out, retval] CURRENCY *pVal);
};
```

This ensures that clients can only read the object's properties and cannot write them. You will also need to edit `Product.h`, removing the `put_` methods, and then remove their bodies from `Product.cpp`. Now the only way to initialize the properties of this object is to use the `Initialize()` C++ method, and since this is not a member of the `IProduct` interface it means that only *internal* code can initialize the object.

Now remove `CComCoClass<>` as a base class. This will make the code slightly smaller, but will also remove the convenience of the `Error()` method. Since the code does not use this, it's not a problem.

```
class ATL_NO_VTABLE CProduct :
    public CComObjectRootEx<CComMultiThreadModel>,
    // the object is noncreatable.
    // public CComCoClass<CProduct, &CLSID_Product>,
    public IDispatchImpl<IProduct, &IID_IProduct, &LIBID_DATAACCESSLib>
```

However, the `CComCoClass<>` template implements an empty category map which your class inherited. Removing the base class means that the object no longer has a category map (to specify what COM categories it implements or requires) and thus the class will not compile. To solve this problem, you need to add the following lines of code:

```
public:
BEGIN_CATEGORY_MAP(CProduct)
END_CATEGORY_MAP()
```

`Product` objects cannot be created externally, so you should not register them. By default the Object Wizard will add a macro to `CProduct` to specify the RGS script (held as a resource) that is used. Replace this macro (shown commented out) with:

```
// DECLARE_REGISTRY_RESOURCEID(IDR_PRODUCT)
DECLARE_NO_REGISTRY()
```

Since the RGS file is no longer needed, you can remove it from the project's resources (look in the `"REGISTRY"` types). Now you should be able to compile the entire project.

Visual Basic Client Test

As a test, let's change the Visual Basic project from the last chapter to use the new versions of `Add()` and `Remove()`. The changes are simple:

```
Private Sub cmdAdd_Click()
    coll.Add txtItem.Text, Val(txtCost.Text)
    cmdAdd.Enabled = False
    txtItem.Text = ""
    txtCost.Text = ""

    Update
End Sub
...
Private Sub cmdRemove_Click()
    Dim item As String
    item = LTrim(lstItems.List(lstItems.ListIndex))
    item = Left(item, InStr(item, " "))
    coll.Remove Val(item)
    cmdRemove.Enabled = False

    Update
End Sub
```

The cmdAdd_Click handler is simpler than before, it just passes the values from the list boxes to the Add() method. The cmdRemove_Click handler is a little more complicated because the parameter passed to Remove() is the ProductID, not the index in the collection. The strings that are added to the list box have the ProductID as the first part of the string. To extract this parameter the code merely trims off any leading spaces and the characters after the first separating space. You should be able to run the application and add or remove items from the collection.

While you are in the Visual Basic IDE, as a final test, try to type the following:

```
Dim prod As New Product ' just a test, delete afterwards
```

You will find that after you type New, the line completion facility of Visual Basic will bring up a list box but it won't contain a Product entry. The reason for this is that Visual Basic knows that this object is noncreatable, so it won't allow you to add the object name. However, Product will show up in the Object Browser because you will want to access Product objects that have been created by the Products object.

Class Factories

As mentioned earlier, the usual way to create an object is to use a class factory object. When your class derives from CComCoClass<> (which is the default for an object created by the Object Wizard) you will automatically get support from CComClassFactory. There will be occasions when you will want to change the class factory that's used by your object. Appendix G explains both how to do this and the options that are available. The basic technique involves the addition of a class factory macro to the class declaration.

One of the options is to create a **singleton** object. Singletons are an accepted pattern, but their use is controversial. It is clear that the singleton behavior is useful, but the actual singleton implementation results in a performance problem. The reason for this is that by their nature they are designed for multiple clients, which can result in a bottleneck. Another problem is that an ATL EXE singleton is only a singleton on a single machine. You can install the object on several machines and use DCOM to choose which one should be used — clearly not a network-wide singleton behavior.

There are ways to alleviate this, which are outlined in Appendix G. In this section I will explain how to create a singleton object that will be used to log messages to a persistent store.

Example: an Event Logging Singleton

The event logging object interface abstracts the logging of an event. The event could be logged to the NT Event Log, to a database, or, as in this case, to a compound file; the implementation is immaterial to the client.

> I have decided to use a compound file because it means that it can be run on Win9x machines. Note that if you decide to use the NT Event Log to log the events then you don't need to use a singleton, because the Event Log Service handles concurrency. Similarly, if the events are logged to a database, you don't need to use a singleton because the database will also handle concurrency issues.

In this example the logger object is a singleton and is thus available to all clients on the local machine. To do this the object should be implemented in an EXE so that only one instance is ever created. An option here is to create an NT service project, meaning that it is run when NT first boots, ensuring that the object is always available. However, this requires an NT machine.

Start by creating an EXE project called `EventLogger` and then add an ATL simple object called `Events`. Make sure that the object's interface is dual and that it uses the **Free** threading model from the **Attributes** tab. The `Events` object will be a collection of `Event` objects so add this simple object with the Object Wizard, also with a dual interface and using the **Free** threading model.

The project will use the free threading model to make it more scaleable — COM will manage a pool of RPC threads to service requests to class factories and objects. All you need to do to implement this is to edit `stdafx.h` and replace the `_ATL_APARTMENT_THREADED` symbol with `_ATL_FREE_THREADED`. This makes sure that the server has an MTA. The **Free** threading model in Object Wizard specifies that the object is safe to use with the MTA. There is another important ingredient: for the object to be a singleton you have to ensure that when multiple clients request a reference, the same EXE instance will be used. ATL ensures this by default by registering the class factories with `REGCLS_MULTIPLEUSE` in `_tWinMain()`.

Setting Events

The `Event` objects have the following read-only properties, which you should add to the `IEvent` interface with ClassView:

Property	Type	Description
Date	DATE	Date that `Events` logged the `Event`
Message	BSTR	The event message
Severity	long	0 = Information, 1 = Error

> Since these properties (and hence the state) of the object are read-only, this object is a prime candidate to use marshal-by-value. This optimization technique will not be covered in this book, but if you are interested, *Professional ATL COM Programming* gives you all the details that you need.

Add the following function and data members to the `Event` object:

```
public:
    void Initialize(DATE dDate, BSTR bstrMsg, long lSeverity);
private:
    DATE m_dDate;
    CComBSTR m_bstrMsg;
    long m_lSeverity;
};
```

Initialize() will be used by Add() to initialize the object with a DATE, BSTR and long before adding it to the collection. The constructor must be modified to set these members to zero. Implement the object's methods and member function like this (notice the handy CHECK_OUT_PARAM() macro!):

```
#define CHECK_OUT_PARAM(p) \
    if (p == NULL) return E_POINTER;

STDMETHODIMP CEvent::get_Date(DATE *pVal)
{
    CHECK_OUT_PARAM(pVal);
    *pVal = m_dDate;
    return S_OK;
}

STDMETHODIMP CEvent::get_Message(BSTR *pVal)
{
    CHECK_OUT_PARAM(pVal);
    return m_bstrMsg.CopyTo(pVal);
}

STDMETHODIMP CEvent::get_Severity(long *pVal)
{
    CHECK_OUT_PARAM(pVal);
    *pVal = m_lSeverity;
    return S_OK;
}

void CEvent::Initialize(DATE dDate, BSTR bstrMsg, long lSeverity)
{
    m_dDate = dDate;
    m_bstrMsg = bstrMsg;
    m_lSeverity = lSeverity;
}
```

Finally, make the Event object noncreatable as you did with the Product object (change the IDL file, modify the object map in EventLogger.cpp, add an empty category map to Event.h, remove the CComCoClass<> base class, remove the registration macro and remove the RGS from the resources).

Collection

The Events collection object will need to be able to obtain information from a source other than an STL container and use it to initialize the Event objects. Because of this, you cannot use ICollectionOnSTLImpl<>. Also, the enumerator will be 'dynamic' — the items will be returned in chronological order and will reflect current items. The upshot of this is that you will have to implement the collection yourself.

Add the following method to IEvents:

Method	Parameters
Add	[in] BSTR bstrMsg, [in] LogSeverity lSeverity

Notice that I have not said to add a Remove() method. This is because the object is only used to add new events or access existing events. Add() logs an event which has a message and a severity which is specified by the following enum. You should add this to the IDL file before IEvents.

```
typedef enum LogSeverity
{
   SEV_INFO  = 0,
   SEV_ERROR = 1
} LogSeverity;
```

This strange syntax is required because MIDL does not allow anonymous enums. Add the following data members to the CEvents class:

```
private:
   CComPtr<IStorage> m_pStg;   // doc file root storage
   CComPtr<IStream> m_pStm;    // stream to hold the current record number
```

The Compounded File

The structure of the compound file (called Data.dat) is shown in the following diagram:

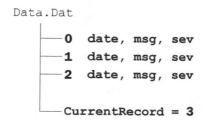

```
Data.Dat
         ┌───── 0  date, msg, sev
         ├───── 1  date, msg, sev
         ├───── 2  date, msg, sev
         │
         └───── CurrentRecord = 3
```

Each event message is added to the root of the compound file as a stream. The name of this stream is a number that is incremented sequentially. The number of the next record that can be added is saved in a stream called CurrentRecord. Hence, when a new record is added, the code can simply read the value in CurrentRecord and then create the new stream.

The compound file is opened in FinalConstruct(). If it does not exist then the code creates the file. When the Events object is destroyed, it closes the compound file so that the data is persisted until the next time the Events object is created. The root storage of this document (equivalent to the HFILE handle of a Win32 file) is saved in the smart pointer m_pStg. When the object is destroyed, the destructor of m_pStg is called which will release the root storage and hence close the file. Smart pointers are covered in Appendix K.

Function Override

Similarly, the pointer to the CurrentRecord stream is held in the m_pStm smart pointer so that it can be accessed in the code. FinalConstruct() is called automatically as part of ATL's two stage construction and is inherited from CComObjectRootBase. Override this function by adding the following code to the public section of the CEvents class definition in Events.h:

```
HRESULT FinalConstruct()
{
   HRESULT hr;
   hr = StgOpenStorage(L"Data.dat", NULL,
               STGM_READWRITE | STGM_SHARE_DENY_WRITE | STGM_TRANSACTED,
               NULL, 0, &m_pStg);
   if (FAILED(hr))
   {
      hr = StgCreateDocfile(L"Data.dat",
               STGM_READWRITE | STGM_SHARE_DENY_WRITE | STGM_TRANSACTED,
               0, &m_pStg);
      if (FAILED(hr))
         return hr;
   }
   hr = m_pStg->OpenStream(L"CurrentRecord", NULL,
               STGM_READWRITE | STGM_SHARE_EXCLUSIVE, 0, &m_pStm);
   if (FAILED(hr))
   {
      hr = m_pStg->CreateStream(L"CurrentRecord",
               STGM_READWRITE | STGM_SHARE_EXCLUSIVE, 0, 0, &m_pStm);
      if (FAILED(hr))
         return hr;
      ULONG count = 0;
      m_pStm->Write(&count, sizeof(ULONG), NULL);
   }
   m_pStg->Commit(STGC_DEFAULT);
   return S_OK;
}
```

The Add() method needs to read the current record number, create a stream and then write the data to it. The following code does this, and needs to be added in Events.cpp:

```
STDMETHODIMP CEvents::Add(BSTR bstrMsg, long lSeverity)
{
   SYSTEMTIME st;
   GetLocalTime(&st);
   DATE dDate;
   SystemTimeToVariantTime(&st, &dDate);

   LARGE_INTEGER li;
   li.LowPart = 0;
   li.HighPart = 0;

   CComPtr<IStream> pStm;

   //only one thread here
   g_csCount.Lock();
   m_pStm->Seek(li, STREAM_SEEK_SET, NULL);
   ULONG ulRec;
   m_pStm->Read(&ulRec, sizeof(ULONG), NULL);
   ulRec++;
   m_pStm->Seek(li, STREAM_SEEK_SET, NULL);
   m_pStm->Write(&ulRec, sizeof(ULONG), NULL);
   m_pStg->Commit(STGC_DEFAULT);
   g_csCount.Unlock();

   CComVariant varDate;
   CComVariant varMsg;
   CComVariant varSev;
   varDate = dDate;
   varMsg = bstrMsg;
   varSev = lSeverity;

   TCHAR strName[20];
   wsprintf(strName, _T("%ld"), ulRec - 1);
```

```
USES_CONVERSION;
g_csData.Lock();
m_pStg->CreateStream(T2OLE(strName), STGM_WRITE | STGM_SHARE_EXCLUSIVE,
                     0, 0, &pStm);
varDate.WriteToStream(pStm);
varMsg.WriteToStream(pStm);
varSev.WriteToStream(pStm);
m_pStg->Commit(STGC_DEFAULT);
g_csData.Unlock();
return S_OK;
}
```

This code reads the current record number from the `CurrentRecord` stream and converts it to a string using `wsprintf()`. If you compile this with UNICODE then `strName` will be UNICODE, otherwise it will be ANSI. `CreateStream()` takes an `LPOLESTR`, i.e. UNICODE, so the ATL `T2OLE()` macro is used to make the conversion. ATL conversion macros are covered in Appendix M.

Refining the Thread

Since the object is free threaded (it runs in an MTA), global data must be protected. You may find that the code for `Add()` is not in an order that makes it easily readable. This is because I have bunched together those calls that access the data file and hence should run within a single thread. I have identified two sections of such code: the first obtains the current record number and the other creates the stream and writes the data. I have chosen to use two critical section objects, so that while one thread is obtaining the record number, another could be writing data.

`g_csCount` and `g_csData` are global objects because they will be used to synchronize with other objects in the project. They need to be declared in `stdafx.h` as `extern`:

```
#include <atlcom.h>
extern CComAutoCriticalSection g_csCount;
extern CComAutoCriticalSection g_csData;
```

and in `EventLogger.cpp`:

```
CComAutoCriticalSection g_csCount;
CComAutoCriticalSection g_csData;
const DWORD dwTimeOut = 5000;
const DWORD dwPause = 1000;
```

Writing to the stream is simplicity itself: the `CComVariant` wrapper class (explained in Appendix K) wraps an automation `VARIANT` and has methods to write its data to a specified stream.

The `Events` object should be available to all users and to make it a singleton you should add the following code to `CEvents`:

```
DECLARE_REGISTRY_RESOURCEID(IDR_EVENTS)
DECLARE_CLASSFACTORY_SINGLETON(CEvents)
DECLARE_PROTECT_FINAL_CONSTRUCT()
```

The object also needs the following property, which you should add to IEvents using the Class View:

Property	Property Type
_NewEnum	LPUNKNOWN

This property is read-only and you should edit the IDL so that the ID of _NewEnum is DISPID_NEWENUM.

Notice that there are no Item or Count properties. These are not required to make the object into a collection and they are not needed in this design. The _NewEnum property will return an enumerator of Event objects, which represent the events that have been logged. However, the enumerator object *is not a singleton*. The reason for this is that the enumerator will hold the current position, representing how many items have been read, so if there are several clients they will need separate current positions.

Custom Enumeration

The enumerator object won't use the ATL enumerator classes, so, we can have greater control over how it works. Create a new ATL simple object called EnumEvents, again with the Free threading model, but this time make sure that it has a custom interface. This is because you will delete the interface that is generated by the Object Wizard and use IEnumVARIANT instead. Since this is not a dual interface, you don't need support for duals in the class.

Once the Object Wizard has finished, edit the IDL to remove the IEnumEvents interface and edit the coclass to look like this:

```
coclass EnumEvents
{
    [default] interface IUnknown;
};
```

The coclass entry in the library section is useful because MIDL will generate the CLSID constant from it.

You now need to edit the header for CEnumEvents by replacing the references to IEnumEvents with IEnumVARIANT. Also, remove the CComCoClass<> base class and add a category map to make the object noncreatable:

```
class ATL_NO_VTABLE CEnumEvents :
    public CComObjectRootEx<CComMultiThreadModel>,
    public IEnumVARIANT
{
public:
CEnumEvents()
    {
    }

// DECLARE_REGISTRY_RESOURCEID(IDR_ENUMEVENTS)
    DECLARE_NO_REGISTRY()

DECLARE_PROTECT_FINAL_CONSTRUCT()

BEGIN_COM_MAP(CEnumEvents)
    COM_INTERFACE_ENTRY(IEnumVARIANT)
END_COM_MAP()
```

```
BEGIN_CATEGORY_MAP(CEnumEvents)
END_CATEGORY_MAP()
```

Use the DECLARE_NO_REGISTRY() macro to prevent registration and remove the IDR_ENUMEVENTS resource. In addition, edit the object map in EventLogger.cpp and the IDL to make this object noncreatable.

It may seem a lot of work to go through to add an interface, but you have no choice because the interface is not oleautomation compatible, and so cannot be successfully described in a type library. This means that you cannot use the interface wizard (Appendix D), and you will have to add the enumerator methods to EnumEvents.h yourself:

```
public:
    STDMETHOD(Next)(ULONG celt, VARIANT* rgVar, ULONG* pCeltFetched),
    STDMETHOD(Skip)(ULONG celt);
    STDMETHOD(Reset)();
    STDMETHOD(Clone)(IEnumVARIANT** ppEnum);
```

The object will need access to the compound file, and so will need to hold storage and stream pointers as data members. In addition, the object needs to keep the current position in the file. Add the following lines to EnumEvents.h:

```
public:
    ULONG m_ulRecPos;
    CComPtr<IStorage> m_pStg;
    CComPtr<IStream> m_pStm;
};
```

I have made these data members public so that I can access them when the object is created without requiring accessor methods. The current position should be initialized to zero in the constructor:

```
CEnumEvents() : m_ulRecPos(0)
{
}
```

The first record in the file is 0, so that makes the Reset() method easy to implement. Simply add this code to EnumEvents.cpp:

```
STDMETHODIMP CEnumEvents::Reset()
{
    m_ulRecPos = 0;
    return S_OK;
}
```

Skip() needs to move the current position. If this goes past the end of the file, the enumerator is set to the last item. This involves reading the number of records in the file and so synchronization is carried out using g_csCount:

```
STDMETHODIMP CEnumEvents::Skip(ULONG celt)
{
    //get the record count
    LARGE_INTEGER li;
    li.LowPart = 0;
    li.HighPart = 0;
    ULONG ulRec;

    g_csCount.Lock();
    m_pStm->Seek(li, STREAM_SEEK_SET, NULL);
    m_pStm->Read(&ulRec, sizeof(ULONG), NULL);
    g_csCount.Unlock();
```

```
    if (m_ulRecPos + celt <= ulRec)
    {
        m_ulRecPos += celt;
        return S_OK;
    }
    m_ulRecPos = ulRec;
    return S_FALSE;
}
```

The Clone() method should make a copy of the enumerator, including state information such as the current position. This code creates a new instance and then initializes the public data members with those in the current object:

```
STDMETHODIMP CEnumEvents::Clone(IEnumVARIANT** ppEnum)
{
    HRESULT hr;
    CComObject<CEnumEvents>* pObj;
    CComObject<CEnumEvents>::CreateInstance(&pObj);
    pObj->m_ulRecPos = m_ulRecPos;
    pObj->m_pStg = m_pStg;
    pObj->m_pStm = m_pStm;
    hr = pObj->QueryInterface(ppEnum);
    if (FAILED(hr))
    {
        delete pObj;
        *ppEnum = NULL;
    }
    return hr;
}
```

Finally, the Next() method needs to access the data in the file. When it reads a record from the file it creates an Event object, initializes it with the data from the record and puts the object into the VARIANT passed from the client. Since this code creates Event objects, the .cpp file should include Event.h:

```
#include "stdafx.h"
#include "EventLogger.h"
#include "EnumEvents.h"
#include "Event.h"
```

```
...
```

```
STDMETHODIMP CEnumEvents::Next(ULONG celt, VARIANT* rgVar,
                                ULONG* pCeltFetched)
{
    if (rgVar == NULL || (celt != 1 && pCeltFetched == NULL))
        return E_POINTER;

    LARGE_INTEGER li;
    li.LowPart = 0;
    li.HighPart = 0;
    ULONG ulRecMax;

    g_csCount.Lock();
    m_pStm->Seek(li, STREAM_SEEK_SET, NULL);
    m_pStm->Read(&ulRecMax, sizeof(ULONG), NULL);
    g_csCount.Unlock();

    ULONG nRem = ulRecMax - m_ulRecPos;    //records remaining in the file
    HRESULT hr = S_OK;
    if (nRem < celt)
        hr = S_FALSE;

    ULONG nMin = min(celt, nRem);
    if (pCeltFetched != NULL)
        *pCeltFetched = nMin;
```

This first part of the function checks the input parameters to make sure that they have valid values — note that the COM specification says that pCeltFetched can be NULL if celt is 1. If there are fewer items in the file than the number requested then the method should return S_FALSE and return all the items that it can.

The next section of the function reads the data from the file by opening the appropriate stream:

```
VARIANT* pelt = rgVar;
for (ULONG pos = 0; pos < nMin; pos++)
{
    //get the data
    CComPtr<IStream> pStm;
    TCHAR strName[20];
    wsprintf(strName, _T("%ld"), pos + m_ulRecPos);
    CComVariant varDate;
    CComVariant varMsg;
    CComVariant varSev;

    USES_CONVERSION;
    g_csData.Lock();
    hr = m_pStg->OpenStream(T2OLE(strName), NULL,
                            STGM_READ | STGM_SHARE_EXCLUSIVE, 0, &pStm);
    if (SUCCEEDED(hr))
    {
        varDate.ReadFromStream(pStm);
        varMsg.ReadFromStream(pStm);
        varSev.ReadFromStream(pStm);
        g_csData.Unlock();
    }
    else
    {
        g_csData.Unlock();
        while (rgVar < pelt)
            VariantClear(rgVar++);
        if (pCeltFetched != NULL)
            *pCeltFetched = 0;
        return hr;
    }
```

This algorithm works well because the record numbers are continuous. If your collection allows a client to remove items then you will have to call IStorage::EnumElements to obtain the names of all the streams and then find the current position.

If the data was successfully read, the code must create an Event object and initialize it:

```
    CComObject<CEvent>* pObj;
    CComObject<CEvent>::CreateInstance(&pObj);
    pObj->Initialize(varDate.date, varMsg.bstrVal, varSev.lVal);
    IDispatch* pDisp;
    pObj->QueryInterface(&pDisp);
    pelt->pdispVal = pDisp;
    pelt->vt = VT_DISPATCH;
    pelt++;
}
m_ulRecPos += *pCeltFetched;
return hr;
}
```

Notice that the newly created object is queried for IDispatch and this is put into the VARIANT.

The final piece of code is to create an enumerator when IEvents::_NewEnum() is
called. To do this you need to include EnumEvents.h in Events.cpp and implement
the method like this:

```
#include "stdafx.h"
#include "EventLogger.h"
#include "Events.h"
#include "EnumEvents.h"

...

STDMETHODIMP CEvents::get__NewEnum(LPUNKNOWN *pVal)
{
    HRESULT hr;
    CComObject<CEnumEvents>* pObj;
    CComObject<CEnumEvents>::CreateInstance(&pObj);
    pObj->m_pStg = m_pStg;
    pObj->m_pStm = m_pStm;
    hr = pObj->QueryInterface(pVal);
    if (FAILED(hr))
        delete pObj;
    return hr;
}
```

This is similar to code that you have already seen. The only point worth noting is that
the storage and stream pointers of the Events object are copied to the enumerator so
that it has access to the file.

Trimming CRT
Before you compile this code, one more thing needs to be dealt with.
Remove _ATL_MIN_CRT as a preprocessor definition for all release builds (open
Project I Settings, select Multiple Configurations and select all of the release builds, then
select the C/C++ tab and, from the Preprocessor category, remove _ATL_MIN_CRT
from the Preprocessor definitions box).

This might appear to be an odd thing to have to do because this symbol is used to
prevent the CRT startup code from being used. However, if you try to compile the
project in a release build with this symbol defined then you will get errors, even
though the CRT is not being used. In fact you do need the CRT startup code, because
one of the things that it does is initialize global objects that have constructors — the
code here has the two CComAutoCriticalSection global objects that you added to
EventLogger.cpp.

Using the Event Logger
To test out the logger object you can change the Products object to log all changes to
the collection. So edit Products.h, include the EventLogger.h header and then
add a member to the CProducts class:

```
#include "product.h"
#include "..\EventLogger\EventLogger.h"

...

private:
    CComPtr<IEvents> m_pLogger;
};
```

The logger object is created in `FinalConstruct()`, which should also be added to the `CProducts` class:

```
HRESULT FinalConstruct()
{
    return m_pLogger.CoCreateInstance(__uuidof(Events));
}
```

`CComPtr<>::CoCreateInstance()` calls `CoCreateInstance()` and then puts the returned interface pointer into the `m_pLogger` smart pointer.

You can then change the `Add()` and `Remove()` methods to log the particular event. So add the following code to the end of `Add()`:

```
STDMETHODIMP CProducts::Add(BSTR strDesc, double dCost, VARIANT* pVar)
{
...
    var = pObj;    // QIs for IDispatch
    pObj->Initialize(++prodID, W2T(strDesc), dCost);
    m_coll.push_back(var);
    var.Detach(pVar);

    TCHAR str[20];
    wsprintf(str, _T(", $%.21f"), dCost);
    CComBSTR bstr = L"Added ";
    bstr += strDesc;
    bstr += str;
    m_pLogger->Add(bstr, SEV_INFO);
    return S_OK;
}
```

Add the following to `Remove()`

```
STDMETHODIMP CProducts::Remove(long lProdID)
{
    VarVector::iterator it;
    it = std::find_if(m_coll.begin(), m_coll.end(), FindProd(lProdID));
    if (it == m_coll.end())
        return E_INVALIDARG;
    m_coll.erase(it);

    CComBSTR bstr, bstr2 = L"Removed ";
    CComQIPtr<IProduct> pProduct = com_cast<IProduct>((*it).pdispVal);
    pProduct->get_Description(&bstr.m_str);
    bstr2 += bstr;
    m_pLogger->Add(bstr2, SEV_INFO);
    return S_OK;
}
```

To look at the contents of the log you can use the following simple Visual Basic application, which assumes that the form has two list boxes (called `lstInfo` and `lstError`) and a command button called `cmdRefresh`. Before entering the code, make sure you have selected the EventLogger 1.0 Type Library from the Project | References dialog.

```
Dim logger As Events

Private Sub cmdRefresh_Click()
    Dim v As Variant
    lstInfo.Clear
    lstError.Clear
    For Each v In logger
        Dim ev As EVENTLOGGERLib.Event
        Set ev = v
```

```
      If ev.Severity = 0 Then
          lstInfo.AddItem Str$(ev.Date) + " " + ev.Message
      Else
          lstError.AddItem Str$(ev.Date) + " " + ev.Message
      End If
   Next
End Sub

Private Sub Form_Load()
   Set logger = New events
End Sub
```

If the Products project is run at the same time, you should see results like this:

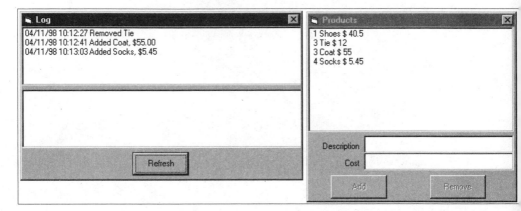

Summary

In this chapter, I have explained how you create objects with ATL. Specifically, I have explained how class factories are implemented and how you can create instances of objects in your own code.

The example from the last chapter has been modified to create objects and add them to the collection. Since these objects should only be used to access data, they have been made noncreatable, meaning that they are externally accessible but not creatable. Although the `CComObject<>` template can be used to make your ATL class concrete, it brings with it the restriction that only the default constructor will be called. Hence, if you want to initialize your ATL object, you must do this after construction. I have shown how you can do this either with an initialization method or by accessing data members directly.

Finally, I developed a singleton object running in an MTA and used this to explain how to protect your code from multithreaded access. I also demonstrated how to write your own enumerator object that has dynamic access to the data that it's enumerating.

4

Automation

Introduction

A long time ago automation was the only way that you could write your own
interfaces. The early development tools supplied for 16-bit OLE2 did not provide a
version of MIDL that would allow you to create 'custom' interfaces. This left you with
two options: you could either make all of your objects use 'standard' interfaces like
`IDataObject` and `IViewObject` or you could create your own `dispinterface`
and talk to it using `IDispatch`. These early tools did include `MkTypeLib`, supplied to
define `dispinterfaces` and compile into type libraries. This made it possible for the
early OLE2 objects to have automation interfaces, and indeed most of the commercial
COM objects and many of the development tools (Visual C++and Visual Basic are two
that come to mind) created and used them.

Later, MIDL became available, but automation had the head start — especially since
VBA and the Office applications were based on it. To alleviate the problems with
automation interfaces (in particular those that occur with late binding) Microsoft
produced `dual` interfaces. These were based on `IDispatch`, so an automation client
could use them, but they also exposed their methods through a vtable and hence
behaved as a custom interface and could be used by C++ clients. A more recent
innovation is type library marshaling — where any interface that can be described in a
type library can be marshaled merely by registering the library.

However, therein lies the problem, only interfaces that *can be described* by a type library
can use type library marshaling, which does restrict you from using some of the richer
aspects of IDL. However, for many applications `dual` interfaces are adequate. Indeed,
if your client is likely to be a scripting client (like the Windows Scripting Host or IE 4)
you *must* give access to your methods through `IDispatch` and hence it is often a good
idea to use a `dual` interface. This is the reason why the Object Wizard defaults to `dual`
interfaces.

This chapter will explore the facilities that ATL gives you to add automation interfaces
to your objects.

IDispatch and Type Libraries

Whenever you create an ATL class through the Object Wizard it will by default be created with a `dual` interface and the interface will be mentioned in the `library` section of the IDL file. Even if the interface is custom, Object Wizard will add the interface to the `library` section because ATL assumes that the interface will be marshaled with type library marshaling. If the interface will not use type library marshaling you should make sure that it is not mentioned in the `library` section (either directly, or indirectly as a parameter of a method of one of the interfaces that is in the `library` section). Alternatively, if none of the interfaces in the type library use type library marshaling then you should ensure that the type library is not registered (see Appendix B), but be aware that this will mean that the Visual Basic IDE will not be able to use the object.

ATL implements `IDispatch` using a class called `IDispatchImpl<>` and the type library created by MIDL. Since the type library is needed, it is added as a resource to your server and registered at the same time as the server. If your objects do not use `dual` interfaces or type library marshaling then you do not need to bind this resource and, so you should remove it, reducing the size of your module. To do this you need to use the **Resource Includes** item on the Visual C++ **View** menu and remove the type library's entry in the **Compile-time directives** box.

If you use `dual` interfaces then the Object Wizard will derive your class from a specialization of `IDispatchImpl<>` based on your object's `dual` interface, and then add both your `dual` and `IDispatch` to the interface map. Why both? Well, by definition a `dual` interface implements `IDispatch`, so this ensures that the methods in the interface are available via both the vtable and `IDispatch`, and can be used by all clients.

What happens if your object implements more than one `dual`? Well, a `dual` implements `IDispatch` and two `dual`s would give you two implementations of this interface. ATL allows you to hide one version (see Appendix A), but you are clearly duplicating code. More serious than this duplication is the fact that scripting clients like VBScript know nothing about `dual` interfaces, all they know about is `IDispatch`, which is the interface that they will ask for. Since ATL provides `IDispatch` through the implementation of one of your `dual` interfaces it means that only the methods of that `dual` will be available to scripting tools. There are ways to get round this as I have mentioned in *Professional ATL COM Programming*, but they are messy, and it is best to avoid the problem altogether.

Before I move onto the next section, it is worth cautioning you. ATL's implementation of `IDispatch` loads the project's type library, and when it does this it specifies the type library version and locale. The locale is passed as a parameter of all the methods of `IDispatch` that use the type library (`GetTypeInfo()`, `GetIDsOfNames()` and `Invoke()`). These methods will ensure that the appropriate type library is loaded *once*, during the first call that any of them receives. This means that even if you have type information for several locales, an instance of a `coclass` is typed to only one of them for its entire lifetime.

The other problem that you should be aware of is that the Object Wizard will derive your class from `IDispatchImpl<>` using the default values for the type library version, that is, version 1.0. If your type library has a different major version number, the type library will not be loaded and the object creation will fail. You should get into the habit of changing the Object Wizard code to specify the actual value of the type library version, i.e. replace:

```
public IDispatchImpl<IMyObject, &IID_IMyObject, &LIBID_PROGLib>
```

with

```
public IDispatchImpl<IMyObject, &IID_IMyObject, &LIBID_PROGLib, 1, 0>
```

If you do this you are more likely remember to change these values when you change the version of the type library.

Error Objects

Error objects are not exclusively for the use of automation objects, but since their ancestry lies in the `ERRORINFO` parameter of `IDispatch` I decided there was good reason to include them here. The most obvious exposure of error objects is through Visual Basic `Err` objects, but you can use them with C++ applications. An error object has the special property that if it is set in one apartment (either in the same process on the same machine as the client, or even on a different machine) it is available in the apartment of the client without any explicit marshaling.

Indeed, error objects are essentially out-of-band data, when set the error object is sent as a hidden extra parameter when the method returns. Error objects are implemented using an undocumented DCOM feature called **channel hooks**. It is possible to write your own channel hooks to extend the marshaling packets sent by DCOM, but it is beyond the scope of this book.

Generating error objects is easy, but you do need to prepare your object for this. Here are the steps

- ❑ When you insert a new ATL object with Object Wizard, check **Support ISupportErrorInfo** from the **Attributes** tab
- ❑ Edit `InterfaceSupportsErrorInfo()` and add to the `arr` array the IID of each subsequent interface that your object supports that can generate error objects.
- ❑ When you return a non-successful `HRESULT` from a method, generate an error object

If you did not originally select error object support when you ran the Object Wizard, you can add it later with these steps:

- ❑ Derive the class from `ISupportErrorInfo` and add this to the interface map
- ❑ Declare `InterfaceSupportsErrorInfo()` in the class and implement it like this

```
STDMETHOD (InterfaceSupportsErrorInfo)(REFIID riid)
{
    static const IID* arr[] =
    {
        // all the interfaces that can generate error objects
        // for example &IID_IMyObject
    };
    for (int i=0; i < sizeof(arr) / sizeof(arr[0]); i++)
    {
        if (InlineIsEqualGUID(*arr[i],riid))
            return S_OK;
    }
    return S_FALSE;
}
```

When a client gets a failure HRESULT it will query for ISupportErrorInfo to see if the object can generate error objects. It will then call InterfaceSupportsErrorInfo() to see if the interface that returned the error can generate error objects. If it can, S_OK is returned, otherwise S_FALSE is.

There are two ways to generate error objects: use the global AtlReportError() or use CComCoClass<>::Error(). Both of these have several overloaded forms, but clearly if your object is noncreatable and you have removed CComCoClass<> then you have no choice other than to use AtlReportError().

Which overloaded form you use depends on the following:

❑ Whether the description string is held as a module resource or you pass it as a TCHAR buffer

❑ Whether you will supply the IID of the interface that generates the error

❑ Whether you pass a reference to a topic in a help file

The most comprehensive of the global versions is:

```
HRESULT WINAPI AtlReportError(const CLSID& clsid, LPCOLESTR lpszDesc,
    DWORD dwHelpID, LPCOLESTR lpszHelpFile, const IID& iid, HRESULT hRes);
```

The clsid is the CLSID of the object that generated the error, and iid is its interface; the error is described by lpszDesc and is detailed in the topic dwHelpID in lpszHelpFile. Finally, this method returns the value passed by hRes, allowing you to use this as the return value of your errant method.

Note that the HRESULT the client receives must be a non-success HRESULT so that it will take the steps to access the error object, if you pass S_OK for hRes then AtlReportError() will return DISP_E_EXCEPTION. The most comprehensive of the Error() methods is:

```
HRESULT WINAPI Error(LPCOLESTR lpszDesc, DWORD dwHelpID,
    LPCOLESTR lpszHelpFile, const IID& iid = GUID_NULL, HRESULT hRes = S_OK);
```

The fact that the server can generate error objects does not mean that the client should try to read them. This is why I said they are passed out-of-band — you only need to include error object code in your client if it needs to read error objects.

The client code is a little more involved; here's what needs to be implemented:

- ❏ When a method returns a non successful HRESULT, query the object for ISupportErrorInfo

- ❏ If the object supports this interface, call InterfaceSupportsErrorInfo() passing the IID of the interface that generated the error

- ❏ If this method returns S_FALSE (note a *success code*) the interface does not generate error objects

- ❏ If this method returns S_OK you can test to see if an error object was generated by calling GetErrorInfo()

- ❏ If this method call returns a NULL interface pointer no error object was generated, otherwise you can call the methods of IErrorInfo to obtain information about the error

If you want to write error object client code I recommend that you look up IErrorObject in the Platform SDK to see what information is passed, and the _com_error class in comdef.h to see how it is used.

One thing that you should be aware of is that there is just one error object per **logical thread**. The logical thread includes the thread in the client that called the object and the thread in the server than runs the object code. Since these can be different threads in different processes, or even on different machines, the term *logical* is used. What this means is that if your object's method calls other methods that set error objects, only the last error object will be returned to the client.

To get round this you will have to centralize your error generating code and, if necessary, aggregate all the generated errors into a single description string.

> *Professional ATL COM Programming* has an example that shows you how to create an object that stores the descriptive strings of each error object that is created, giving access to them through an enumerator.

Extended Error Objects

OLE DB implements an object called CLSID_EXTENDEDERRORINFO that implements IErrorRecords in addition to IErrorInfo. IErrorRecords allows you to add error records to the error object, but rather than adding whole strings the errors are added using an ID that identifies a format string, with one or more parameters inserted. The client can then access the record by calling GetErrorInfo() and the error object returns the error record using an error object with the IErrorInfo interface.

However, this does not actually contain the error information (the error is represented by the error ID and the inserted parameters) so when the client calls `IErrorInfo::GetDescription()` a separate object called a **lookup service** is used. This object implements a method called `GetErrorDescription()` that is passed the error ID and the insert parameters. This method has the responsibility of formating the description string. The lookup service object should be registered by adding the `ExtendedErrors` key to the CLSID key of the object that generated the error. This new key should have a key that is the CLSID of the lookup service object. For example, look at this RGS script:

```
NoRemove CLSID
{
    ForceRemove {97ABD11F-8E11-11D2-88C3-00104BDC361E} = s 'MyObj Class'
    {
        ExtendedErrors = s 'Extended Error Service'
        {
            {97ABD120-8E11-11D2-88C3-00104BDC361E} = s 'MyObj Lookup'
        }
        InprocServer32 = s '%MODULE%'
        {
            val ThreadingModel = s 'Apartment'
        }
    }
}
```

I really like this idea, because it means that error objects can be used to give an error stack trace. However, neither extended error objects, nor lookup services are supported in ATL at present other than as a client of the extended error object in the `AtlTraceErrorRecords()` method (see Appendix I).

If you would like to use extended errors the code is fairly simple. The interfaces are defined in `oledb.h` and the UUIDs are in `msdaguid.h`. When an error occurs your method needs to create an instance of `CLSID_EXTENDEDERRORINFO` and call `AddErrorRecord()` for all the error records (of type `ERRORINFO`) that you want to insert. You can then make this the current error object by querying for the `IErrorInfo` interface and passing it as the parameter to `SetErrorObject()`.

Example: Using Error Objects

Let's change the example so that it will use error objects. As I said earlier, to support error objects an object should implement `ISupportErrorInfo`. Since we have already created the ATL classes, you will have to add this interface by hand. The process is quite easy. Open `Products.h` and derive `CProducts` from `ISupportErrorInfo`:

```
class ATL_NO_VTABLE CProducts :
    public CComObjectRootEx<CComSingleThreadModel>,
    public CComCoClass<CProducts, &CLSID_Products>,
    public ISupportErrorInfo,
    public IDispatchImpl<IProdCollection, &IID_IProducts,
        &LIBID_DATAACCESSLib>
```

then add this interface to the interface map:

```
BEGIN_COM_MAP(CProducts)
    COM_INTERFACE_ENTRY(IProducts)
    COM_INTERFACE_ENTRY(IDispatch)
    COM_INTERFACE_ENTRY(ISupportErrorInfo)
END_COM_MAP()
```

Finally, add this method:

```
// ISupportErrorInfo
public:
    STDMETHOD (InterfaceSupportsErrorInfo)(REFIID riid)
    {
        static const IID* arr[] =
        {
            &IID_IProducts
        };
        for (int i=0; i < sizeof(arr) / sizeof(arr[0]); i++)
        {
            if (InlineIsEqualGUID(*arr[i],riid))
                return S_OK;
        }
        return S_FALSE;
    }
```

The loop is here to allow you to add other interface IDs if you add interfaces to the object at a later stage.

Now you can go through all the interface methods in the class and wherever a non-successful HRESULT is returned you can return an error object. For example, here is the relevant code in Remove():

```
for (it = m_coll.begin(); it < m_coll.end(); it++)
{
    CComVariant var = *it;
    CComQIPtr<IProduct> pProd = var.pdispVal;
    long prodID;
    pProd->get_ProductID(&prodID);
    if (lProdID == prodID)
    {
        CComBSTR bstr, bstr2;
        CComPtr<IDispatch> pDisp = (*it).pdispVal;
        CComPtr<IProduct> pProduct = com_cast<IProduct>(pDisp);
        pProduct->get_Description(&bstr.m_str);
        bstr2 = L"Removed ";
        bstr2 += bstr;
        m_pLogger->Add(bstr2, 0);
        m_coll.erase(it);
        // break;
        return S_OK;
    }
}
return Error(L"ProductID is invalid", IID_IProducts, E_INVALIDARG);
```

To use error objects in the Product object a similar procedure needs to be carried out. Derive CProduct from ISupportErrorInfo, add ISupportErrorInfo to the interface map, and add the inline method InterfaceSupportsErrorInfo(). The only difference between this and what you did for CProducts is the following line of code in InterfaceSupportsErrorInfo() :

```
static const IID* arr[] =
{
    &IID_IProduct
};
```

Then you can change the CHECK_OUT_PARAM() macro in Product.cpp to:

```
#define CHECK_OUT_PARAM(p) \
    if (p == NULL) \
        return AtlReportError(CLSID_Product, _T("out pointer is invalid"), \
                IID_IProduct, E_POINTER);
```

If you have a class that derives from `CComCoClass<>` then you can use `Error()` instead:

```
#define CHECK_OUT_PARAM_E(p) \
   if (p == NULL) \
      return Error(_T("out pointer is invalid"), \
               IID_IProduct, E_POINTER);
```

How do we test out these changes? The change to the `Product` object can only be tested with C++ because Visual Basic ensures that a valid pointer is always passed for [out] parameters. I will leave it as an exercise for you to write a small C++ project to test this out. Testing the `Remove()` method is easy: create a Visual Basic project that uses the `Products` object and add some invalid code like this:

```
Private Sub Form_Load()
   Dim ev As New Products
   ev.Remove 99 ' there is no product 99
End Sub
```

When you run this you will get the following dialog:

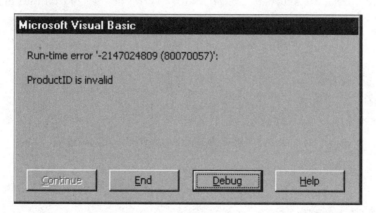

Of course, this is not too user friendly, so instead you can use the Visual Basic `Err` object:

```
Private Sub Form_Load()
   On Error GoTo error_handler
   Dim ev As New Products
   ev.Remove 99
   Exit Sub
error_handler:
   MsgBox Err.Description, vbOKOnly, "Error from " + Err.Source
End Sub
```

Notice that the `Err` object is the error object thrown by the `Products` object.

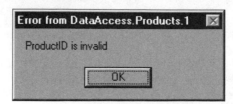

Connection Points

COM has formalized event subscription and generation using objects called connection points. An event consists of the event-generating object calling a COM method on the client that catches it. This COM method is the event handler and the interface it is part of is known as the **sink interface** from the client's point of view (because it *sinks* events), and an **outgoing interface** from the point of view of the object that generates the event (because it calls *out* on this interface).

Thus if a client wants to catch events it must implement a sink object that implements the sink interface. The object that generates events (the connectable object) implements the `IConnectionPointContainer` interface. To see if the connectable object can generate events on a specified outgoing interface it calls `IConnectionPointContainer` to obtain the connection point object for the outgoing interface. The connectable object returns a `IConnectionPoint` interface pointer and to subscribe to the events the client passes the `IUnknown` pointer of the sink object to `IConnectionPoint::Advise()`.

ATL supports connection points through two facilities. Firstly, there is an option on the **Attribute** tab of the Object Wizard: **Support Connection Points**. Secondly, ClassView is equipped with the connection point wizard. In fact, if you forget to add connection point support with the Object Wizard then the connection point wizard will do it for you, so I will concentrate on this wizard.

The connection point wizard is run through the context menu of an ATL class in ClassView. It replaces the proxy generator that existed in previous versions of Visual C++. When you run this wizard it will attempt to read the type library for the project — if this does not exist you are given the option to load another type library. If you have specified connection point support with the Object Wizard then it will add the definition of an outgoing interface to the IDL of the project. If you want to use this interface you must ensure that you have added the event methods to it and compiled the IDL *before* you run the connection point wizard. Remember, although you define the outgoing interface in the IDL your object does not implement it; your object calls methods on this interface using code ('proxy' code) generated by the connection point wizard.

ATL allows you to generate events on either a custom interface or a `dispinterface`, but not `dual` interfaces. The reason for this is that for a `dual` ATL cannot know if the client has implemented `IDispatch` or a vtable to catch the event. The connection point wizard will ignore all `dual` interfaces defined in your type library. Note that Visual Basic and C++ clients can use custom sink interfaces or `dispinterfaces`, but scripting clients (like the windows scripting host and IE) will only sink events on a `dispinterface`.

To use a custom interface instead of a `dispinterface` you need to do edit the IDL file:

❑ Find the `coclass` for the object and change the line which has the [default, source] attribute to have `interface` rather than `dispinterface`

❑ Find the definition of the event interface in the `library` section and change it from `dispinterface` to `interface`; you will also need to derive the interface from `IUnknown` and remove the two lines `properties:` and `methods:`

After this you will be able to add methods to this interface with ClassView.

Furthermore, the connection point wizard knows that the interface you are looking for is an outgoing interface, so it will only show those interfaces that have been marked with [source]. The only way that you can do this is to add this attribute to the interface in the `coclass` entry in the IDL. Thus if you add an outgoing interface by hand to the IDL you have to make sure that it is marked as [source] in one of the `coclasses`.

Connection Points and DCOM

There are a few things that ought to be mentioned about connection points. When you make or break the connection there is a lot of traffic between the object and its client. It takes five round trips to make the connection and four to break it. This occurs because the connection point mechanism is generic — remember, it was designed for controls which are inproc, so method calls are fast. You have to decide whether this amount of traffic is justified, especially if the connectable object is on another machine. Bear in mind that typically the client will only make or break a connection to a connectable object *once* during its lifetime, but that an object may have many clients and make these calls for *all* of them.

The alternative is to devise your own connection point mechanism by defining an interface with `Advise()` and `Unadvise()` methods that add or remove interface pointers from an array. You will have to implement this array and the event generation code yourself, because the connection point wizard only understands connection points. If this is too much work, then stick with connection points.

Another issue that you need to be aware of is that the client that implements the sink object will pass an interface pointer to the connectable object. When the connectable object generates an event it does so by calling methods on the sink object. If the client and connectable object are on different machines this means that the account under which the connectable object is running must have permissions to access the client process. This is the reverse of what you are normally used to (the client should have the correct permissions to access the server). To set these permissions you can either use an `AppID` for the client process (also requiring the sink object to be registered) or you can call `CoInitializeSecurity()`.

If the client is a DLL, which is typical if you want a control to sink events, then you do not have these options. Instead, you can do one of two things. The first is that you can ensure that the server identity has the same name and password as the account the client is running under. This does *not* mean you should use the Launching User identity — this will fail on Windows NT 4 because it would require delegation, which it doesn't support. You don't have to use the same account for both the client and server — the accounts can be local to each machine.

The other option is to use a middleman object implemented in an EXE server on the client. This works because the middleman can be configured to allow the client to have access to it and run under an account that the connectable object will give access to. Since it is implemented in an EXE it can also be configured to specify which accounts can access it, and so give access to the remote object.

> **Professional ATL COM Programming covers all the issues involved with security and connection points and offers solutions to the common problems.**

Example: Adding Connection Points to the Events Object

In this example, I will add connection point support to the `Events` object so that when a new `CEvent` object is added to the collection any connected clients will be informed. The first task is to add the outgoing interface to the `Events` object. As I mentioned earlier, if you had used the Object Wizard to add connection point support this interface would have been added for you. However, doing this manually is quite simple.

Run the GUID Generator (Project, Add To Project, Components and Controls, Visual C++ Components) to create a GUID in registry format (make sure you copy this to the clipboard).

> **If you use this tool often you can run it quicker by adding it to the Tools menu. To do this use the Customize item on the Tools menu and from the Tools tab add the new tool. The process that you should add to the Command box is GUIDGEN.EXE from Common\Tools\ directory.**

Add the following to the `Library` section of the IDL before `Events` coclass.

```
[
    uuid(468FD22D-77B5-11D2-88A9-00104BDC361E)
]
dispinterface DLoggerEvents
{
properties:
methods:
};
```

The `uuid()` is the one generated with the GUID Generator.

You do not have to compile the IDL at this point because ClassView will update itself when you save the file, so use it to add the following method to DLoggerEvents:

```
[id(1)] void NewEvent([in]long lEventID);
```

The idea is that the client will be informed about the Event object that has been logged using the ID of the stream used to hold it. The client will need to obtain the Event object using this ID, so you need to add an Item() method to the IEvents interface. To do this add the following with ClassView:

```
HRESULT Item([in] long lEventID, [out, retval] IEvent** pOut);
```

Next you need to edit the IDL by hand to make two changes. The first is to change the id() of the newly created Item() method from whatever ClassView gave you to id(DISPID_VALUE). The second change is to move the definition of IEvent to the position *above* the definition of IEvents, because IEvent is referenced in Item().

The connection point wizard requires one more thing. The outgoing interface must be marked with the IDL [source] attribute. The only place that you can use this on an interface is when declaring an interface in a coclass, so add the following:

```
coclass Events
{
    [default] interface IEvents;
    [default, source] dispinterface DLoggerEvents;
};
```

This indicates that the Events object will generate events on the DLoggerEvents dispinterface, i.e. it is the outgoing interface.

Now you need to implement Item(), so open Events.cpp, add Event.h to the headers included at the top of the file and then implement the method like this:

```
STDMETHODIMP CEvents::Item(long lEventID, IEvent **pOut)
{
    if (pOut == NULL)
        return Error(L"out pointer is invalid", IID_IEvents, E_POINTER);

    WCHAR strName[20];
    CComPtr<IStream> pStm;
    CComVariant varDate;
    CComVariant varMsg;
    CComVariant varSev;

    swprintf(strName, L"%ld", lEventID);
    HRESULT hr;
    g_csData.Lock();
    hr = m_pStg->OpenStream(strName, NULL, STGM_READ | STGM_SHARE_EXCLUSIVE,
                                                        0, &pStm);
    if (SUCCEEDED(hr))
    {
        varDate.ReadFromStream(pStm);
        varMsg.ReadFromStream(pStm);
        varSev.ReadFromStream(pStm);
        g_csData.Unlock();
    }
    else
    {
        g_csData.Unlock();
        return Error(L"cannot get item", IID_IEvents, hr);
    }
```

```
    CComObject<CEvent>* pObj;
    CComObject<CEvent>::CreateInstance(&pObj);
    pObj->Initialize(varDate.date, varMsg.bstrVal, varSev.lVal);
    hr = pObj->QueryInterface(pOut);
    if (FAILED(hr))
    {
        delete pObj;
        return Error(L"cannot create the object", IID_IEvents, hr);
    }
    return hr;
}
```

Notice that I have added error object support to this object. For this to work you need to carry out some additional steps (detailed in the previous section): Derive CEvents from ISupportErrorInfo, add ISupportErrorInfo to its interface map, and add the inline method InterfaceSupportsErrorInfo() (with &IID_IEvents).

Now let's get down to adding connection point support. First, ensure that the IDL is compiled. Once you have done this, right click on CEvents in ClassView and select **Implement Connection Point**. You should find the DLoggerEvents interface is given in the list box. If the interface is not present you have missed out one of the steps given previously (most likely either the dispinterface is not marked as the outgoing interface for the Events object, or you have not compiled the IDL).

Make sure that you check the box next to the DLoggerEvents and click on **OK**. This will generate and add the 'proxy' class CProxyDLoggerEvents<> to the project and derive CEvents from it. Remember that I said that the connection point wizard will add connection point support to your class for you? Open Events.h and you'll see that your class now derives from IConnectionPointContainerImpl<>, and this has been added to the interface map:

```
BEGIN_COM_MAP(CEvents)
    COM_INTERFACE_ENTRY(IEvents)
    COM_INTERFACE_ENTRY(IDispatch)
    COM_INTERFACE_ENTRY(ISupportErrorInfo)
    COM_INTERFACE_ENTRY_IMPL(IConnectionPointContainer)
END_COM_MAP()
```

Notice that the entry uses the deprecated COM_INTERFACE_ENTRY_IMPL(). You should replace it with COM_INTERFACE_ENTRY().

> **This is one bug in the connection point wizard — even if your class already has connection point support it will add this macro to the map.**

You will also notice that a connection point map has been added:

```
public :
BEGIN_CONNECTION_POINT_MAP(CEvents)
    CONNECTION_POINT_ENTRY(DIID_DLoggerEvents)
END_CONNECTION_POINT_MAP()
```

However, the IID that the wizard uses is wrong, it should be `DIID_DLoggerEvents` (as shown in the above code).

> **Check the IID specified in the macro. If you have** `IID_DLoggerEvents` **add the** `D` **prefix. This bug in the connection point wizard appears to have been fixed with service pack 1 of Visual C++ 6.**

Deriving from the proxy class does two things: it adds a connection point for the `DLoggerEvents` interface to the class, and it provides code that you can use to generate an event. We will leave this as it is, but note that you do not have to use the wizard to add connection point and event generation code. As Appendix A points out you can derive your class from `IConnectionPointImpl<>` for the outgoing interface and then write your own code to iterate through all the cached sink interfaces and call the appropriate method. The proxy class is convenient because it does both actions for you.

Let's generate an event, so edit the `Add()` method thus:

```
    pStm.Release();
    Fire_NewEvent((long)ulRec - 1);
    return hr;
}
```

I release the stream first before firing the event because a client that gets the event will most likely want to call `IEvents::Item()` on the event ID to get information about the event. COM is synchronous, so the client will attempt to call `Item()` *before* `Add()` has returned. Since `pStm` has opened the stream with exclusive access the client will be refused access. I have used a smart pointer, so the stream gets released when the smart pointer goes out of scope (i.e. when the method returns), which is why I didn't have to worry about this before. I get round this problem now by explicitly calling `CComPtr<>::Release()`.

Before showing you a client that uses these events, there is one more thing you can do. You have marked `DLoggerEvents` as the default outgoing interface of the object, but some clients (for example Visual Basic when you drop a control on a form, but not when you use an object with `WithEvents`) will not read the type information of the object. Instead they will query it and ask it to specify its outgoing interface. To support this, your object should support the `IProvideClassInfo2` interface, so derive `CEvents` from `IProvideClassInfo2Impl<>`:

```
class ATL_NO_VTABLE CEvents :
    public CComObjectRootEx<CComMultiThreadModel>,
    public CComCoClass<CEvents, &CLSID_Events>,
    public ISupportErrorInfo,
    public IDispatchImpl<IEvents, &IID_IEvents, &LIBID_EVENTLOGGERLib>,
    public CProxyDLoggerEvents< CEvents >,
    public IConnectionPointContainerImpl<CEvents>,
    public IProvideClassInfo2Impl<&CLSID_Events, &DIID_DLoggerEvents>
{
```

and add the interface to its interface map:

```
BEGIN_COM_MAP(CEvents)
    COM_INTERFACE_ENTRY(IEvents)
    COM_INTERFACE_ENTRY(IDispatch)
    COM_INTERFACE_ENTRY(ISupportErrorInfo)
    COM_INTERFACE_ENTRY(IConnectionPointContainer)
    COM_INTERFACE_ENTRY(IProvideClassInfo2)
END_COM_MAP()
```

Example: A Visual Basic Project that Handles Events

This example uses the project that you developed in the last chapter to show the logged events. Open this project and change the declaration of the `logger` object to:

```
Private WithEvents logger As Events
```

This tells Visual Basic that the object can generate events, prompting it to read the type info of the object to determine the default outgoing interface that the object uses (Visual Basic cannot handle events from other outgoing interfaces). From this it will generate the handler methods. If you open Object list box in the code view you will see that Visual Basic has added the `logger` object. If you select this Visual Basic will add the following:

```
Private Sub logger_NewEvent(ByVal lEventID As Long)
End Sub
```

This is the handler for the `NewEvent()` event generated by the `logger` object.

Add a label to the form called `lblRecent` (to show the most recent event) and implement the handler like this:

```
Private Sub logger_NewEvent(ByVal lEventID As Long)
    Dim ev As EVENTLOGGERLib.Event
    Set ev = logger.Item(lEventID)
    Dim s As String
    s = Str$(ev.Date) + " " + ev.Message
    If ev.Severity = 0 Then
        lblRecent = "Info: " + s
    Else
        lblRecent = "Error: " + s
    End If
    lstInfo.AddItem s
End Sub
```

This reads the event that was generated and puts information about it into the label as well as updating the appropriate list box. To test this out you can run the application and use the other Visual Basic example from the last chapter to add and remove a few items.

Implementing Dispinterfaces

It is not only Visual Basic applications that can catch events, C++ clients can too. If the outgoing interface is a custom one there are no problems, you just create an object that implements that interface and make the connection to it. To help you, ATL defines a method called `AtlAdvise()` that will query for `IConnectionPointContainer`, obtain the connection point object, and make the connection. The method looks like this:

```
HRESULT AtlAdvise(IUnknown* pUnkCP, IUnknown* pUnk,
    const IID& iid, LPDWORD pdw);
```

The parameters are:

- ❑   pUnkCP is the object you are trying to connect to
- ❑   pUnk is the sink object that your code implements to catch the event
- ❑   iid is the outgoing interface on which you will catch events
- ❑   pdw is a pointer to a DWORD that will be filled with a value used to identify the connection when you want to break it

When you have finished with the connection you can break it with AtlUnadvise():

```
HRESULT AtlUnadvise(IUnknown* pUnkCP, const IID& iid, DWORD dw);
```

Notice that this passes the DWORD cookie obtained in AtlAdvise(). These two methods take COM pointers. If you have smart pointer that has been initialized you can call the CComPtr<>::Advise() member:

```
Advise(IUnknown* pUnk, const IID& iid, LPDWORD pdw);
```

This method simply passes these parameters and the interface wrapped by the smart pointer to AtlAdvise(). There is no corresponding Unadvise() method, and CComPtr<> does not provide the DWORD to hold the value returned from IConnectionPoint::Advise().

One problem you may encounter when handling events is when the outgoing interface is a dispinterface. The ATL Wizard allows you to implement dual interfaces but not dispinterfaces. Since a dispinterface is just an implementation of IDispatch that implements a specified group of methods, and a dual also implements IDispatch, you can implement the former with the latter. For example, imagine you have a dispinterface called DDisp and a dual called IMyObject that has the same methods with the same DISPIDs. If your ATL object implements IMyObject it can specify that this can be used to implement DDisp by adding the following entry to the interface map:

```
BEGIN_COM_MAP(CMyObject)
    COM_INTERFACE_ENTRY(IMyObject)
    COM_INTERFACE_ENTRY_IID(DIID_DDisp, IMyObject)
    COM_INTERFACE_ENTRY(IDispatch)
END_COM_MAP()
```

There is another way to do this. ATL has two templates called `IDispEventImpl<>` and `IDispEventSimpleImpl<>` that you can use to implement a `dispinterface`. They have these names because the most common reason to implement a `dispinterface` is to provide handlers for events generated by a connection point. Both templates are explained fully in Appendix A. Basically, to implement `dispinterface` methods you need to give information about them. `IDispEventImpl<>` uses a type library (this will be used in this example) and `IDispEventSimpleImpl<>`uses information in the sink map (an example of this is shown in the appendix).

`IDispEventImpl<>` parameters are an ID, the name of your class, the IID of the `dispinterface` and the LIBID and version of the type library. The first parameter is present because this class is actually designed to allow your object to handle events generated by controls in a composite control (see Appendix J), allowing you to specify which control you are providing methods for (several controls could generate events on the same `dispinterface`). However, if you are not providing handlers for a control, don't worry, just use any unique number, but make sure that you use the same ID in the entries in the sink map. For example:

```
public IDispEventImpl<99, CMyObject, &DIID_DDisp, &LIBID_PROGLib, 1, 0>
```

Here `LIBID_PROGLib` is the *registered* type library that describes the dispinterface `DDisp`. Note the version: the default values of the template are version `0.0` which guarantees that the attempt to load the type library will fail, thus you must always explicitly mention the actual version.

The sink map for the above example would look like this:

```
BEGIN_SINK_MAP(CMyObject)
    SINK_ENTRY_EX(99, DIID_DDisp, 1, GetData)
END_SINK_MAP()
```

The entry indicates that the method on `DDisp`, which has the `DISPID` of 1, is implemented by the method called `GetData()`in your class. This method should have the same return value and parameters as the `dispinterface` method, and in addition must use the `__stdcall` calling convention, so if the `dispinterface` method is this:

```
methods:
    [id(1)] double GetData([in] long lVal);
```

then your class should implement:

```
double __stdcall GetData(long lVal);
```

Example: Using IDispEventImpl<> With MFC

I know this book is about ATL, but bear with me because most of this code will be in ATL rather than MFC. MFC is used here to provide the application framework, so this does not violate my assertion (see Appendix D) that you should try to avoid using MFC in ATL projects, because this is an MFC project using ATL!

In this example I will show you an MFC project which will sink the events generated by the Events object. To do this, create a new MFC EXE application called LoggerEvents and use the AppWizard to specify that it is based on a dialog box. Remove the **OK** and **Cancel** buttons and replace them with a list box that has the ID of IDC_LISTEVENTS that does not sort, nor allows selection. Next insert a new ATL object and notice that Object Wizard will specify that ATL support is required and give a dialog saying "Do you want to add ATL support to your MFC Project?". Reply **Yes** to this.

When the Object Wizard dialog appears add a simple ATL object called LoggedEvent that has a custom interface. The reason for using a custom interface is that you don't really need it, and making it custom reduces the work you need to do when you remove it from the class and replace it with IUnknown. Do this now and change the interface map as well. Remember also to remove the interface from the IDL file and replace the mention of ILoggedEvent in the coclass with IUnknown.

This object is only created within the project, so make it noncreatable by removing the base class CComCoClass<> and replace the registration macro with DECLARE_NO_REGISTRY(). In addition, since no objects are exposed from the class you can remove the object map in LoggerEvents.cpp.

While you are in this file you can remove much of the code that the Object Wizard has added. The reason is that this code is used to expose class factories, and since the sink object is noncreatable, you will not have a class factory. So, remove the following methods:

```
CLoggerEventsModule::Unlock()
CLoggerEventsModule::Lock()
CLoggerEventsModule::FindOneOf()
```

Then remove the line _Module.RevokeClassObjects() from CLoggerEventsApp::ExitInstance(), and edit InitATL() to look like this:

```
BOOL CLoggerEventsApp::InitATL()
{
    m_bATLInited = TRUE;
#if _WIN32_WINNT >= 0x0400
    HRESULT hRes = CoInitializeEx(NULL, COINIT_MULTITHREADED);
#else
    HRESULT hRes = CoInitialize(NULL);
#endif

    if (FAILED(hRes))
    {
        m_bATLInited = FALSE;
        return FALSE;
    }
```

```
    _Module.Init(NULL, AfxGetInstanceHandle());
    LPTSTR lpCmdLine = GetCommandLine();
    return TRUE;
}
```

Since you do not need the extra members of CLoggerEventsModule, change _Module to be an instance of CComModule and make a similar change to stdafx.h.

```
// in Loggerevents.cpp
CComModule _Module;

// in stdafx.h
//class CLoggerEventsModule : public CComModule
//{
//public:
//    LONG Unlock();
//    LONG Lock();
//    LPCTSTR FindOneOf(LPCTSTR p1, LPCTSTR p2);
//    DWORD dwThreadID;
//};
//extern CLoggerEventsModule _Module;
extern CComModule _Module;
```

Once you have done this you can add the sink map to the sink object. Add the following line to LoggedEvent.h so that the file will have the interface and library constants:

```
#import "..\EventLogger\EventLogger.tlb" no_namespace, no_implementation,
named_guids
```

To provide an implementation of the dispinterface you need to derive CLoggedEvent from:

```
public IDispEventImpl<99, CLoggedEvent,
    &DIID_DLoggerEvents, &LIBID_EVENTLOGGERLib, 1, 0>
```

And add a sink map:

```
BEGIN_SINK_MAP(CLoggedEvent)
    SINK_ENTRY_EX(99, DIID_DLoggerEvents, 1, OnNewEvent)
END_SINK_MAP()
```

This specifies that the event with a DISPID of 1 is handled by the OnNewEvent() method, this is declared as:

```
public:
    void __stdcall OnNewEvent(long lEventID)
    {
    }
```

I'll come back to this in a moment, but first you will need to create the connectable object and an instance of the sink object to handle the events. Open `LoggerEventsDlg.h` and add the following near the top:

```
#import "..\EventLogger\EventLogger.tlb" no_namespace, no_implementation,
                                                              named_guids
#include "LoggedEvent.h"
```

This adds the constant definitions for the `Events` object and the class definition of `CLoggedEvent`. Next, add these members to the class:

```
protected:
    CComPtr<IEvents> m_pEvents;
    CComObjectNoLock<CLoggedEvent>* m_pSink;
};
```

Note that I use a smart pointer to hold the `IEvents` interface pointer because I am using COM to get the interface reference. The second pointer is to the sink object that will be created by the class, so you do not need to hold an interface pointer, just a pointer to the object. These objects are created in `OnInitDialog()` in `LoggerEventsDlg.cpp`:

```
m_pEvents.CoCreateInstance(__uuidof(Events));
m_pSink = new CComObjectNoLock<CLoggedEvent>;
m_pSink->AddRef();
m_pSink->DispEventAdvise(m_pEvents, &DIID_DLoggerEvents);
return TRUE;
```

This code obtains a reference to the `Events` object and then creates an instance of the sink object (I call `AddRef()` through the object pointer to keep it alive). Finally, I call `DispEventAdvise()` inherited through `IDispEventImpl<>` to create the connection. You will also have to add the following to the top of the file:

```
#import "..\EventLogger\EventLogger.tlb" no_namespace,  implementation_only,
                                                              named_guids
```

The connection needs to be broken when the dialog is closed, so open ClassWizard, select `CLoggerEventsDlg` from the **ObjectIDs** box and `WM_CLOSE` from the **Messages** box, and then click **Add Function**. Implement this method like this:

```
void CLoggerEventsDlg::OnClose()
{
    if (m_pSink)
    {
        m_pSink->DispEventUnadvise(m_pEvents, &DIID_DLoggerEvents);
        m_pSink->Release();
    }
    CDialog::OnClose();
}
```

The `m_pEvents` smart pointer will ensure that the `Events` reference is released when the application closes. When the event is generated, the `OnNewEvent()` method will be called on the sink object. This should handle the event by adding an entry into the list box. To do this, the object needs to be initialized with a pointer to the list box, as well as a pointer to the `Events` object so that the sink object can get information about it.

Open `LoggedEvent.h` and edit the class to have the following data members and initialization method:

```
public:
   void Initialize(IEvents* pEvent, CListBox* pListbox)
   {
       m_pEvents = pEvent;
       m_pListbox = pListbox;
   }
private:
   CComPtr<IEvents> m_pEvents;
   CListBox* m_pListbox;
};
```

Initialize these pointers to NULL in the constructor.

You can now initialize the sink object in `OnInitDialog()`:

```
m_pSink = new CComObjectNoLock<CLoggedEvent>;
m_pSink->AddRef();
CListBox* pListBox = (CListBox*)GetDlgItem(IDC_LISTEVENTS);
m_pSink->Initialize(m_pEvents, pListBox);
m_pSink->DispEventAdvise(m_pEvents, &DIID_DLoggerEvents);
```

The final task is to implement the event handler:

```
void __stdcall OnNewEvent(long lEventID)
{
   CComPtr<IEvent> pEvent;
   if (SUCCEEDED(m_pEvents->raw_Item(lEventID, &pEvent)))
   {
       DATE dDate;
       pEvent->get_Date(&dDate);
       CComBSTR bstrDesc;
       pEvent->get_Message(&bstrDesc);
       long lSeverity;
       pEvent->get_Severity(&lSeverity);

       SYSTEMTIME st;
       VariantTimeToSystemTime(dDate, &st);

       CString str;
       str.Format(_T("%04d-%02d-%02d %02d:%02d:%02d %S "),
           st.wYear, st.wMonth, st.wDay,
           st.wHour, st.wMinute, st.wSecond, bstrDesc.m_str);
       if (lSeverity == 0)
           str += _T("Info");
       else
           str += _T("Error");

       m_pListbox->AddString(str);
   }
}
```

The only significant thing to point out here is that I am calling `IEvents::Item()` using the header generated by `#import`. `#import` generates a 'friendly' wrapper methods using `_com_ptr`, but it reuses the `Item()` name (remember a COM interface is called by its position in the vtable, not by the C++ method name). I could have used this method, but since I did not want to use `_com_ptr` I decided to call the COM method directly. The vtable that `#import` generates have methods prefixed with `raw_` so to call the COM method `IEvents::Item()` you need to call `raw_Item()`.

You should be able to compile the project and run it. To test it out run the Visual Basic Products example developed in the last chapter and add and remove a few items. You should see something like this:

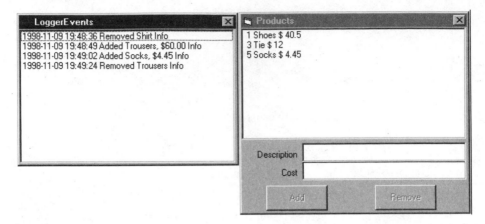

Summary

This chapter has covered three important topics. Firstly, it introduced you to error objects. These are used to convey rich error information from the object to a client when an error occurs. Error objects are the nearest that COM has to C++ exceptions. They require adding support for ISupportErrorInfo as well as their generation and initialization. ATL does all the work for you, hiding from you most of the code so that generating an error object is as simple as calling a method.

I have also covered connection points. These were originally designed for bi-directional communications between controls and their containers, but you can use them for non-control objects. ATL has extensive support for connection points as well as the ClassView connection point wizard which will add connection point and event generation code from a type library description of the outgoing interface.

Finally, I have shown you how to implement a dispinterface using ATL. As an example of this I developed code that sinks events from an outgoing dispinterface, and as a bonus I have shown how you can use this code in an MFC project.

OLE DB

Introduction

Everyone has data of some kind; indeed, these days your PC will be full of it. You will have data held formally in relational databases and accessed using SQL. You will have data in email systems accessed through MAPI. In addition to these, you will have other data sources that won't be so formalized or structured. For example, as a developer you'll create lots of data in the mere process of developing code. The source files that make up your projects are data, and when you put your code under source control you're putting it into a database. If you think about it, you could even view the FAT (or NTFS) file system as a database — it just holds information about the files on your disk.

The big problem with these different databases is that, to access the data, you have to use an API specific to that database type, which can be quite arcane. **ODBC (Open Database Connectivity)** was the first attempt to unify access to databases, and there are now ODBC drivers for many types of databases, including data sources like text files and Excel spreadsheets. ODBC abstracts database access to a series of C API calls. **OLE DB (Object Linking and Embedding Database)** takes this a step further; it abstracts database access to calls through OLE DB COM interfaces.

There are OLE DB providers available from Microsoft and third parties for most of the popular data sources, including ODBC, so if you have an ODBC driver for a data source you can access it through OLE DB. Most of the time, however, you won't use OLE DB directly. Instead, you will use a library like **ADO (Active Data Objects)**. This sits on top of OLE DB and gives a simpler interface to your data, which can be used by a wider range of clients (ADO presents an automation interface).

ATL Consumer Templates

This is where the ATL consumer templates come in. If you use OLE DB directly, you will need to write a fair amount of code, much of which is unintelligible. ATL will hide the majority of this code from you, and if you use the Object Wizard it will even obtain information about your data source and its schema automatically, using this to generate even simpler wrapper classes.

The following diagram shows the arrangement of the various components.

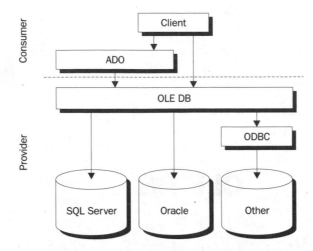

The ATL OLE DB consumer classes use COM but, as the name suggests, it is not *server* code, so you don't need object registration or class factories. You can either use the ATL classes by hand (but this requires that you know the schema of the database) or you can use the Object Wizard (which will use OLE DB to read the schema and allow you to choose the table that you want to access). However, the Object Wizard will only work in certain types of project (a Win32 application or DLL) which contains particular files (a CPPand an IDL file with the same name as the project). There are ways to trick the Object Wizard (see Appendix E), but the simplest way to get round this is to generate the consumer classes in a dummy project and then copy them to the project where you will use them.

In the examples in this chapter, I will use OLE DB consumer classes in the Products object. This is an ATL project and so fulfils all the criteria needed to run the Object Wizard.

OLE DB Consumers

The OLE DB templates take up approximately one third of the code in ATL, so clearly they are an important part of the library. The Object Wizard allows you to create OLE DB providers as well as OLE DB consumer classes, but I'll deal only with using the ATL consumer classes here.

Several objects are required to get access to an OLE DB data source. The first is a **data source object**, which represents the connection to the data source. This object is used to create **session** objects, through which you can create transactions, access tables and execute queries. To make a query you need a **command** object, containing the query in whatever form the data source supports. (The ODBC providers, for example, use SQL queries, but an **OLAP (Online Analytical Processing)** provider will have commands based on **Multidimensional Expressions — MDX**.) When the command is executed, data is returned via a **Rowset** object, representing zero or more rows of results. You can iterate through this to get individual rows using an **accessor** object, which gives you access to a single row, as illustrated in the diagram below:

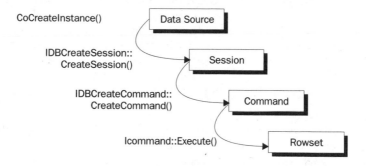

Properties

OLE DB objects have properties, which you use to specify the behavior that you want from them. For example, a data source object will have properties that hold authentication information: the DBPROP_AUTH_USERID property contains the user ID, and DBPROP_AUTH_PASSWORD contains the password. Different OLE DB providers will require different properties to be set, often with provider-specific data. For example, the data source property, DBPROP_INIT_DATASOURCE, takes a string that represents the data source name (DSN) for an ODBC OLE DB provider, but is the path to the MDB file for the Jet OLE DB Provider.

In essence, properties are used to handle the differences between the various OLE DB providers. Once you've set the required properties the OLE DB code you write is generic for all providers. The skill, of course, is in determining which properties you should set, and what values you should use. When you use Object Wizard to create consumer classes, it will set the appropriate properties for you to make a connection to the data source. It will also present all data source properties so that you have the option of fine-tuning the access.

Session, rowset and command objects also have properties; command properties are interesting because these specify the functionality that you want with the resultant rowset. For example, if you want to update, insert or delete records in a rowset then you need to set DBPROP_IRowsetChange property on the command object that will create the rowset. This indicates that when the rowset is created you want to use the IRowsetChange interface. In addition you need to set the DBPROP_UPDATABILITY property on the command object to indicate which of these actions (update, insert or delete) you wish to perform. If the rowset supports the interface (and these actions) you will be able to call its methods. Restricting the properties according to the command that you will perform allows you to get the rowset object with only the functionality you require.

If you need to pass a parameter to a query then you need to put a placeholder in the command text (for example SQL providers use a ?) and create a buffer to hold the data that the command object will use to replace this. The buffer is passed to the ICommand::Execute() command that will perform the query and return a reference to the rowset object that contains the results.

Once you have a rowset you'll want to access the data in it, and to do this you have to create bindings. These associate memory in your process with a column that will be returned from the rowset. Your code can then access the data through this memory. The actual data is accessed from the rowset using an accessor object, which needs to know about the binding.

ATL Consumer Classes

ATL simplifies all of this through the CDataSource, CSession, CCommand<>, CRowset and CAccessor<> classes. The Object Wizard OLE DB consumer wizard will allow you to select an OLE DB provider and will read its properties. It will use this information to generate two classes to allow you to access the data source. One class is the **user record class** and represents a row. It has the suffix Accessor, but it does not implement an accessor object. Instead, it holds the buffers used for binding to accessors or parameters.

The accessor is implemented by the other class created for you. This class is general purpose, because in addition to implementing the accessor, it also holds a CSession object representing the database session and implements methods to access the command and rowset objects for queries. The Wizard will generate a method called OpenDataSource() that creates a data source object with appropriate properties and uses this to create a session object that is cached in the CSession object.

For example, here is a typical class generated for you by the Wizard:

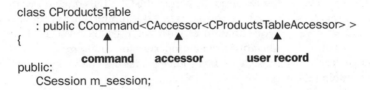

```
class CProductsTable
    : public CCommand<CAccessor<CProductsTableAccessor> >
{
                    command    accessor    user record
public:
    CSession m_session;
```

The command class is used both to create and execute a query and to give you access to the results. Depending on the options you select in Object Wizard, you will either get CCommand<>, to execute a query, or CTable<>, to access all rows and all columns on a table. The Wizard will even generate a method called Open() that will open the data source, create a session and execute a command. The command class derives from a recordset class, so you can use its methods to access more rows from the result of the query through the user record class's data members.

The accessor class determines the columns that we want to access in the data source. The Wizard will use CAccessor<>, which uses entries in the user record to determine the data that will be read. You can determine the table structure at runtime, in which case you can use one of the other accessor classes that ATL provides.

The inheritance hierarchy of the previous example is:

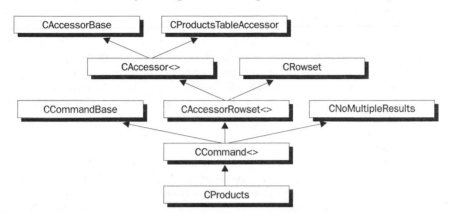

Thus CProducts derives from CCommand<>, CAccessor<>, CAccessorRowset<> and CProductsAccessor, as well as their various base classes.

You can use the CProducts class like this:

```
CProducts db;
db.Open();      // create session and execute a command
                // to get a rowset
while (db.MoveNext() == S_OK) // read a row
    cout << "db.m_ProductID << ", "
         << db.m_Description << endl;
```

Here, CProducts derives from CRowset so you can call CRowset::MoveNext() to get individual rows. It also derives from the CProductsAccessor user record class, which has data members for each of the columns returned from the query.

In addition to the data members holding column data, the user record class needs to have information that will be used by the accessor to bind to its data members. If the command takes parameters, it needs binding information for those too. This information is held in a COLUMN map, a PARAM map and, perhaps, an ACCESSOR map. Clearly the command must be specified somewhere, and in absence of your code explicitly mentioning one (through a parameter of one of the overloaded Open() methods) the default command will be used — the Object Wizard will generate a command that simply selects all fields in the table and adds it to the user record class using the DEFINE_COMMAND() macro.

Here is the user record class created for access to the Products table.

```
class CProductsAccessor
{
public:
    TCHAR m_Description[51];
    LONG m_ProductID;
    CURRENCY m_UnitCost;

BEGIN_COLUMN_MAP(CProductsAccessor)
    COLUMN_ENTRY(1, m_ProductID)
    COLUMN_ENTRY(2, m_Description)
    COLUMN_ENTRY_TYPE(3, DBTYPE_CY, m_UnitCost)
END_COLUMN_MAP()
```

```
DEFINE_COMMAND(CProductsAccessor,
            _T("SELECT ProductID, Description, UnitCost ")
            _T("FROM Products"))
};
```

If you want to use a different command then you can edit the string in the
DEFINE_COMMAND() macro, or you can create a separate CCommand<> object based
on another user record class. You can then execute this through the session object
created via CProducts::OpenDataSource(). The example code in this chapter will
show you several ways to do this.

ATL also provides a template called CTable<> that you can use in place of
CCommand<>. If you use this (the Object Wizard will if you choose a table rather than a
command), your user record class won't have a defined command. This is because you
will be accessing entire rows from the table, effectively doing a SELECT * FROM ...
query. Since there is no command, CTable<> has a version of Open() that takes the
table name rather than the command text. Using CTable<> is more efficient at
accessing a table than the corresponding SELECT * in a CCommand<>.

Accessors

ATL provides several accessor classes, the choice of which depends on how much you
know about the database. In the previous section, I mentioned CAccessor, which is
used when you know about the database and the structure of its tables. It is the
simplest of the accessor templates to use since you can use it as a parameter to
CCommand<> or CTable<>. It will get the binding and parameter information it needs
from the user record class that you pass as its parameter.

The binding information that links columns in a rowset to the data members is
mentioned in the COLUMN map. Each COLUMN_ENTRY() macro gives the index of a
column and the name of the data member that will be used to hold the column value
(see Appendix I for more information). If the type of the column is not one of the more
common types, then you can use one of the other COLUMN_ENTRY() macros to specify
the type and size of the column data type.

CTable<> is a pain to use if you have tables with many columns and you're only
interested in a few of them. This is because all of the columns declared in the COLUMN
map will be bound to the user record class data members. You can restrict the binding
by removing columns from the map, so if you just want to retrieve the description
strings from the Products table you can use:

```
BEGIN_COLUMN_MAP(CProductsAccessor)
   COLUMN_ENTRY(2, m_Description)
END_COLUMN_MAP()
```

Notice that the correct column number is used. The problem with this is that to get the
other columns at another time you will have to declare a new user record with a
COLUMN map that includes the columns you require. CAccessor<> comes to the
rescue here, because it allows you to specify more than one accessor for the table. To
do this you replace the COLUMN map with an ACCESSOR map (in fact a COLUMN map is
just an ACCESSOR map that declares a single accessor).

The ACCESSOR map can have a default accessor, but this is not essential. If there is a default accessor then this will be used when MoveNext() is called, and you can access the data immediately through the user record. If there's no default accessor (also called the auto accessor), or if you want to use one of the other accessors then after calling MoveNext() you should call GetData(), giving the index of the accessor you want to use.

For example:

```
BEGIN_ACCESSOR_MAP(CProductsAccessor, 3)
    BEGIN_ACCESSOR(0, false)
        COLUMN_ENTRY(2, m_Description)
    END_ACCESSOR()
    BEGIN_ACCESSOR(1, false)
        COLUMN_ENTRY(1, m_ProductID)
        COLUMN_ENTRY(2, m_Description)
    END_ACCESSOR()
    BEGIN_ACCESSOR(2, false)
        COLUMN_ENTRY(1, m_ProductID)
        COLUMN_ENTRY(2, m_Description)
        COLUMN_ENTRY_TYPE(3, DBTYPE_CY, m_UnitCost)
    END_ACCESSOR()
END_ACCESSOR_MAP()
```

The second parameter to BEGIN_ACCESSOR_MAP() gives the number of accessors. The first parameter of BEGIN_ACCESSOR() gives the (zero-based) index of the accessor, while the second indicates whether the accessor is an auto accessor . In this example, there is no auto accessor, so to use this user record you need to call GetData():

```
while (db.MoveNext() == S_OK)
{
    db.GetData(1);
    cout <<  printf db.m_ProductID << ", "
        << db.m_Description << endl;
}
```

If you don't know the structure of the database at design time then you can use one of the other accessor templates (CDynamicAccessor, CDynamicParameterAccessor or CManualAccessor). However, although they give you more control over the parameters and columns that you can bind to, you're left with the responsibility of finding out what types the columns are and you'll have to do much of the binding work yourself.

Parameters

As mentioned earlier, if the command takes a parameter then your code needs to hold the value of the parameter in a buffer. This information must then be passed to the Execute() method of the command object so that it knows the type and size of the parameter. For CAccessor<> based classes you can use a PARAM map to provide this information. Here is an example I will use later in this chapter:

```
DEFINE_COMMAND(CProductsTableAccessor,
    _T("SELECT ProductID, Description, UnitCost ")
    _T("FROM Products WHERE ProductID = ?"))
BEGIN_PARAM_MAP(CProductsTableAccessor)
    COLUMN_ENTRY(1, m_ProductID)
END_PARAM_MAP()
```

As you can see, the command takes one parameter that is part of the SELECT query. The PARAM map indicates that the value of the parameter will be in the m_ProductID user record member, so before you execute the query (most likely through a call to Open()) you must make sure that this data member has been set. In this example, the COLUMN map binds the m_ProductID to the ProductID. This data member contains the input parameter (because it is mentioned in the PARAM map) and also takes a return value from the query (because it is mentioned in the ACCESSOR or COLUMN map).

If you don't know the command's parameters at design time, you can use CDynamicParameterAccessor to allow you to get information about parameters and set them at runtime.

Bookmarks

There are situations where you will want to mark a position in a rowset so that you can come back to it later. This is done using a **bookmark**. To do this you need to add a CBookmark<> member to the user record and indicate that this is a bookmark by adding a BOOKMARK_ENTRY() into the COLUMN or ACCESSOR map. For example:

```
CBookmark<0> m_bookmark;

BEGIN_COLUMN_MAP(CProductsAccessor)
    BOOKMARK_ENTRY(m_bookmark)
    COLUMN_ENTRY(1, m_ProductID)
    COLUMN_ENTRY(2, m_Description)
    COLUMN_ENTRY_TYPE(3, DBTYPE_CY, m_UnitCost)
END_COLUMN_MAP()
```

The parameter to the CBookmark<> template is the size of the bookmark in bytes. If you pass 0 (or miss out the parameter) then the size is determined dynamically at runtime.

When you move through the rowset, the bookmark will be initialized with data to indicate the current position. If you want to save this position you can do so by declaring another CBookmark<> object in your code and initializing it with the value of the CBookmark<> in your user record. At a later stage you can move back to that position using CRowset::MoveToBookmark():

```
CProducts db;
db.Open();
CBookmark<> position;

while (db.MoveNext() == S_OK)
{
    cout <<" db.m_ProductID << ", "
        << db.m_Description << endl;
    if (lstrcmp(db.m_Description, _T("Shirt")))
        position = db.m_bookmark;
}

// now move back to the shirt entry:
if (position.GetSize() != 0)
{
    db.MoveToBookmark(position);
    // now do something with the shirt...
}
```

Clearly, the bookmark is only valid for a particular rowset, so don't be tempted to cache the value and pass it to another rowset.

Example: Adding Database Support

In this example I'll replace the collection implementation of Products to use a database — a simple Access 97 database called Products.mdb. Since an Access database is being used you'll need to remove the ICollectionOnSTLImpl<> implementation and replace it with the collection interface. To do this, remove the three typedefs for VarVector, VarEnum and IProdCollection from Products.h and modify the inheritance of CProducts as shown below:

```
class ATL_NO_VTABLE CProducts :
    public CComObjectRootEx<CComSingleThreadModel>,
    public CComCoClass<CProducts, &CLSID_Products>,
    public ISupportErrorInfo,
    public IDispatchImpl<IProducts, &IID_IProducts, &LIBID_DATAACCESSLib>
```

You will also need to remove all the code in the constructor — you no longer have a STL container and, in any case, the data will be held in the database. Remember that the object has three properties that were previously implemented by ICollectionOnSTLImpl<>. You now need to implement these yourself, so add the following public methods to the header:

```
STDMETHOD(get_Item)(long lProdID, VARIANT *pVal);
STDMETHOD(get__NewEnum)(LPUNKNOWN *pVal);
STDMETHOD(get_Count)(long *pVal);
```

and the following empty implementations and #include to Products.cpp:

```
#include <OleDBErr.HOLEDBERR.H>

STDMETHODIMP CProducts::get_Count(long *pVal)
{
    return S_OK;
}

STDMETHODIMP CProducts::get__NewEnum(LPUNKNOWN *pVal)
{
    return S_OK;
}

STDMETHODIMP CProducts::get_Item(long lProdID,
                                 VARIANT *pVal)
{
    return S_OK;
}
```

The OleDBErr.h header file defines the symbols for the various errors that the OLE DB templates will return.

These methods, and the Add() and Remove() methods, will have to be changed to use the database. The first action is to generate some consumer classes, so run the Object Wizard and select **Consumer** from the **Data Access** category. Next, you need to go through the steps of specifying the database, so click on **Select Datasource** button. You will be given a list box containing the currently installed OLE DB Providers, one of which is called **Microsoft Jet 3.51 OLE DB Provider**. This option can be used to gain access to Access databases, so select it and then, in the next dialog, browse for Products.mdb.

Your OLE DB provider might have a different version number to this.

The source code for this chapter has a sample database that you can use but, if you wish, you can use Access 97 to create `Products.mdb` and add a few records to it. This should have a single table called `Products` with three columns, as shown below:

Name	Data type	Index
ProductID	Number	Primary
Description	Text[50]	
UnitCost	Currency	

Notice that there is a tab called All. This lists all the properties that can be set, most of which will get values from the other tabs but you can easily select a property and change its value if you choose. In this example, just leave the properties at the values set by Object Wizard. Once the data source properties are initialized, you can click on the OK button. The Wizard will open the database to get information about all the tables, queries and stored procedures in the database. The consumer class will be based on just one of these, so select the `Products` table and click on the OK button.

Object Wizard now has all the information about the `Products` table that it needs to be able to create the user record, so you are shown the initial Object Wizard dialog again. The Object Wizard chooses a **Short Name** of `Products` by default, but this will mean that the consumer class it will create will clash with the class name of the collection. To avoid this, change the **Short Name** to `ProductsTable`. Also, ensure that the **Type** is **Command** and select all the check boxes in the **Support** frame.

When you close the Object Wizard, it generates the consumer class and user record for you and `#includes atldbcli.h` in `stdafx.h`. Open `ProductsTable.h` and take a look at the `OpenDataSource()` method. This initializes the session object by opening a `CDataSource` object with:

```
hr = db.Open(_T("Microsoft.Jet.OLEDB.3.51"), &dbinit);
```

The first parameter specifies the OLE DB provider that will be used, while the second parameter gives the initial values of the data source properties. One of these properties is `DBPROP_INIT_DATASOURCE`, which contains the path to the MDB file you gave to the Object Wizard. Of course, if you want to use this object on another machine then you will have to ensure that the MDB is in the same folder on that machine. If you can't guarantee this, edit this method to take a path to the actual database file. This path could be initialized during the installation of the application by an administrator and held in a persistent store like the registry. (This is not a problem if you use the ODBC provider.)

Include `ProductsTable.h` in `Products.h` so that you can use the consumer classes. Next, you need to make `CProducts` implement `get_Count()` to return the number of records in the `Products` table. This will use the SQL `COUNT()` function and so will only return one value. Rather than using the `CProductsTableAccessor` user record, create a new user record in `ProductsTable.h`:

```
class COutParamAccessor
{
public:
    LONG m_Param;

BEGIN_COLUMN_MAP(COutParamAccessor)
    COLUMN_ENTRY(1, m_Param)
END_COLUMN_MAP()
};
```

I've called this `COutParamAccessor` because I will use it as a general user record to return a `LONG` value from a query. This user record will be used again, later in the project.

Now you can implement the method in `Products.cpp` like this:

```
#define CHECK_OUT_PARAM(p) \
    if (p == NULL) \
        return Error(_T("out pointer is invalid"), IID_IProducts, E_POINTER);

STDMETHODIMP CProducts::get_Count(long *pVal)
{
    CHECK_OUT_PARAM(pVal);
    HRESULT hr;
    *pVal = 0;

    CProductsTable db;
    db.OpenDataSource();
    CCommand<CAccessor<COutParamAccessor> > count;
    hr = count.Open(db.m_session,
        _T("SELECT COUNT(ProductID) FROM Products"));
    if (SUCCEEDED(hr))
        hr = count.MoveNext();
    if (FAILED(hr))
    {
        TCHAR str[40];
        wsprintf(str, _T("Cannot access the database")
            _T(" 0x%08x"), hr);
        CComBSTR bstr = str;
        m_pLogger->Add(bstr, 1);
        return Error(L"Cannot access the database", IID_IProducts, hr);
    }
    else
        *pVal = count.m_Param;
    return hr;
}
```

Notice that I'm not using the command defined by the Object Wizard. Instead, I've created a new command object based on some embedded SQL. The query is performed by calling `Open()` and the results are obtained via `COutParamAccessor` by calling `MoveNext()`. If the call fails, I create an error object and log the error to the error logger.

Now let's look at database access that will need a parameter: get_Item(). This method is passed the ProductID and should return the corresponding Product object. The query should ask for the entire row to be returned if the ProductID field is the same as the parameter passed to get_Item(). To do this you need to edit CProductsTableAccessor so that the command has a WHERE clause.

Edit the code after END_COLUMN_MAP() in ProductsTable.h so that it reads:

```
DEFINE_COMMAND(CProductsTableAccessor,
               _T("SELECT ProductID, Description, UnitCost ")
               _T("FROM Products WHERE ProductID = ?"))
```

This will be used as the default command by calling Open() without a value for the command string. Now we can add the following code to CProducts::get_Item:

```
STDMETHODIMP CProducts::get_Item(long lProdID, VARIANT *pVal)
{
    CHECK_OUT_PARAM(pVal);
    HRESULT hr;

    CProductsTable db;
    db.m_ProductID = lProdID;
    hr = db.Open();
    if (SUCCEEDED(hr))
        hr = db.MoveNext();
    if (hr == DB_S_ENDOFROWSET || FAILED(hr))
    {
        TCHAR str[50];
        wsprintf(str, _T("Cannot get product #%ld"), lProdID);
        CComBSTR bstr = str;
        m_pLogger->Add(bstr, SEV_ERROR);
        return Error(str, IID_IProducts, E_INVALIDARG);
    }
```

(The rest of the code for this method is shown later.) Since there is a parameter in the SQL defined above (the ?) we need to initialize it with the product ID that we're looking for. To do this, the m_ProductID member of the user record is initialized with this value. To indicate that there is a parameter (which should be read when the command is executed) and which data member will be used to hold it, you need to add a parameter map to the user record (CProductsTableAccessor in ProductsTable.h):

```
BEGIN_PARAM_MAP(CProductsTableAccessor)
    COLUMN_ENTRY(1, m_ProductID)
END_PARAM_MAP()
```

Notice that after calling MoveNext() I check for a failed HRESULT to see if either an error occurred or a value of DB_S_ENDOFROWSET has been returned. This is an OLE DB status code, *but it is not a failure code*. The reason it is not a failure is that it indicates that the method succeeded, but the query returned an empty rowset. Of course, since get_Item() assumes that lProgID refers to an existing row, we return an error code.

If the query is successful then a new `Product` object should be created. Complete `CProducts::get_Item` with the following code:

```
CComObject<CProduct>* pObj;
CComObject<CProduct>::CreateInstance(&pObj);
CComVariant var;

var = pObj;
double dCost;
VarR8FromCy(db.m_UnitCost, &dCost);
pObj->Initialize(db.m_ProductID, db.m_Description, dCost);
var.Detach(pVal);
return S_OK;
}
```

`Add()` involves two queries. The first query is used to get a unique `ProductID` for the new item. In the previous version of this code, I calculated the highest value of `ProductID` of existing entries and incremented that. You can do something similar in this version using the SQL `MAX()` function. Since we already have a user record that will return a single number value, we can use that. `CProducts::Add` needs to be changed so replace the previous code with the following:

```
STDMETHODIMP CProducts::Add(BSTR strDesc, double dCost, VARIANT* pVar)
{
    CHECK_OUT_PARAM(pVar);

    USES_CONVERSION;
    HRESULT hr;
    CProductsTable db;
    db.OpenDataSource();
    CCommand<CAccessor<COutParamAccessor> > max;
    max.m_Param = 0;      // just in case there are no records
    m_mutex.Lock();
    hr = max.Open(db.m_session,
                  _T("SELECT MAX(ProductID) FROM Products"));
    if (SUCCEEDED(hr))
        hr = max.MoveNext();
```

Now, `max.m_Param` has the maximum `ProductID` used so far, so this can be used to calculate a new `ProductID`. Notice the call to `m_mutex.Lock()`. This is used to mark the start of a guarded section of code — I want to make sure that the code is thread safe, and this is one area where there might be a problem.

This first query obtains a value from the database to determine what value will be used for the `ProductID` of the new record that is inserted into the database in a following query. Without this locking there is a possibility that, once the first query has been performed, another thread could be scheduled to run the same code. In that case it will get the same value for the `ProductID`. If the insertion query is run it will add a new record. When the first thread is scheduled to run again, it will attempt to add a record using a `ProductID` (which is an index field) that already exists, so the insertion will fail. Marking a section of code as a guarded block indicates that all the code in the section should be treated as *atomic*. This means that no other thread should run the code before the current thread has finished the entire guarded block (this assumes that no code other than `DataAccess.dll` will alter the database). Note that the execution of `ICommand::Execute()` (deep within the bowels of `Open()`) can be regarded as atomic but the rest of the code in `Open()` can't.

To guard the code I use a Win32 mutex kernel object. I could have chosen to use a critical section, but this would mean that the code would be safe from access only within the current process. A mutex is a machine wide object, so when one thread in one process owns the mutex, no other thread will be able to access it. This solution works if the users of the database are all on the same machine. In a distributed environment, where clients can be on different machines, it won't work. In this case, you'll have to put the logic of both queries within a stored procedure. The database will ensure that the stored procedure is executed atomically.

The mutex is wrapped by the following simple class:

```
#ifndef __MUTEX_H_
#define __MUTEX_H_

class CMutex
{
public:
    CMutex(LPCTSTR strName)
    {
        m_hMutex = CreateMutex(NULL, FALSE, strName);
    }
    ~CMutex()
    {
        CloseHandle(m_hMutex);
    }
    void Lock()
    {
        WaitForSingleObject(m_hMutex, INFINITE);
    }
    void Unlock()
    {
        ReleaseMutex(m_hMutex);
    }
private:
    HANDLE m_hMutex;
};

#endif //__MUTEX_H_
```

This creates a mutex object in the constructor with a specified name. If a mutex already exists with this name then that mutex will be opened. The Lock() method will wait until the mutex is available (i.e. no other thread owns it), at which point this thread will own it. The Unlock() method releases ownership of the mutex.

Create a new header file, type in this code and save it as Mutex.h. Add this file to the project by right clicking on the **Header Files** folder and then selecting **Add Files to Folder**. Add an include for this header file to the top of Products.h, then add a data member and initialize it in the constructor:

```
CProducts() : m_mutex("Products") {}

...

private:
    CComPtr<IEvents> m_pLogger;
    CMutex m_mutex;
};
```

Now that you have a `ProductID`, you have all of the required data to add the item to the database. To insert a new record we need a new user record that has the parameter information that we'll use in the `INSERT` query, so this should be added to `ProductsTable.h`:

```
class CInsertProductsAccessor
{
public:
   TCHAR m_Description[51];
   LONG m_ProductID;
   CURRENCY m_UnitCost;

BEGIN_PARAM_MAP(CInsertProductsAccessor)
   COLUMN_ENTRY(1, m_ProductID)
   COLUMN_ENTRY(2, m_Description)
   COLUMN_ENTRY_TYPE(3, DBTYPE_CY, m_UnitCost)
END_PARAM_MAP()
};
```

You can now use this to create a new command and insert the record. Next, the code below should be added to `CProducts::Add` (remember it has already obtained the maximum `ProductID` from the database):

```
CCommand<CAccessor<CInsertProductsAccessor> > insert;
if (SUCCEEDED(hr))
{
   if (SysStringLen(strDesc) >= sizeof(insert.m_Description))
   {
      m_mutex.Unlock();
      return Error(L"Description too large", IID_IProducts,
               E_INVALIDARG);
   }
   insert.m_ProductID = max.m_Param + 1;
   VarCyFromR8(dCost, &insert.m_UnitCost);
   lstrcpy(insert.m_Description, W2T(strDesc));
   hr = insert.Open(db.m_session,
               _T("INSERT INTO Products ")
               _T("VALUES(?, ?, ?)"));
}
m_mutex.Unlock();

if (FAILED(hr))
{
   TCHAR str[50];
   wsprintf(str, _T("Cannot add the product %S ")
               _T("0x%08x"), strDesc, hr);
   CComBSTR bstr = str;
   m_pLogger->Add(bstr, SEV_ERROR);
   return Error(L"Cannot add the product", IID_IProducts, hr);
}
```

The code first checks that the product description isn't bigger than the buffer used by the user record, and then initializes the user record with the data for the new record. Finally, calling `Open()` on the new command does all the work of creating the command, binding the parameters and then executing the command. Since the command doesn't return any data there's no need to call `MoveNext()`.

The final task in this code is to create a new `Product` object and return it. You've seen this code before, I've just rearranged it and deleted some lines that are no longer needed:

```
CComObject<CProduct>* pObj;
CComObject<CProduct>::CreateInstance(&pObj);
CComVariant var;

var = pObj;
pObj->Initialize(insert.m_ProductID, W2T(strDesc), dCost);
var.Detach(pVar);

WCHAR str[20];
swprintf(str, L", $%.2lf", dCost);
CComBSTR bstr = L"Added ";
bstr += strDesc;
bstr += str;
m_pLogger->Add(bstr, SEV_INFO);
return S_OK;
}
```

The next thing to do is implement `Remove()`. The SQL for this is simple: you use `DELETE` and a `WHERE` clause to specify which record to delete. This means that you need to pass a single parameter in the query, but you don't need to receive any data back. For this, you need a new user record in `ProductsTable.h`:

```
class CInParamAccessor
{
public:
   LONG m_Param;

BEGIN_PARAM_MAP(CInParamAccessor)
   COLUMN_ENTRY(1, m_Param)
END_PARAM_MAP()
};
```

Notice that this has a `PARAM` map, rather than a `COLUMN` map.

The majority of the code in `Remove()` will have to be changed. The first part of the `Remove()` method needs to check that the record exists. I do this because, if I try to execute the `DELETE` query with an invalid `ProductID`, the OLE DB provider will happily perform the query and return `S_OK` without removing any records. Since I want to tell the user that the `ProductID` that they've passed was invalid, this check has to be made:

```
STDMETHODIMP CProducts::Remove(long lProdID)
{
   HRESULT hr;
   CProductsTable db;
   db.m_ProductID = lProdID;
   m_mutex.Lock();
   hr = db.Open();
   if (SUCCEEDED(hr))
      hr = db.MoveNext();
   if (hr == DB_S_ENDOFROWSET || FAILED(hr))
   {
      m_mutex.Unlock();
      TCHAR str[50];
      wsprintf(str, _T("Cannot get the product %ld"), lProdID);
      CComBSTR bstr = str;
      m_pLogger->Add(bstr, SEV_ERROR);
         return Error(L"Cannot get the product",
                     IID_IProducts, E_INVALIDARG);
   }
```

Notice again the use of the mutex object. This is because there will be two queries, the second of which is dependent on the first, and I don't want another thread to preempt this thread before both queries have been run. In this query I use CProductsTableAccessor so I don't have to create a new command and can call Open() directly through the CProductsTable object.

Now I know whether the record exists, I can delete it if it does:

```
CCommand<CAccessor<CInParamAccessor> > del;
del.m_Param = lProdID;
CDBPropSet propset(DBPROPSET_ROWSET);
propset.AddProperty(DBPROP_UPDATABILITY, DBPROPVAL_UP_DELETE);
hr = del.Open(db.m_session,
               _T("DELETE FROM Products WHERE ProductID = ?"), &propset);

m_mutex.Unlock();
if (FAILED(hr))
{
    CComBSTR bstr = L"Delete failed";
    m_pLogger->Add(bstr, SEV_ERROR);
    return Error(L"Delete failed", IID_IProducts, E_INVALIDARG);
}

CComBSTR bstr;
bstr = L"Removed ";
bstr += db.m_Description;
m_pLogger->Add(bstr, SEV_INFO);
return S_OK;
}
```

This uses the new user record and passes the ProductID of the record through m_Param. Notice that the call to Open() is passed the pointer to a CDBPropSet structure. This is used to indicate that the query will require specific behavior from the OLE DB object (in this case, the ability to delete records). The rest of the code is straightforward.

The final thing to do is implement the enumerator. As with the EventLogger project, you will need to add a new enumerator object. The steps are generally the same as for the EnumEvents object: create an object called EnumProducts with a custom interface, the Both threading model and Support ISupportErrorInfo checked. Delete the definition of IEnumProducts from the IDL file and use IUnknown as the [default] interface for the EnumProducts coclass (also mark this as noncreatable):

```
[
    uuid(AD8EFF02-8DC1-11D2-8B04-00902707906A),
    helpstring("EnumProducts Class"),
    noncreatable
]
coclass EnumProducts
{
    [default] interface IUnknown;
};
```

Next make the object noncreatable by editing CEnumProducts to remove the CComCoClass<> base class and replace IEnumProducts with IEnumVARIANT:

```
class ATL_NO_VTABLE CEnumProducts :
    public CComObjectRootEx<CComMultiThreadModel>,
    public ISupportErrorInfo,
    public IEnumVARIANT
```

You also need to change the interface map and the registration macro, and add an empty category map:

```
DECLARE_NO_REGISTRY()
DECLARE_PROTECT_FINAL_CONSTRUCT()

BEGIN_COM_MAP(CEnumProducts)
    COM_INTERFACE_ENTRY(IEnumVARIANT)
    COM_INTERFACE_ENTRY(ISupportErrorInfo)
END_COM_MAP()

BEGIN_CATEGORY_MAP(CEnumProducts)
END_CATEGORY_MAP()
```

Since the object isn't registered, you can remove the RGS for the object from the project (through ResourceView, delete the IDR_ENUMPRODUCTS REGISTRY item and, through FileView, select and delete EnumProducts.rgs). Then open DataAccess.cpp and edit the object map to make CEnumProducts noncreatable:

```
BEGIN_OBJECT_MAP(ObjectMap)
OBJECT_ENTRY(CLSID_Products, CProducts)
OBJECT_ENTRY_NON_CREATEABLE(CProduct)
OBJECT_ENTRY_NON_CREATEABLE(CEnumProducts)
END_OBJECT_MAP()
```

Since the object supports rich error objects, you have to make sure that the InterfaceSupportsErrorInfo() method specifies that IEnumVARIANT returns error objects. Change the code in EnumProducts.cpp to:

```
static const IID* arr[] =
{
    &IID_IEnumVARIANT
};
```

Now you're ready to write the enumerator code. As with EnumEvents, you'll need to implement the enumerator methods yourself, so add these to the EnumProducts.h header:

```
// IEnumVARIANT
public:
    STDMETHOD(Next)(ULONG celt, VARIANT* rgVar, ULONG * pCeltFetched);
    STDMETHOD(Skip)(ULONG celt);
    STDMETHOD(Reset)();
    STDMETHOD(Clone)(IEnumVARIANT** ppEnum);
```

and their implementations to `EnumProducts.cpp`:

```
STDMETHODIMP CEnumProducts::Next(ULONG celt, VARIANT* rgVar,
                                  ULONG* pCeltFetched)
{
    if (rgVar == NULL || (celt != 1 && pCeltFetched == NULL))
        return AtlReportError(CLSID_EnumProducts, L"out pointer invalid",
                              IID_IEnumVARIANT, E_POINTER);
    HRESULT hr = S_OK;
    return hr;
}

STDMETHODIMP CEnumProducts::Skip(ULONG celt)
{
    HRESULT hr = S_OK;
    return hr;
}

STDMETHODIMP CEnumProducts::Reset()
{
    HRESULT hr = S_OK;
    return hr;
}

STDMETHODIMP CEnumProducts::Clone(IEnumVARIANT** ppEnum)
{
    HRESULT hr = S_OK;
    return hr;
}
```

This object needs to make queries on the database, so to give access to it I derive the class from `CProductsTable` (note the additional `#include` lines as well):

```
#include "resource.h"                        // main symbols
#include "..\EventLogger\EventLogger.h"
#include "ProductsTable.h"

/////////////////////////////////////////////////////////////////////////////
// CEnumProducts
class ATL_NO_VTABLE CEnumProducts :
    public CComObjectRootEx<CComMultiThreadModel>,
    public ISupportErrorInfo,
    public IEnumVARIANT,
    public CProductsTable
```

This will allow an instance to hold information about the previous queries that have been performed, specifically to maintain the rowset. This is important for `Next()` because it means that the code does not have to perform a new query every time `Next()` is called.

The object should also have a reference to the `Events` object so that I can log any problems. I could call `CoCreateInstance()` to get another reference to this object, but this will clearly take time. I already have a reference to this object in the `Products` object, so I can pass its pointer to the newly created `EnumProducts` object when it's created in `get__NewEnum()`. To pass this pointer I use a C++ *member function* called `Initialize()` (this is *not* a COM method because I don't want external users to be able to call it).

Use ClassView to add this `public` member function to `CEnumProducts`:

```
HRESULT Initialize(IEvents* pLogger);
```

Then add the following data member:

```
private:
    CComPtr<IEvents> m_pLogger;
};
```

Implement the method like this:

```
HRESULT CEnumProducts::Initialize(IEvents* pLogger)
{
    HRESULT hr;
    m_pLogger = pLogger;

    hr = OpenDataSource();
    if (FAILED(hr))
    {
        TCHAR str[40];
        wsprintf(str, _T("Cannot open the database 0x%08x"), hr);
        CComBSTR bstr = str;
        m_pLogger->Add(bstr, SEV_ERROR);
    }
    return hr;
}
```

The first part of the code copies the pointer passed as a parameter and, since
`m_pLogger` is a smart pointer, the assignment operator will ensure that `AddRef()` is
called. The next part calls `OpenDataSource()` through the `CProductsTable` base
class to create the session.

> For a simple implementation like this, this code is fine. However, you
> should be aware of some potential problems. The session object is
> created in `Initialize()` when the enumerator object is created, and the
> session is destroyed when the enumerator is released. This means that a
> database connection remains open for the lifetime of the enumerator,
> which can be a resource problem. To solve this you could use a database
> cursor to hold the current position and only open a session when you
> actually need access to the database. The techniques for doing this are
> beyond the scope of this book.

Whenever a new enumerator is created, there won't be an open rowset — I'll use this
fact later. An implementation detail of this object is that the object maintains the data
required for the *subsequent* call to `Next()`. Hence, `Reset()` is implemented like this:

```
STDMETHODIMP CEnumProducts::Reset()
{
    HRESULT hr;
    Close();

    CDBPropSet propset(DBPROPSET_ROWSET);
    propset.AddProperty(DBPROP_IRowsetLocate, true);
    hr = CCommand<CAccessor<CProductsTableAccessor> >
     ::Open(m_session,
     _T("SELECT ProductID, Description, UnitCost ")
     _T("FROM Products ORDER BY ProductID"), &propset);
    MoveFirst();
    return hr;
}
```

The code calls Close() to ensure that there isn't an open rowset and then it calls
Open(), which is inherited from CProductsTable. However, since there are several
Open() methods in the base classes, the code explicitly mentions the inheritance
branch. The command that is performed is given as the second parameter and a
CDBPropSet initialized with a DBPROP_IRowsetLocate property passed as the
third parameter. This is required to traverse through the rowset with calls like
MoveFirst() and MoveNext(), using parameters.

Since I've implemented Reset() to perform the query every time it is called, the
enumerator is dynamic — when records are added, deleted or changed the change can
be obtained after the next call to Reset(). The call to MoveNext() will obtain the
values for the first row, which will be cached until the next call to Next().

The Skip() method needs to move the current position by a specified number of
records. Notice that in the following code I check to see if m_spRowset has a value; if
it doesn't then the object hasn't been used yet, so I call Reset().

```
STDMETHODIMP CEnumProducts::Skip(ULONG celt)
{
    HRESULT hr;
    if (!m_spRowset)
        Reset();
    hr = MoveNext(celt - 1, true);
    if (hr == DB_E_BADSTARTPOSITION)
    {
        Reset();
        return S_FALSE;
    }
    return hr;
}
```

The next task, which is to implement Next(), is the longest. This method needs to
read the requested number of rows from the database and use each to initialize a
Product object.

This code should call `Reset()` under two conditions. The first of these is if the object has not been used yet (`Reset()` hasn't been called), in which case `m_spRowset` is NULL. The second condition is if a previous call to `Next()` reached the end of the rowset. To indicate this second case the code will set `m_ProductID` to a value of -1. Since I read the results for the *subsequent* call to `Next()` and cache the result if `m_ProductID` has a value of -1 the method should return immediately and indicate that there are no more items:

```
STDMETHODIMP CEnumProducts::Next(ULONG celt, VARIANT* rgVar,
ULONG* pCeltFetched)
{
    if (rgVar == NULL || (celt != 1 && pCeltFetched == NULL))
        return AtlReportError(CLSID_EnumProducts,
                              L"out pointer invalid", IID_IEnumVARIANT,
                              E_POINTER);
    HRESULT hr = S_OK;

    if (m_ProductID == -1)
    {
        Reset();   // for next time
        if (pCeltFetched != NULL)
            *pCeltFetched = 0;
        return S_FALSE;
    }

    if (!m_spRowset)
        hr = Reset();

    if (FAILED(hr))
    {
        CComBSTR bstr = L"Database error";
        m_pLogger->Add(bstr, SEV_ERROR);
        if (pCeltFetched != NULL)
            *pCeltFetched = 0;
        return AtlReportError(CLSID_EnumProducts, bstr, IID_IEnumVARIANT, hr);
    }
```

The following code creates a `Product` object and initializes it with the values cached in the data members inherited from the user record:

```
VARIANT* pelt = rgVar;
ULONG pos;
for (pos = 0; pos < celt; pos++)
{
    CComObject<CProduct>* pObj;
    CComObject<CProduct>::CreateInstance(&pObj);
    double dCost;
    VarR8FromCy(m_UnitCost, &dCost);
    pObj->Initialize(m_ProductID, m_Description, dCost);
    IDispatch* pDisp;
    pObj->QueryInterface(&pDisp);
    pelt->pdispVal = pDisp;
    pelt->vt = VT_DISPATCH;
    pelt++;
```

The next action is to get the next record for the next pass through the loop (or the next call to Next()):

```
        hr = MoveNext();
        if (hr == DB_S_ENDOFROWSET)
        {
            pos++;
            m_ProductID = -1;
            if (celt != pos)
                hr = S_FALSE;
            else
                hr = S_OK;
            break;
        }
        if (FAILED(hr))
        {
            CComBSTR bstr = L"Database error";
            m_pLogger->Add(bstr, SEV_ERROR);
            while (rgVar < pelt)
                VariantClear(rgVar++);
            if (pCeltFetched != NULL)
                *pCeltFetched = 0;
            return AtlReportError(CLSID_EnumProducts, bstr,
                            IID_IEnumVARIANT, hr);
        }
    }
    if (pCeltFetched != NULL)
        *pCeltFetched = pos;
    return hr;
}
```

If MoveNext() returns a status code that shows that the end of the rowset has been reached there's no point in continuing the loop, so pos is incremented to reflect the actual number of items in the array. The code checks to see if the requested number of items have been obtained and returns S_OK if they have, otherwise S_FALSE is returned. If the call to MoveNext() fails then there is a problem with the database, and in this situation I abort the entire method, cleaning up any objects that may have been put in the array.

The final task is to implement Clone(). This should create an EnumProducts object that has the same value as the object that creates it. In other words, the cloned object must have the same rowset and be at the same position in the rowset as the creator object. On the surface, Clone() is simple:

```
STDMETHODIMP CEnumProducts::Clone(IEnumVARIANT** ppEnum)
{
    HRESULT hr;
    CComObject<CEnumProducts>* pObj;
    CComObject<CEnumProducts>::CreateInstance(&pObj);
    hr = pObj->QueryInterface(ppEnum);
    if (FAILED(hr))
    {
        delete pObj;
        *ppEnum = NULL;
        return AtlReportError(CLSID_EnumProducts, L"cannot clone enumerator",
                        IID_IEnumVARIANT, hr);
    }
    return pObj->InitializeClone(this, m_pLogger);
}
```

This code simply creates a new object; but notice the function call at the end. This is a
C++ method (again, *not* a COM method) used to pass the current object's state to the
cloned object. Use ClassView to add this `public` method to `CEnumProducts`:

```
HRESULT InitializeClone(CEnumProducts* pCreator, IEvents* pLogger);
```

and implement it in `EnumProducts.cpp`:

```
HRESULT CEnumProducts::InitializeClone(CEnumProducts* pCreator,
    IEvents* pLogger)
{
    m_pLogger = pLogger;
    m_spRowset = pCreator->m_spRowset;
    if (m_spRowset)
       Bind();

    m_ProductID = pCreator->m_ProductID;
    m_UnitCost = pCreator->m_UnitCost;
    lstrcpy(m_Description, pCreator->m_Description);
    return S_OK;
}
```

First, I copy the reference to the `Events` object, then I initialize the rowset by copying
the `m_spRowset` smart pointer. If this is non-NULL (there is an open rowset) `Bind()`
is called to make the object allocate its internal buffers for the rowset. These buffers,
and the rowset interface pointer itself, are released the next time `Reset()` is called.
Finally, I initialize the user record data members so that the next time `Next()` is called
there is data that can be used.

The `EnumProducts` object is now finished, except for the following `#include`
statements:

```
#include "Product.h"
#include "ProductsTable.h"
#include <OLEDBERR.H>
```

Now you can go back to `CProducts` and implement `get__NewEnum()`:

```
STDMETHODIMP CProducts::get__NewEnum(LPUNKNOWN *pVal)
{
    HRESULT hr;
    CComObject<CEnumProducts>* pObj;
    CComObject<CEnumProducts>::CreateInstance(&pObj);
    hr = pObj->QueryInterface(pVal);
    if (FAILED(hr))
    {
        delete pObj;
        return Error(L"Cannot return enumerator", IID_IProducts, hr);
    }
    pObj->Initialize(m_pLogger);
    return hr;
}
```

Remember to `#include EnumProducts.h` at the top of `Products.cpp`.

As you can see, I pass a reference to the `Events` object to the newly created
`CEnumProducts` object through the C++ method `Initialize()`.

You should now be able to compile the project and test it out with the Visual Basic example code developed in the last few chapters. These programs should behave in almost exactly the same way as before but with one slight difference — when `Products` is restarted the product list will contain the same items that were present before the application was closed. This is because persistence is achieved via the database.

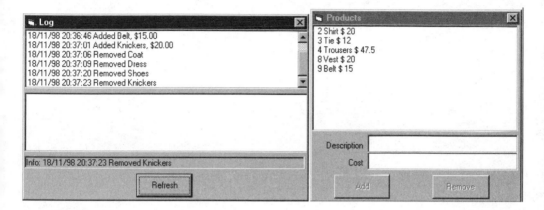

Summary

This chapter has introduced you to the OLE DB consumer classes in ATL 3.0. Databases are extremely important for business applications and anything that makes database access easier is welcomed. OLE DB goes part of the way by abstracting all data source access into a collection of standard interfaces but, because they are generic, access to a database can be quite complex. However, this is also their strength because it means that code written to use one OLE DB data source can be adapted quickly to use another.

The ATL classes abstract database access further by wrapping the OLE DB API into a simpler and easier to use class library. This has been demonstrated in the changes I've made to the `Products` example where I replaced the STL implementation of the collection with an OLE DB data source (in this case Access).

6

Windows and Controls

Introduction

Up to this point in this book, the objects you've come across have had no user interface. This is deliberate because many of the objects that you're likely to come across in a business environment won't have a user interface. However, there are situations where you will want a visual interface, and the most usual case is ActiveX controls.

This chapter covers two broad subjects: in the first half I'll cover the ATL windowing classes and in the second half I'll cover the control classes. The windowing classes are provided to implement window and dialog procedures and have support for handling messages. They don't have to be used as part of a COM object. Indeed, you can write Win32 applications without any COM support using these classes. However, the situation in which you're most likely to use these classes is when you write a control.

ActiveX controls cannot be used on their own; they must be created by, and used within, a control container. There are many containers available, some with more functionality than others. The more control functionality that you expose to a container, and the closer the integration with the container, the more interfaces the control should support. This is the situation where ATL's interface implementations become most apparent. When you create a control class with the Object Wizard, you'll find the interface map crammed full of interfaces, and you don't have to write a single line of code to get this support.

The example in this chapter will develop a control that gives access to the Products collection to allow you to add and remove items.

Windows

ATL provides a class called CWindow. This does not implement a window — its purpose is to wrap a HWND - so it may appear misnamed. The class has many methods, most of which mirror the equivalent Win32 function. If all it does is wrap the Win32 functions then why does it exist? Well, although its methods have the same name as the corresponding Win32 functions, you'll notice that they don't take a HWND parameter. The reason for this is that the encapsulated HWND is used. CWindow will check this to make sure that it refers to an existing window, causing an assertion failure in debug builds if it doesn't. CWindow differs from the MFC CWnd in that it doesn't take part in a window's window procedure — that is the responsibility of another class, as you'll see later. Appendix J lists the methods of CWindow and explains which are wrapper methods and which have no equivalent in Win32.

You can use CWindow like this:

```
// uses atlwin.h and atlbase.h
CWindow hWnd;
hWnd = ::FindWindow(NULL, _T("My Window"))
if (hWnd.IsWindow())
    hWnd.ShowWindow(SW_HIDE);
```

This uses the Win32 FindWindow() function to look for a window with the caption "My Window" and if this exists it hides it. Note that CWindow has an assignment operator, which is how it is initialized with a value from FindWindow(). You should be aware that CWindow also has an HWND conversion operator, so any function that takes a HWND parameter can be passed a CWindow.

Creating a Window

CWindow has a Create() method which allows you to create a window of a registered window class, so if you want to create an edit box you can use code like this:

```
CWindow hEdit;
RECT rect = {0, 0, 100, 100};
hEdit.Create(_T("EDIT"), hParent, rect,
             _T("Contents"),
             WS_CHILD | WS_BORDER | WS_VISIBLE,
             0, IDC_EDIT);
```

Create() does have default parameters, but here I've provided values for most of them. It will return the HWND of the created window (which will be NULL if the creation failed — I've ignored it here). The first parameter is the name of the Windows class, the second the HWND of a parent window. That is followed by a RECT structure specifying the position of the window and the title to give it. The next two parameters specify the style of the window and because the window is a child (it includes the WS_CHILD style attribute), another parameter is required to give its ID.

To manipulate this control you can use the various methods in CWindow. So, to get and set the text in this window, you can use:

```
CComBSTR bstr;
hEdit.GetWindowText(bstr.m_str);
bstr += L" more text";
hEdit.SetWindowText(W2T(bstr));
```

Window Messages

GetWindowText() is pretty generic and most windows will respond to it. If you want to do things that are specific to a particular window class then you'll need to send it a message. For example, to get the starting and ending character positions of the selection in an edit box, you need to send the EM_GETSEL message:

```
int iStart, iEnd;
hEdit.SendMessage(EM_GETSEL, (WPARAM)&iStart, (LPARAM)&iEnd);
```

AtlCon

Sending messages to windows like this is rather grungy but, unfortunately, there's no support in the core ATL library to wrap code around a specific window's messages. However, don't fear, help is available — although it is rather hidden from you! Visual C++ comes with an ATL example called AtlCon, which has a header file called AtlControls.h. This file is clearly a part of ATL, but perhaps it wasn't finished in time to be included in the core library, so it's currently unsupported. However, I find it so useful that I've copied it to my Atl folder under the VC98 folder. (You may decide to be more cautious and merely add the path to the AtlCon folder in your INCLUDE path.)

This file declares an ATLControls namespace with CWindow-based wrapper classes for all of the Win32 and common controls (described in Appendix J). For example, one of these classes is called CEdit, which wraps the code to create and manipulate an edit control. Using this class, the previous code can be written like this:

```
CEdit hEdit;
RECT rect = {0, 0, 100, 100};
hEdit.Create(hParent, rect, _T("Contents"),
             WS_CHILD | WS_BORDER | WS_VISIBLE,
             0, IDC_EDIT);
hEdit.AppendText(_T(" more text"));
```

The Create() method doesn't need a class name because CEdit will provide that, otherwise the other parameters are the same as CWindow. Here you can see that I'm adding text to the control using the AppendText() method. This class also provides code for control messages:

```
int iStart, iEnd;
hEdit.GetSel(iStart, iEnd);
```

Common Controls

As you can see, this code is far easier to read than the previous version. The situation where you will find these classes most useful is when you want to use the Win32 Common Controls. If you've used these controls before, you'll know that you initialize and access them either by sending messages, or by using macros (that, in fact, will send a message for you). However, some of the messages can take large structures as parameters, making it quite confusing as to what values you should pass. The `AtlControls` classes help here because they provide methods for specific actions and ensure that the correct parameters are passed with an appropriate message.

ListView Control

For example, in the following code I have a dialog that has a ListView control. The dialog is initialized by handling the `WM_INITDIALOG` message (I'll explain how in the next section) with the following code, where I call `CWindow::GetDlgItem()` to get the handle of the control and then use the `CListViewCtrl` wrapper class:

```
CListViewCtrl lv;
lv = GetDlgItem(IDC_LISTPANE);

RECT rect;
lv.GetClientRect(&rect);
LVCOLUMN lvc = {LVCF_TEXT | LVCF_WIDTH, 0,
                (rect.right - rect.left)/2, NULL,
                0, 0, 0, 0};
lvc.pszText = _T("Name");
lv.InsertColumn(0, &lvc);

lvc.mask |= LVCF_SUBITEM;
lvc.pszText = _T("Data");
lvc.iSubItem = 1;
lv.InsertColumn(1, &lvc);
```

The code then sets up the columns that the ListView will use by initializing a `LVCOLUMN` and passing this to `InsertColumn()`. Items can be added to the control using:

```
int item = lv.AddItem(itemIndex, 0, strName);
lv.SetItemText(item, 1, strData);
```

This is considerably easier than trying to determine the various `LVITEM` parameters to use and then sending appropriate messages.

Writing Window Procedures

`CWindow` and the classes in the `AtlControls` namespace are fine when you want to manipulate controls on a window or in a dialog but they can only be used on windows that already have a window procedure. This means that you can send messages to the window and it will handle the message according to the documentation. These wrapper classes don't allow you to receive messages. Consequently, you cannot respond to messages sent by the system when some system event occurs (for example, the window is created or the user clicks on it) or when a child control sends a notification message (for example, the user expands a branch in a tree control). To be able to accept a Windows message you need to implement a window procedure and register it (either by registering a new window class, or by subclassing or superclassing an existing one).

CWindowImpl<>

ATL provides a template called CWindowImpl<> to do this work for you. I won't go into the details of how this class works because, in most cases, you don't need to know about the implementation details. This template takes two parameters. One is the name of a class that will be used to wrap a HWND — CWindow will be used by default. The other is a class that defines the window traits — which effectively consist of the style and extended style that will be used by default when creating the window. CWindowImpl<>::Create() can be passed a style and an extended style, and these will be combined with these traits.

> *Professional ATL COM Programming* explains in great depth how the ATL windowing classes work.

CWindowImpl<> registers a window class for you. The window procedure of this class will forward messages to your class by calling a method called ProcessWindowMessage(). You don't need to implement this method. Instead, you should add an ATL MSG map, which will implement it for you. Details of all the macros you can use in a message map are given in Appendix A. An example of a simple map is shown below:

```
BEGIN_MSG_MAP(CMyWindow)
    MESSAGE_HANDLER(WM_LBUTTONDOWN, LButtonHandler)
END_MSG_MAP()

LRESULT LButtonHandler(UINT uMsg, WPARAM wParam, LPARAM lParam,
                       BOOL& bHandled)
{
    DWORD fwKeys = wParam;
    WORD xPos = LOWORD(lParam);
    WORD yPos = HIWORD(lParam);
    ATLTRACE("Left button click at (%d, %d)\n", xPos, yPos);
    if (fwFlags & MK_CONTROL != 0)
        ATLTRACE("Ctrl Key Pressed\n");
    if (fwFlags & MK_SHIFT != 0)
        ATLTRACE("Shift Key Pressed\n");
    return 0;
}
```

This map indicates that, when the left button is clicked on the window, the LButtonHandler() method will be called. The class that implements this map should, at the very least, be derived from CMessageMap, which indicates that it can handle messages. However, note that this base class does not implement a window procedure, so you'll have to route the messages using another class (a derived class could use the CHAIN_MSG_MAP() macro) or derive your class from CWindowImpl<>, which itself derives from CMessageMap.

Once a class derives from CMessageMap you can use the ClassView message map wizard to add messages to a map and implement their handlers. However, you'll only want to use this wizard for a few messages. The reason for this is that it only knows about the common messages and won't allow you to add range handlers (which handle a range of messages).

Notice the parameters of the message handler given in the previous example. What is apparent from this is that no message cracking (obtaining actual parameters from the message's lParam and wParam) is performed. In the LButtonHandler() example, I've cracked the message parameters myself. If you've moved from MFC to ATL, message parameter cracking is one feature that you'll miss!

CDialogImpl<>

ATL also provides a class called CDialogImpl<>, which derives from CMessageMap and implements a dialog procedure. This means that a class that derives from this template can have a message map that handles messages from the dialog and any of its child controls. The dialog should have a dialog resource created in the resource editor, and should be held in a member called IDD (that is usually a member of an anonymous enum):

```
enum { IDD = IDD_MYDIALOG };

BEGIN_MSG_MAP(CMyDialog)
    MESSAGE_HANDLER(WM_INITDIALOG, OnInitDialog)
END_MSG_MAP()
```

Your dialog class can be used to create either modal or modeless dialogs. You specify which by calling an appropriate method in CDialogImpl<>. If you want to create a modal dialog then you should call DoModal(), which blocks the current thread until the dialog is closed. In this case you will most likely implement the dialog class to have data members initialized by the code that called DoModal(). The dialog class can use these to initialize the dialog controls with OnInitDialog(), which is called when the WM_INITDIALOG message is received. When the dialog is closed, you'll get the BN_CLICKED notification if the OK button is clicked. You can use this to copy data from the controls back into the data members, so that the code that called DoModal() can access this data when it returns.

For example, a dialog could have these message handlers:

```
public:
CComBSTR Name;
BEGIN_MSG_MAP(CGetNameDlg)
    MESSAGE_HANDLER(WM_INITDIALOG, OnInitDialog)
    COMMAND_ID_HANDLER(IDOK, OnOK)
END_MSG_MAP()

LRESULT OnInitDialog(UINT, WPARAM, LPARAM, BOOL& bHandled)
{
    USES_CONVERSION;
    CWindow wnd = GetDlgItem(IDC_NAME);
    wnd.SetWindowText(W2T(Name));
    return 0;
}

LRESULT OnOK(WORD, WORD, HWND, BOOL& bHandled)
{
    CWindow wnd = GetDlgItem(IDC_NAME);
    wnd.GetWindowText(&Name.m_str);
    EndDialog(0);
    return 0;
}
```

and the dialog would be called like this:

```
CGetNameDlg dlg;
dlg.Name = m_Name;
dlg.DoModal();
m_Name = dlg.Name;
```

If you want to create a modeless dialog then you should call
`CDialogImpl<>::Create()` when you want the dialog to appear and
`DestroyWindow()` when you no longer need it. In this case, you can initialize child
controls in the `WM_INITDIALOG` handler (as before). However, since you'll want to get
control values as they change, you'll have to have more code in the dialog class and
provide some mechanism to inform the parent window (perhaps by posting a
message).

ActiveX Controls

If your class derives from `CDialogImpl<>` then you can use any of the Win32 or
Common Controls and the wrapper classes in `AtlControls.h` to manipulate them. If
you want to use ActiveX controls on your dialog then you should use
`CAxDialogImpl<>` as a base class. In addition to the functionality of
`CDialogImpl<>` this class will create ActiveX controls using a dialog template and
initialize them by passing data through a call to `IPersistStreamInit::Load()`.

`CAxDialogImpl<>` uses the ATL hosting classes, so you also need to include
`AtlHost.h`. If you use Object Wizard to create a dialog class then it will derive it from
`CAxDialogImpl<>`. If you don't what to use any ActiveX controls you can simply
change the base class to `CDialogImpl<>`. The ClassView message map wizard will
then be able to recognize that a dialog is based on a template and will read this to
allow you to handle notification or command messages. As mentioned previously, this
will be a reduced set of messages.

If the dialog has ActiveX controls, they will send notifications to the dialog using COM
events, so your dialog must be able to sink these. When you do this through the
ClassView message handler wizard, it will derive your dialog class from
`IDispEventImpl<>`, add a `SINK` map and add an appropriate event handler to the
class (details are given in Appendix A). You may have more than one ActiveX control,
and you may decide to handle the same event from each of them. This is not a problem
because the entries in the sink map associate the control ID with the event and the
event handler. For example:

```
BEGIN_SINK_MAP(CMyDialog)
    SINK_ENTRY(IDC_FIRSTCTL, DISPID_CLICK, OnClickOne)
    SINK_ENTRY(IDC_SECONDCTL, DISPID_CLICK, OnClickTwo)
END_SINK_MAP()
```

However, this doesn't apply to Win32 controls on a dialog. Notification messages sent
by these will be handled in the dialog's *message* map. The `WM_COMMAND` and
`WM_NOTIFY` messages pass the ID of the control that generated the message. If you
have more than one instance of a control type then the message map macros will
'crack' `WM_COMMAND` and `WM_NOTIFY` messages sufficiently to get the ID of the source
of the message. This allows you to handle the messages from different controls with
different handlers. So, if you have a dialog with **Add** and **Remove** buttons, your
message map can handle button clicks with:

```
BEGIN_MSG_MAP(CMyDialog)
    COMMAND_HANDLER(IDC_ADD, BN_CLICKED, OnClickedAdd)
    COMMAND_HANDLER(IDC_REMOVE, BN_CLICKED, OnClickedRemove)
END_MSG_MAP()
```

You get a similar 'cracking' for notification messages sent by Common Controls.

One thing that may be apparent from this description is that ATL has some quite sophisticated classes to create and manipulate windows. These do not necessarily need to be part of a control or any COM object. The implication is that you can use ATL to write Win32 applications that have windows.

This is indeed the case. All you have to do is ensure that the correct headers are included. The following code is a simple Win32 application, created with the AppWizard and with added ATL code to display a dialog. I've used the resource editor to create a simple dialog (choose Insert | Resource, select Dialog and then, when you've created the resource, add the RC file to the project). This code shows how to create the dialog:

```
#include "stdafx.h"
#include <atlbase.h>
CComModule _Module;
#include <atlwin.h>
#include "resource.h"

int APIENTRY WinMain(HINSTANCE hInstance, HINSTANCE, LPSTR lpCmdLine,
                     int nCmdShow)
{
    _Module.Init(NULL, hInstance);
    CSimpleDialog<IDD_ABOUT> dlg;
    dlg.DoModal();
    return 0;
}
```

Here, IDD_ABOUT is the dialog template that you added to the project. As you can see, this combined with the AtlControls classes means that you can write a Win32 application without the overhead of MFC and without having to write any window or dialog procedures.

Subclassing and Superclassing Windows

ATL allows you to **subclass** and **superclass** windows. These are methods of code reuse in Win32 programming and are possible because of the ability to obtain the pointer to the window procedure of any registered window class. You can either create a new class that uses this window procedure as well as providing some message handling (superclassing), or take an existing instance of a registered Windows class and intercept the messages that it should handle (subclassing). In both cases, you have the choice of passing the message to the original window procedure, to handle the message yourself, or to do both.

CContainedWindow<>

ATL carries out subclassing and superclassing through CWindowImpl<> and a class called CContainedWindow<>. If you use the Object Wizard control option Add Control Based On then it will create an instance of CContainedWindow<> as a data member in your class and use this to create and encapsulate the superclassed window. When you use this class you don't need to derive from it as its purpose is to forward the messages for the contained window to your window's message map. To do this you initialize instances of this class with a pointer to an instance of your window class. However, since this means that your message map is likely to handle messages for two different windows, ATL has to use a way to distinguish between the messages. To do this it uses alternative message maps.

Alternative Message Maps

An alternative message map is effectively a sub-message map, in that the main part of the map handles messages sent to the main window and the alternative maps handle messages sent to contained windows. The alternative message maps are named according to an ID that you pass to the constructor of a contained window object. For example:

```
CContainedWindow m_Names;
CContainedWindow m_Products;

CContainerWindow :
    m_Names(_T("LISTBOX"), this, 1),
    m_Products(_T("LISTBOX"), this, 2)
{
    m_bWindowOnly = true;
}

BEGIN_MSG_MAP(CContainerWindow)
    MESSAGE_HANDLER(WM_CREATE, OnCreate)
    MESSAGE_HANDLER(WM_LBUTTONDOWN, MainLBtnHandler)
ALT_MSG_MAP(1)
    MESSAGE_HANDLER(WM_LBUTTONDOWN, NamesLBtnHandler)
ALT_MSG_MAP(2)
    MESSAGE_HANDLER(WM_LBUTTONDOWN, ProductsLBtnHandler)
END_MSG_MAP()
```

This has three entries to handle `WM_LBUTTONDOWN` messages. The first handles the left button click on the main window, and the other two handle the same message but for two contained list boxes. This example superclasses the list boxes by calling `CContainedWindow::Create()` in the `WM_CREATE` handler (these superclassed windows must be created somewhere).

To subclass a window, it must already be created (for example a control on a dialog box), in which case you pass its `HWND` to `CContainedWindow::SubclassWindow()`. (More details are given in Appendix J.)

Controls

A control usually has a visual representation and will therefore have a window. However, it won't always have its *own* window. What do I mean by this? Well, windows are quite expensive resources, and containers that create many controls that create their own windows put a burden on system resources. So, as an optimization, a container can create a single window, passing a portion of this to newly created controls. A control that can accept a portion of a container-created window is known as a **windowless** control because it does not own the window. All containers will support **windowed** controls and most will support windowless controls. Consequently, although it makes sense for your control to be windowless but, if the container doesn't support this, create a window and be windowed if the container doesn't support this.

Windowed Controls

ATL contains code to allow your control to be either windowed or windowless. If you don't want your control to be windowless you can set a `bool` value called `m_bWindowOnly` (inherited through `CComControlBase`) to `true`. If you want to base a control on another class by superclassing or if you use a composite control, then your control should not be windowless. This is because the control must create the window to superclass but the window created by the container won't be the window that the control will want to superclass.

121

Windowless Controls

If your control is windowless it can still handle messages, because the container will pass messages to it by calling the control's `IOleInPlaceObjectWindowless::OnWindowMessage()`. ATL implements this by routing the message through the message map.

Control Interfaces

Controls are tightly coupled to the container that creates them. Because of this, a control must implement many interfaces. ATL contains implementations for all of the required interfaces, many of which are implemented in the general base class `CComControlBase` that your control inherits through `CComControl<>`. Centralizing code like this is useful, because many of these interfaces use values stored in common data members.

Drawing Controls

The most noticeable thing about a control is its user interface. Composite controls are based on a dialog template and, to a large extent, the drawing is carried out by these. HTML controls use DHTML, held as a resource in the DLL, to draw the user interface, and controls that superclass Win32 controls will allow the superclassed window to draw itself. However, lite and full controls (which don't superclass another window) do not do any drawing for you, so you have to provide this code.

As I mentioned earlier, a control can either be windowed and create its own window, or windowless and use a portion of a window created by the container. ATL integrates the two and provides a `WM_PAINT` handler called `CComControlBase::OnPaint()` that is used in both cases. You don't see this and it's not even mentioned in your control's message map. This is because it is declared in the message map of `CComControl<>` (which is derived from `CComControlBase`) and your control's message map will chain unhandled messages to this map (Appendix A describes message chaining). Your drawing code is called by `OnPaint()`, as will be made clear in a moment.

WM_PAINT Handler

The `WM_PAINT` handler is not the only situation when a control will draw itself — there are two others. Firstly, a container will call the control's `IViewObject::Draw()` method when it wants to obtain a visual representation of the control. Secondly, full controls support `IDataObject` and some containers will call `GetData()` to cache a metafile in a compound document or ask for a metafile when the control is printed.

ATL will ensure that all of these requests are handled by the same drawing code and, although you can write your own `WM_PAINT` handler (`IViewObject::Draw()` or `IDataObject::GetData()`) it makes sense to use ATL's and centralize the drawing code in one place.

ATL_DRAWINFO Structure

ATL's implementation of these methods will pack information about the drawing context into a structure called `ATL_DRAWINFO` and pass this to a method called `OnDrawAdvanced()`. The data passed to this method has had very little processing. You can override it but it's usually best not to because the default implementation will normalize the device context to ensure that it is scaled to pixels with the origin in the top left hand corner. Thus, the device context has the same properties, wherever it originated from. This normalized device context is then passed to the control's `OnDraw()` method, where you should put your drawing code.

The Object Wizard will add some sample code to your class to implement `OnDraw()`, but all it does is draw a rectangle and print some text in the center. In most cases, you will just want to draw the control directly into the device context passed through the `ATL_DRAWINFO` parameter of this method. However, you should pay particular attention to the cases where a control is printed or when a metafile is required by the container. In these cases, you may decide to use different drawing code. This is particularly true if you have controls embedded in your control (for example, on a composite control) because you'll have to take the steps required to get these child controls to either print themselves, or to get your code to provide a representation.

To determine whether `OnDraw()` is being called to print your control, you can pass the `hdcDraw` member of the `ATL_DRAWINFO` structure to the Win32 `GetDeviceCaps()` in order to get the `TECHNOLOGY` capability of the context. If the control is being drawn on the screen, you'll get `DT_RASDISPLAY`, otherwise you will get `DT_METAFILE` or `DT_RASPRINTER`. In the latter case, you'll be able to get additional information about the printer from the `ptd` member of `ATL_DRAWINFO`.

Another thing to be aware of is that the default font brushes and pens used by the container for a printer's device context (or metafile device context to be passed to the printer) will not be the same as those in the screen device context. Consequently, you should review carefully how you want the control to appear and if, for example, the font style is important, you should make sure that you select the appropriate font in your `OnDraw()`, even if the default used by the screen context is suitable. In addition, check the size of the device context and scale your drawing to this — do not use absolute units. The Object Wizard generated `OnDraw()` does this:

```
HRESULT OnDraw(ATL_DRAWINFO& di)
{
    RECT& rc = *(RECT*)di.prcBounds;
    Rectangle(di.hdcDraw, rc.left, rc.top, rc.right, rc.bottom);

    SetTextAlign(di.hdcDraw, TA_CENTER|TA_BASELINE);
    LPCTSTR pszText = _T("ATL 3.0 : Ctrl");
    TextOut(di.hdcDraw,
            (rc.left + rc.right) / 2,
            (rc.top + rc.bottom) / 2,
            pszText,
            lstrlen(pszText));

    return S_OK;
}
```

Finally, make sure that you test your control with every container that you intend it for. I've found that some containers clip the drawn image and there's no consistency between containers as to which edges this will occur on. The answer is to test, test and test again!

Redrawing the Control

Now that you've written the drawing code, there's one important issue to consider: the control is drawn when the container tells it to draw itself, so what happens if the control decides that it needs to redraw itself? Controls have methods and properties, and when a container calls one of its methods or changes a property, the control's visual representation may well change. To force the control to be redrawn, the control can call the ATL method `FireViewChange()`. This does two things. Firstly, it causes the control to be redrawn, by either invalidating the control's entire window (if it's windowed) or telling the container that the control's section of the window is invalid (if it's windowless). The other thing that this does is to tell the container that the control's view has changed, so the container has a chance to respond.

A related situation occurs when the image of a control is cached in a compound document. If the internal state of the control affects this cached image, you need to inform the container when the state changes so that the container can ask for an updated metafile. To do this, you need to call `SendOnDataChange()` which will inform the container that, when it saves a compound document with the control embedded in it, it should ask for a metafile image of the control. (You'll probably also want to call `SetDirty()` at the same time to indicate that the container should also read the new value of the control's state to save in the document.)

Finally, be wary about what GDI functions you call in `OnDraw()`. If this is used for metafile rendering, you should only use functions that can be put in a metafile. Appendix J lists the functions you can use.

> *Beginning ATL COM Programming* contains an example that shows the steps you need to take for a control to correctly show itself in loaded and activated states on compound documents.

Resizing Controls

You should pay particular attention to the size of your control and what happens when it is resized. The reason for this is that, during design time, you will have made very careful decisions about the layout of the control and if the container decides to change the size then the overall look and feel will change.

The first thing you should be aware of is that your object will inherit a data member called `m_bAutoSize`. If this is set to `true` it indicates that the control will tell its container what size it should be and won't allow the container to change this. You will most likely use this with composite controls, because these controls are based on a dialog template and you will have determined the child control sizes and positions using the resource editor.

> In general, unless you're willing to write dialog control resizing and repositioning code, you will always set `m_bAutoSize` to `true` for composite controls.

The HTML control contains the Internet Explorer control which is made the same size as your control; when your control changes size so does the Internet Explorer control. The user interface in an HTML control is drawn based on DHTML code (that is typically bound as a resource in your module) and so this code should respond to changes in the control size.

Content Sizing

ATL controls use content sizing, which means that the container can pass a size to the control and the control has the option of returning the size that it actually wants to be. There are two sizes maintained by the ATL control classes, m_sizeExtent and m_sizeNatural. Both of these are set by default to 2 x 2540 HIMETRIC units (which translates to 2 inches), but you can specify the default size of the control yourself in its constructor. If the control is a composite control, the code generated by the Object Wizard will calculate m_sizeExtent from the dialog template size using CComCompositeControl::CalcExtent().

You use m_sizeNatural to specify the natural size of the control, which is the size that the control would prefer to be. A container should try to use this size if possible. The control can set m_bDrawFromNatural to true if it needs to specify that, when it is drawn, the natural size should always be used. The container may try to resize the control, in which case the size is placed in m_sizeExtent. Your control can set m_bResizeNatural to true if it wants the natural size to be changed to this new size.

Properties and Persistence

Most controls will have internal state, and will need to initialize this state when loaded and save it when unloaded. At a minimum, the control should support IPersistStream (or the derived interface IPersistStreamInit). However, some containers (like Microsoft Office applications) require the control to support IPersistStorage. ATL lite controls only support IPersistStreamInit, whereas full controls also support IPersistStorage. As the name suggests, IPersistStreamInit persists data as a stream of bytes. ATL has code in CComVariant to convert any of the VARIANT data types to a stream. The IPersistStorage implementation also saves data in a stream. It creates this stream (named Contents) in the storage that the control is passed from the container.

> IPersistStorageImpl<> only has a minimal implementation of IPersistStorage and this doesn't follow the protocols suggested by the COM specification. It is adequate for most situations but it won't work when a control is asked to persist itself under low memory conditions.

The other important persistence interface is `IPersistPropertyBag`. Unlike the other two interfaces, this is a 'random access' interface, where properties are saved or loaded individually by name. This interface is used by Internet Explorer to support the `<PARAM>` tag, and by Visual Basic to persist control properties in the FRM file for a form. If a control doesn't support this interface, Visual Basic will use `IPersistStream` and save the data in a FRX file; you won't be able to use the `<PARAM>` tag in Internet Explorer. If you want your control to support this interface, you have to make the changes by hand — derive from `IPersistPropertyBagImpl<>` and add the interface to the interface map.

Property Maps

ATL implements all of these persistence interfaces using the property map (more details of this are given in Appendix A). Two types of data are supported: COM properties and raw data. COM properties are properties on your control and hence have methods in the IDL with `[propget]` and `[propput]` attributes. The ATL persistence interface implementations merely call the appropriate `get_` and `put_` method to get or set the property value (and, if necessary, read or write it to a stream). Raw data can only be integer values and must be data members in the class.

> There are ways to persist non-integer raw data, but it requires your class to override the `Save()` and `Load()` methods of the ATL implementations. An explanation of how to do this is given in *Professional ATL COM Programming*.

Ambient Properties

Ambient properties are implemented by containers. Their purpose is to maintain a constant look and feel across all the controls on a container and the container itself. When an ambient property changes, the control will be informed by the container calling your control's `IOleControl::OnAmbientPropertyChange()` method. By default, this does nothing so, to be able to respond to changes in ambient properties, you need to provide an implementation. You should first check the `DISPID` passed as a parameter to see if it is a property that you're interested in.

However, `OnAmbientPropertyChange()` is not passed the actual value of the property; you have to read it from the container. ATL helps here with a method called `GetAmbientProperty()` which will return a `VARIANT` with the property value, or one of many methods that begin with `GetAmbient` (for example `GetAmbientFont()`) which will return a particular ambient property. If you want to respond to several ambient properties then you'll need to add code for each of these in your implementation of `OnAmbientPropertyChange()`. For example:

```
STDMETHOD(OnAmbientPropertyChange)(DISPID dispid)
{
    switch (dispid)
    {
    case DISPID_AMBIENT_BACKCOLOR:
        GetAmbientBackColor(m_clrBackColor);
        FireViewChange()
        break;
```

```
case DISPID_AMBIENT_FORECOLOR:
   GetAmbientForeColor(m_clrForeColor);
   FireViewChange()
   break;
}
return S_OK;
}
```

One property that you may be particularly interested in is the UserMode ambient
property. If this is FALSE, the control is being used in a tool (such as Visual Basic) in
design mode. You can make use of this to give different behavior for the control at
design time and runtime.

Stock Properties

A stock property is a property that has a specific DISPID that all containers know
about — the BackColor property, for example. You can add support for stock
properties by using the **Stock Properties** tab in Object Wizard, which allows you to
specify which property you want to support. The wizard will derive the class from
CStockPropImpl<> and add an appropriate member variable for each one (details of
the changes the Object Wizard makes and how you can do it yourself are given in
Appendix J).

CStockPropImpl<> will implement the get_ and put_ methods for the property.
The put_ method first informs the container that the property is about to change,
which allows the container to choose whether this particular property can change. If
the container allows it, the code will change the member variable and then call
FireViewChange() so that the control has the opportunity to redraw itself. Next, it
informs the container that the control's state has changed (so that it knows it will have
to read the state again if it wants to save the control's state) as well as this particular
property.

Property Pages

Some properties are quite complex (Font properties for example, which require
several parameters to describe). A control might have several related properties, or a
property may have a numeric value that is meaningless as a number (for example
dates, which are held as doubles and colors which are held as 32-bit integers). A
property page can be used to simplify all of these situations.

You can use one of the standard property pages, or you can design your own — ATL
provides an Object Wizard type to do this. When you add a property to the property
map you can use the final parameter of PROP_ENTRY() to specify the CLSID of the
property page used to edit the property. You can use CLSID_NULL if the property
does not have to appear on a property page. If there are several properties that use a
single page then you can use the PROP_PAGE() macro to specify the CLSID of a page
that will be used for one or more properties.

The standard property pages are:

CLSID	Description
CLSID_StockColorPage	The familiar color page which allows you to select a color from a swatch or by specifying the RGB values
CLSID_StockFontPage	The standard font selection page
CLSID_StockPicturePage	A page that allows you to select a picture file from disk (BMP, DIB, CUR, ICO, WMF, EMF, GIF, JPG), which it will show in a preview pane

When you write your own property page, you are essentially creating a dialog. This means that most of the page's code will be to handle the notification messages from the various controls on the page's surface.

When the page is shown you will most likely want to initialize its controls with data from the properties in the object. The property page class created for you by the Object Wizard has a data member called m_ppUnk, which is an array of IUnknown pointers to objects that are using this particular property page. In most cases, you should merely access the first entry. To obtain the property values, you can call QueryInterface() to obtain the appropriate dual interface and then access the properties using their get_ methods.

Property pages have an **Apply** button that a user can click to write the values to the control. Normally this is disabled, but when a user changes a value in the property page you can enable this button by calling SetDirty() with an argument of TRUE. The Object Wizard will generate a method called Apply() that is called when the user clicks on the **Apply** button. You can use this to write the changed values to the control through the values in the m_ppUnk array.

A control can tell the container to show its property pages to the user by accessing its IOleControlSite interface. ATL caches the container's IOleClientSite, so you can call QueryInterface() on this to obtain the IOleControlSite interface:

```
CComQIPtr<IOleControlSite> spControlSite(m_spClientSite);
spControlSite->ShowPropertyFrame();
```

Communicating with the Container

The last section showed how you can get a container to show a control's property pages. Normally controls appear on a client site in the container, but they can further integrate themselves with the container by calling various container interfaces. The control caches an IOleClientSite and an IOleInPlaceSite pointer, which you can call to get access to these other interfaces. Specifically, you can call IOleClientSite::GetContainer() to get access to the IOleContainer interface and through this get access to the other objects in the container. Through IOleInPlaceSite::GetWindowContext() you can get access to the IOleInPlaceFrame and IOleInPlaceUIWindow interfaces on the container.

IOleInPlaceFrame can be used to merge menus with the container's menus. The control does this by passing an empty menu to InsertMenus(), which the container fills with its File, View and Window menus. The control can then add its own menu items into this menu and call SetMenu(). When the control deactivates it can call RemoveMenu().

In addition, IOleInPlaceFrame can be used to tell the container to hide its modeless windows (for example when the control wants to show its own) by calling EnableModeless(). The control can also tell the container to display status text in its status bar by passing a string to SetStatusText().

Example: A Control to Access the Products

In this example, I'll develop a control to access the Products collection, with the criteria that it should be usable in clients like Visual Basic and Internet Explorer. To do this, create a new DLL project called Controls. Use the default settings and insert a **Composite Control type ATL object**. It is better to use the full version rather than the lite version because it gives the control many interfaces, widening the possible number of clients — the unneeded interfaces will be removed at a later stage. Clearly, if you're only going to target Internet Explorer then you could use the lite version. Call this control ProductAccess and use all the default values.

The Object Wizard will create a dialog template for you, so resize it to a manageable size (2 inches square) and insert a list box called IDC_ITEMS which doesn't sort items. Add two edit boxes called IDC_DESC and IDC_COST (which is number only) and two buttons called IDC_ADD and IDC_REMOVE, both of which are disabled. Your template will look something like this:

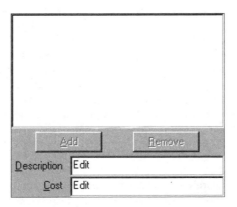

The Object Wizard will add a small bitmap as a resource (the familiar ATL pile of cubes), which will be used in tools such as Visual Basic that have a toolbox for controls. You can edit this to a suitable image if you like, bearing in mind that the background should be light gray (RGB of 192, 192, 192).

Composite controls don't show you the **Miscellaneous** tab, but will ensure that the `Control` and `Insertable` keys are added to the RGS file so that containers using the OLE Insert Object common dialog will show them (for example, Word). Some containers don't use this and instead show the controls that have suitable category IDs, so add a category map to `ProductAccess.h`:

```
BEGIN_CATEGORY_MAP(CProductAccess)
    IMPLEMENTED_CATEGORY(CATID_Insertable)
    IMPLEMENTED_CATEGORY(CATID_Control)
END_CATEGORY_MAP()
```

also, add

```
#include <comcat.h>
```

Unfortunately, this still won't allow the control to be inserted into all containers: to be able to insert it into an Excel spreadsheet, you also need an `Insertable` key in the versioned `ProgID`. To do this, you need to edit the RGS file (don't you wish all containers would use the same criteria to determine if a control is insertable? Hopefully, in the future all containers will use component categories):

```
Controls.ProductAccess.1 = s 'ProductAccess Class'
{
    CLSID = s '{78BFF990-845B-11D2-BD81-00104B7D75C0}'
    'Insertable'
}
```

This control is a composite control and you don't really want to have to write code to resize and reposition embedded controls. To avoid this, add the following to the constructor:

```
m_bAutoSize = TRUE;
```

If you don't do this then Visual Basic programmers will be able to resize the control, which will just create a large unused area on the form or clip it.

Now you need to write the message handlers, so click on **Add Windows Message Handler** through ClassView and select `IDC_DESC`. This is the description edit box and you should add a handler for `EN_CHANGE` and call it `OnChangeEditBoxes()`. This handler is called when the text is changed in this text box, but you can use this to respond to the change event from *both* edit boxes, so edit the header and change the `COMMAND_HANDLER()` to a `COMMAND_CODE_HANDLER()`:

```
COMMAND_CODE_HANDLER(EN_CHANGE, OnChangeEditBoxes)
```

Now the `EN_CHANGE` notification set by all edit boxes will be handled by `OnChangeEditBoxes()`. This handler is implemented to check to see if there is text in *both* edit boxes; if so the **Add** button is enabled, otherwise it is disabled:

```
LRESULT OnChangeEditBoxes(WORD wNotifyCode, WORD wID,
                          HWND hWndCtl, BOOL& bHandled)
{
   CWindow hDesc, hCost;
   hDesc = GetDlgItem(IDC_DESC);
   hCost = GetDlgItem(IDC_COST);
   bool bEnable = (hDesc.GetWindowTextLength() > 0
                   && hCost.GetWindowTextLength() > 0);
   CWindow hAdd;
   hAdd = GetDlgItem(IDC_ADD);
   hAdd.EnableWindow(bEnable);
   return 0;
}
```

Although you're handling the message, you don't need to set bHandled to true
because this will be done for you by default. You only need to change the value of this
parameter if you want to indicate that you want the default message handler to handle
the message, as you'll see later.

The **Remove** button should only be enabled if the user selects an item in the list box, so
add a handler to IDC_ITEMS for the LBN_SELCHANGE message:

```
LRESULT OnSelChangeItems(WORD wNotifyCode, WORD wID,
                         HWND hWndCtl, BOOL& bHandled)
{
   CWindow hRemove;
   hRemove = GetDlgItem(IDC_REMOVE);
   hRemove.EnableWindow();
   return 0;
}
```

Now you can add BTN_CLICKED handlers for the two buttons: **Add** and **Remove**.
Before you add the code for these, you will need to access the Products collection, so
include the following in the ProductAccess.h header file:

```
#include "..\DataAccess\DataAccess.h"
#include "..\EventLogger\EventLogger.h"
```

Note that I'm assuming that the other two projects folders are in the same folder as the
Controls folder. You may have to adjust your include path (select the **Options** item
on the **Tools** menu and edit the **Directories** tab).

The control needs to create instances of these two objects, so add the following smart
pointers as data members of CProductAccess:

```
private:
   CComPtr<IProducts> m_pProducts;
   CComPtr<IEvents> m_pLogger;
};
```

The objects should be created in the `FinalConstruct()` method, which you should add to the class:

```
HRESULT FinalConstruct()
{
    HRESULT hr;
    hr = m_pLogger.CoCreateInstance(__uuidof(Events));
    if (FAILED(hr))
        return hr;
    hr = m_pProducts.CoCreateInstance(__uuidof(Products));
    if (FAILED(hr))
    {
        CComBSTR bstr = L"Cannot create Products";
        m_pLogger->Add(bstr, SEV_ERROR);
        return hr;
    }
    return hr;
}
```

Notice that the CLSID of these objects is obtained through two classes called `Events` and `Products`, which were added to the headers by MIDL (this is described in Appendix K). The CLSID is added with `__declspec(uuid())` so that you can retrieve it later with `__uuidof()`. Note that it's only the most recent version of MIDL (supplied in Visual C++ 6) that allows you to do this.

Now that you have access to the `Products` object, you can use this to initialize the list box control. The composite control is based on a dialog, so your control will receive dialog notification messages. You should add a handler for `WM_INITDIALOG` and use this to initialize the controls. I've decided to put the code for the control's methods in the CPP file, but you'll find that the message handler wizard will add code inline within the class definition in the header. It's a simple task to move method implementations to the CPP file.

I'll use the wrapper classes in `AtlControls.h` in the handlers, so add an include for this in `ProductsAccess.h`. (As I said before, I've moved this to my `VC98\Atl\Include` directory. If your copy is in a different directory you can add this to the include path.)

```
#include <AtlControls.h>
using namespace ATLControls;
```

Implement the handler like this:

```
LRESULT CProductAccess::OnInitDialog(UINT uMsg, WPARAM wParam,
                                     LPARAM lParam, BOOL& bHandled)
{
    USES_CONVERSION;
    HRESULT hr;
    CListBox hListBox;
    hListBox = GetDlgItem(IDC_ITEMS);

    CComPtr<IUnknown> pUnk;
    CComPtr<IEnumVARIANT> pEnum;
    hr = m_pProducts->get__NewEnum(&pUnk);
    if (FAILED(hr))
    {
        CComBSTR bstr;
        bstr = L"Cannot get the enumerator";
        m_pLogger->Add(bstr, 1);
        return 0;
    }
```

```
      pUnk.QueryInterface(&pEnum);

      CComVariant vars[5];
      ULONG ulFetched;
      while(SUCCEEDED(pEnum->Next(5, vars, &ulFetched)))
      {
         ULONG idx;
         for (idx = 0; idx < ulFetched; idx++)
         {
            CComPtr<IDispatch> pDisp;
            CComPtr<IProduct> pProd;
            pDisp = vars[idx].pdispVal;
            pDisp-> QueryInterface (&pProd);

            CComBSTR bstrDesc;
            pProd->get_Description(&bstrDesc.m_str);
            long ID;
            pProd->get_ProductID(&ID);

            int item;
            item = hListBox.AddString(W2T(bstrDesc));
            hListBox.SetItemData(item, ID);
            vars[idx].Clear();
         }
         if (ulFetched == 0)
            break;
      }
      return 0;
   }
```

Notice that I only add the product description to the list box, but the product ID is saved as item data so that I can access it later in the LBN_DBLCLK handler. Add this handler now with ClassView — it will be implemented by presenting the product details in a dialog. So, after you've added the handler, add a dialog with the Object Wizard, call it ProductDetails and add three read-only edit boxes called IDC_ID, IDC_DESC and IDC_UNITCOST. Since you don't need a Cancel button, you can remove it, its handler method and its entry in the message map. This dialog doesn't use ActiveX controls so you can change the base class to CDialogImpl<> and remove the #include for AtlHost.h. The dialog should look like this:

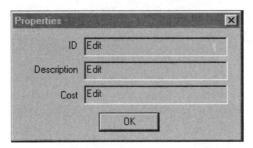

Next, add three public data members to CProductDetails:

```
public:
   CComBSTR m_bstrDesc;
   long m_lProductID;
   double m_dCost;
};
```

Initialize the last two to –1 in the constructor to indicate that they have invalid data.

```
CProductDetails() : m_lProductID(-1),
                    m_dCost(-1)
```

You can then implement the WM_INITDIALOG handler to copy the data in these variables to the controls on the dialog:

```
LRESULT OnInitDialog(UINT uMsg, WPARAM wParam,
                     LPARAM lParam, BOOL& bHandled)
{
    USES_CONVERSION;
    CWindow hEdit;
    if (m_lProductID != -1)
    {
        TCHAR str[20];
        wsprintf(str, _T("%ld"), m_lProductID);
        hEdit = GetDlgItem(IDC_ID);
        hEdit.SetWindowText(str);
    }
    if (m_bstrDesc.Length() > 0)
    {
        hEdit = GetDlgItem(IDC_DESC);
        hEdit.SetWindowText(W2T(m_bstrDesc));
    }
    if (m_dCost != -1)
    {
        TCHAR str[20];
        _stprintf(str, _T("$%.02f"), m_dCost);
        hEdit = GetDlgItem(IDC_UNITCOST);
        hEdit.SetWindowText(str);
    }
    return 1;
}
```

In this code, I make sure that the edit boxes are only set if the member variables have been initialized by the caller code. I have no choice here but to use _stprintf() to format the cost because the Windows wsprintf() cannot format floating point values. This means that you'll have to use the C runtime, so you will need to remove the _ATL_MIN_CRT symbol from release builds (this process was explained in Chapter 3. You need to use the C/C++ tab on the **Project Settings** dialog). In addition, you will need to include stdio.h in stdafx.h (this header is included in atlbase.h *only* for debug builds).

```
extern CComModule _Module;
#include <atlcom.h>
#include <atlhost.h>
#include <atlctl.h>
#include <atlwin.h>
#include <stdio.h>
```

Now you can implement the LBN_DBLCLK handler, so open ProductAccess.cpp, add ProductDetails.h as an include and then add this code (note that this implementation has been moved from the header file, as was the OnInitDialog() method above):

```
LRESULT CProductAccess::OnDblclkItems(WORD wNotifyCode, WORD wID,
                                      HWND hWndCtl, BOOL& bHandled)
{
    HRESULT hr;
    CListBox hListBox;
    hListBox = GetDlgItem(IDC_ITEMS);
    int item = hListBox.GetCurSel();
    if (item == LB_ERR)
        return 0;

    long id;
    id = static_cast<long>( hListBox.GetItemData(item));
```

This gets the product ID by reading the item data from the selected item. Once the ID has been obtained, we can try to get the selected item from the Products object:

```
CComVariant var;
hr = m_pProducts->get_Item(id, &var);
if (FAILED(hr))
{
    // item has disappeared
    MessageBox(_T("Item has been deleted"),
               _T("Information"),
               MB_OK | MB_ICONWARNING);
    return OnInitDialog(0, 0, 0, bHandled);
}
```

If the code can't get the item then someone has removed it since the list box was last updated, so the user is informed and the list box is updated. Otherwise, the item is obtained from the Products collection:

```
CComPtr<IDispatch> pDisp;
CComPtr<IProduct> pProd;
pDisp = var.pdispVal;
pDisp->QueryInterface(&pProd);

CComBSTR bstrDesc;
pProd->get_Description(&bstrDesc.m_str);
pProd->get_ProductID(&id);
CURRENCY cy;
pProd->get_UnitCost(&cy);
```

The final code creates a dialog object and initializes it with data from the selected Product object. The actual dialog window is created with a call to DoModal():

```
CProductDetails dlg;
dlg.m_lProductID = id;
dlg.m_bstrDesc = bstrDesc;
VarR8FromCy(cy, &dlg.m_dCost);
dlg.DoModal();
return 0;
}
```

The next task is to write a handler for the Add button:

```
LRESULT CProductAccess::OnClickedAdd(WORD wNotifyCode, WORD wID,
                                     HWND hWndCtl, BOOL& bHandled)
{
    CWindow hAdd;
    hAdd = GetDlgItem(IDC_ADD);
    hAdd.EnableWindow(FALSE);

    CWindow hDesc, hCost;
    hDesc = GetDlgItem(IDC_DESC);
    hCost = GetDlgItem(IDC_COST);

    USES_CONVERSION;
    CComBSTR bstr;
    hCost.GetWindowText(bstr.m_str);
    double dCost;
    dCost = atof(W2A(bstr.m_str));
    bstr.Empty();
    hDesc.GetWindowText(bstr.m_str);
```

This code reads the data from the edit boxes. Notice that I use atof() to convert the string obtained from the control into a double. I would have used an appropriate _t macro to accommodate compiling with the UNICODE symbol, but there doesn't appear to be a wide char equivalent of atof(), so the ANSI version must be used.

The following code adds the item to the `Products` collection:

```
HRESULT hr;
CComVariant var;
hr = m_pProducts->Add(bstr, dCost, &var);
if (FAILED(hr))
{
    bstr += L": cannot add this item";
    m_pLogger->Add(bstr, SEV_ERROR);
    MessageBox(W2T(bstr.m_str), _T("Products"), MB_OK | MB_ICONWARNING);
}
else
{
    CListBox hListBox;
    hListBox = GetDlgItem(IDC_ITEMS);
    hListBox.ResetContent();
    OnInitDialog(0, 0, 0, bHandled);
    hDesc.SetWindowText(_T(""));
    hCost.SetWindowText(_T(""));
}
return 0;
}
```

Notice that I call `OnInitDialog()` to update the display. This will also ensure that, if any other clients change the database, those changes will be reflected. If the database table has many items then this may be a problem because the control will take a long time to fill. I'll address this issue in the *Delayed Loading* section.

The **Remove** handler is similar:

```
LRESULT CProductAccess::OnClickedRemove(WORD wNotifyCode, WORD wID,
                                        HWND hWndCtl, BOOL& bHandled)
{
    CWindow hAdd;
    hAdd = GetDlgItem(IDC_REMOVE);
    hAdd.EnableWindow(FALSE);

    CListBox hListBox;
    hListBox = GetDlgItem(IDC_ITEMS);
    long id;
    id = static_cast<long>( hListBox.GetItemData(hListBox.GetCurSel()));
```

As before, this code first obtains the ID of the selected item. After that, you need to determine if the item exists:

```
HRESULT hr;
CComVariant var;
hr = m_pProducts->get_Item(id, &var);
if (FAILED(hr))
{
    TCHAR str[30];
    wsprintf(str, _T("item %ld doesn\'t exist"), id);
    CComBSTR bstr = str;
    m_pLogger->Add(bstr, SEV_ERROR);
    MessageBox(str, _T("Products"), MB_OK | MB_ICONWARNING);
    hListBox.ResetContent();
    OnInitDialog(0, 0, 0, bHandled);
    return 0;
}
```

There is an ulterior motive to this check, because I want to copy the data in the `Product` object to the appropriate controls on the composite control:

```
hr = m_pProducts->Remove(id);
if (FAILED(hr))
{
    TCHAR str[30];
    wsprintf(str, _T("cannot remove item %ld"), id);
    CComBSTR bstr = str;
    m_pLogger->Add(bstr, SEV_ERROR);
    MessageBox(str, _T("Products"), MB_OK | MB_ICONWARNING);
}
else
{
    USES_CONVERSION;
    CWindow hDesc, hCost;
    hDesc = GetDlgItem(IDC_DESC);
    hCost = GetDlgItem(IDC_COST);

    CComPtr<IProduct> pProd;
    CComBSTR bstr;
    var.pdispVal->QueryInterface(&pProd);
    pProd->get_Description(&bstr.m_str);
    hDesc.SetWindowText(W2T(bstr.m_str));

    CURRENCY cy;
    pProd->get_UnitCost(&cy);
    bstr.Empty();
    VarBstrFromCy(cy, LOCALE_USER_DEFAULT, 0, &bstr.m_str);
    hCost.SetWindowText(W2T(bstr.m_str));
}
hListBox.ResetContent();
OnInitDialog(0, 0, 0, bHandled);
return 0;
}
```

You should be able to compile and test this control either by using the ActiveX Test Container or by loading the HTML file that the Object Wizard created for you.

When you run this under Internet Explorer, you will find that a gray background will be momentarily shown. This is because the `OnDraw()` method provided by `CComCompositeControl<>` rather inconveniently fills the background with `GRAY_BRUSH` and then prints `"ATL Composite Control"` in the center. This is simple to remedy by adding the following to the class header:

```
HRESULT OnDraw(ATL_DRAWINFO& di)
{
    return S_OK;
}
```

Now `OnDraw()` does nothing. However, as you may recall from earlier on in this chapter, if you want to support printing of this control or caching a metafile in a compound document, then you should put the code in `OnDraw()`:

```
int caps = GetDeviceCaps(di.hdcdraw, TECHNOLOGY);
if (caps != RAS_DISPLAY)
{
    // put printing and metafile code here
}
```

Removing Functionality

The control you have just made is a full control. I specified that you should use this to get the interfaces required by the widest possible number of containers. However, the Object Wizard will provide many interfaces that you don't need, so let's remove them. When you do this, you will remove appropriate `Impl` base classes, as well as interfaces in the interface map.

This control doesn't have a property page and it doesn't generate events, so you can remove support for the following two interfaces:

```
ISpecifyPropertyPages
IProvideClassInfo2
```

(Remember, if you remove `IProvideClassInfo2` from the interface map then you also need to remove `IProvideClassInfo`.)

Although the control is not windowless you need to use `IOleInPlaceObjectWindowlessImpl<>` because the implementations of interfaces such as `IOleWindow` depend on it.

This example doesn't have any data, but if you want it to be used in Microsoft Office applications then you need to support `IPersistStream` and `IPersistStorage`. Similarly, if you want to use the control in Visual Basic, you need to support at least `IPersistStreamInit`. Since you need persistence interfaces, you also need to have a property map, so all of this code must remain.

Finally, you need to have `IDataObject` if the control is to be used in Office applications, because it allows the control to return a metafile rendering that is stored in compound documents. A similar metafile is obtained from your control if the compound document is printed by such an application, but note that Visual Basic and Internet Explorer will use `IViewObject::Draw()`.

Delayed loading

I mentioned earlier that updating the list box whenever you add or remove items could take a long time if there are many items in the table. It is possible to code round this problem but there isn't space in this chapter to show all the code, so I'll just describe the steps that you need to take.

Firstly, when you successfully remove an item from the collection you can call `CListBox::DeleteString()` to remove an individual item from the list box rather than removing all items. In a similar way, you need to use `CListBox::AddString()` (and `CListBox::SetItemData()` using the `ProductID` in the `Product` object returned by `IProducts::Add()`) when you add an item. This will prevent the entire table being loaded when you add or remove a single item, but it doesn't solve the problem that the list box will be filled when the composite control is first created.

To solve this problem, you need to implement a delayed fetch algorithm. In order to do this you need to be more intimate with how the list box works. The mechanism is as follows: when the composite control is first created, the list box should be filled with one more item than can be shown, meaning that the vertical scrollbar will be shown. When the user clicks on the down button of the scrollbar, the composite control should then read the next batch of items and add them to the list box. In addition, you should also handle keyboard clicks.

Note that I said that you should do this when the down button is clicked. The reason is that you only want to do this when the last item is shown at the bottom of the list box. In this situation, the user won't be able to click between the thumb and the down button (to send the `SB_PAGEDOWN` scroll code) or drag the thumb further down.

To handle the click on the down arrow you need to catch the `WS_VSCROLL` message that is sent to the list box. However, your composite control can only handle *notification* messages sent by the list box to its parent (`WM_COMMAND` and messages starting with `LBN_`). To get round this, you need to superclass the list box.

To do this you should remove the list box from the dialog template and then add a CContainedWindow<> member variable for the list box. This object should be initialized in the constructor to give it an alternative message map ID.

```
CContainedWindow m_ctlListBox;
CProductAccess()
   : m_ctlListBox(_T("LISTBOX"), this, 1);
{
   m_bWindowOnly = TRUE;
   CalcExtent(m_sizeExtent);
   m_bAutoSize = TRUE;
}
```

The actual control window can be created in the WM_INITDIALOG handler, but remember that you do have the messy task of determining the size and position of the list box. For example:

```
// positioned at top left hand corner of the control
// 100 pixels wide and high
RECT rect = {0, 0, 100, 100};
m_ctlListBox.Create(m_hWnd, rect, NULL,
                 WS_BORDER | WS_VSCROLL | WS_CHILD | WS_VISIBLE);
```

The WS_VSCROLL style is added to make sure that the vertical scrollbar is shown.

The WM_VSCROLL handler can test for SB_LINEDOWN to catch when the user clicks on the down arrow key. The code should detect if the user is at the bottom of the items in the list. If you know how many items there are in the list box, you can do this by obtaining the total number of items in the box and the index of the top item that you can see:

```
LRESULT OnVScroll(UINT uMsg, WPARAM wParam,
                 LPARAM lParam, BOOL &bHandled)
{
   if (LOWORD(wParam) == SB_LINEDOWN)
   {
      CListBox hListBox = m_ctlListBox;
      int total = hListBox.GetCount();
      int toppos = hListBox.GetTopIndex();
      if (toppos + NUMITEMS == total)
      {
         // get items and add them to the
         // list box
      }
   }
   bHandled = false;
   return 0;
}
```

Here, NUMITEMS is the number of items that can be viewed in the list box, so the bottom item has an index of (toppos + NUMITEMS). I've set bHandled to false to indicate that, although I've handled the message, I want the default message handler to handle the message as well and hence scroll down to the items I've added.

I have missed out the code to add the new items but it is fairly straightforward — you need to read the items from the last position that was read. This could involve caching the enumerator object obtained from `IProducts::get_NewEnum()` or by saving an index and using `IEnumVARIANT::Skip()`.

However, when you read items from the database you may read items that you've already added to it through this control. In this case, the item will already be in the list box. So, when you read an item from the database, you must check that it's not in the list box by reading through all these items and checking the `ProductID` cached as item data.

Finally, you may also consider adding a **Reset** button, which will empty the list box and fill it to the initial state when the control was first loaded. This will allow the users to reset the control to obtain any changes to the database, and also to order the items according to the order determined by the enumerator.

Summary

ActiveX controls are ubiquitous, and help you to provide reusable visual components. However, to provide all the functionality needed by a control, including all the communications with the control container, you may need to implement many interfaces. ATL has implementations for all the required interfaces. The Object Wizard control types will derive from the appropriate templates, generating support code so that you can compile the code and get a fully-working control.

Controls are usually visual components, so you will need to do some drawing. For this reason, ATL has windowing classes that will allow you to create your own Windows class, or to subclass or superclass an existing one. It also provides dialog classes that allow you to base a control on a dialog template, or to create a modal or modeless dialog. The great thing about these classes is that you don't have to use them with ATL controls — you can use them to create dialogs and windows in non-COM code. In addition, you can find classes for all the Win32 and common controls in the `AtlControls.h` header included with the `AtlCon` example on your Visual C++ disks. These classes are invaluable if you intend to write dialog or composite control code.

This chapter includes an example that wraps access to the `Products` collection using an ActiveX control. The control has all of the interfaces that are required for it to be used with containers like Visual Basic, Internet Explorer and Microsoft Office applications.

ATL Maps

A **COM server** has to provide the mechanism to create objects of one or more COM class through objects called class factories. It should also be able to register and unregister these classes and any interfaces that they use.

A **COM object** should be able to support at least two interfaces — IUnknown is required but to be useful it must have at least one more interface. Interfaces define functionality, and when an object supports a particular interface a client knows that the object supports that particular functionality. In addition, if several objects support the same interface then you have **componentization** — where a client can choose between several **components** to provide the functionality.

To allow clients to have access to an object's interfaces it must implement QueryInterface() to return pointers to its interfaces when requested – once an object (an instance of a **coclass**) returns a particular interface pointer from QueryInterface() it must *always* return a pointer for that interface (and for IUnknown, it must *always* be the same pointer).

The object may take part in bi-directional communications. If it generates events it can implement IConnectionPointContainer to return connection point objects for one or more sink interfaces; and if it sinks events it must be able to specify the event handlers that will be used. Some objects (particularly control containers) support IServiceProvider to return interfaces to the services that it supports. In addition, a COM object can support COM categories; it should register its use of these during its registration. Other objects (in particular, but not exclusively, controls) can support IPersistXxx interfaces so that they can have their state initialized or be persisted.

ActiveX controls often have visual views and so will contain a window or a portion of a window. If this is the case, some mechanism to handle received Windows messages is required. An ActiveX control may therefore have message handlers.

All these things I have described involve variable amounts of data:

- ❑ a server can create *one or more* COM classes
- ❑ an object has *at least two* interfaces

- ❏ an object may implement COM categories
- ❏ a control can have message handlers
- ❏ an object may persist its properties

To enable you to provide this variable data ATL provides maps. A map is merely a collection of macros that implement a function or populate an array. The advantage of using a map is that information is presented in a clear, coherent way in one place in your code. This makes the information easy to read and alter - ATL also provides wizards to change the entries in various maps.

There are downsides: some maps are implemented with static arrays, restricting what you can place in them. In this case you cannot call non-static member functions. Non-static data members can still be used, this involves calculating their offset from the this pointer.

Maps have the following general format:

```
BEGIN_xxx_MAP(class)
    ENTRY_MACRO(parameters)
END_xxx_MAP()
```

xxx indicates the type of the map:

- ❏ COM to specify the interfaces implemented by an object
- ❏ MSG to specify message handlers
- ❏ SINK to specify event handlers
- ❏ CATEGORY to list implemented or required categories
- ❏ CONNECTION_POINT to specify the connection point objects implemented in the object
- ❏ OBJECT to indicate the objects implemented in the server
- ❏ SERVICE to indicate the services implemented by the object
- ❏ PROP to specify which COM properties and class data members are persisted

class is the name of your ATL class (the OBJECT map is an exception, see below). The information in the map is entered using various macros, which will have zero or more parameters.

In the following sections I will list all the maps that you can use in ATL, the map macros and their parameters.

Object Map

Unlike all the other maps in this section, the object map is not part of a class. Its purpose is to list all the ATL classes in the server that implement COM classes. The parameter passed to this macro is the name of an array that will be used to store _ATL_OBJMAP_ENTRY items. The ATL AppWizard uses the name ObjectMap **by default**, but the choice is arbitrary. A pointer to the first entry of this map is used to initialize the global _Module object, which caches it. All future access to the map is through this pointer, so if you do need to change ObjectMap to another name there is only one other place that you need to edit the code: in the call to _Module.Init() in DllMain() or WinMain().

The object map is put in your main .cpp file (the file containing DllMain() or WinMain()) by the AppWizard and is altered with the Object Wizard, although you may choose to change some items by hand. There are two types of entries that you can have in the object map:

Entry	Description
OBJECT_ENTRY Parameters: clsid, class	This specifies the ATL class, class in the current project that implements the COM class identified with clsid.
OBJECT_ENTRY_NON_CREATEABLE Parameter: class	This specifies that instances of the COM class implemented by the ATL class in your project can only be created by code in the current project.

The parameters for these macros are:

- ❑ clsid: the CLSID of the object
- ❑ class: the name of the ATL class that implements the object

This map does a lot of work; it specifies:

- ❑ the code that will be used to register or unregister the COM coclass registry entries
- ❑ a method to create the class factory object for the COM class
- ❑ a method to create instances of the COM class
- ❑ a method used to register and unregister the required and implemented categories of the object
- ❑ a method that will be used for once-only class-level initialization and clean up
- ❑ a method that will provide a description of the object

This information is managed though static members of the ATL class specified. The OBJECT_ENTRY() macro uses the class parameter to get access to these members.

The Object Wizard will add appropriate members to your class, but if you want to change them you should not edit members of the map. Instead, you can either use appropriate macros or override methods in your class.

At first glance, the second of these macros looks a little strange. Why would you need to mark an object as not being externally creatable? Why not just leave it out of the map? There are two main reasons, the first is registration, and the second is resource initialization. The major reason an object is registered is to allow COM to find the object server when an external client requests an instance. However, there are other reasons for registration. Your object may have `coclass` specific data that needs to be made persistent, requiring default values to be put in the registry when the object is first registered. The `OBJECT_ENTRY_NON_CREATEABLE()` macro gives access to the appropriate registration method in the ATL class (if it exists). If the object does not have any registry entries then you can add the `DECLARE_NO_REGISTRY()` macro in the object's ATL class, but if you do this it is prudent also to remove the ATL provided RGS script for this object from the project resources.

The other reason for adding a non-creatable object to the object map is to register its `ObjectMain()` function. Every ATL object can have one of these; the default implementation, inherited from `CComObjectRootBase`, does nothing. When a server is first loaded it will iterate through all the entries in the object map and call `ObjectMain()` for each of the objects passing a parameter of `true`. When the server unloads it will call each `ObjectMain()` with a parameter of `false`. You can use this to perform a once-only initialization and clean-up of class-level resources.

If you decide to make an object externally noncreatable then it is a good idea to edit the project's IDL and give the `coclass` for the object the `noncreatable` attribute. This ensures that although scripting languages can still use the type information about the object, they will know that they cannot create instances. Another option is to remove `CComCoClass<>` as a base class of your ATL class, however in addition to removing object creation code this will also remove the `Error()` methods, enforcing you to use the more verbose `AtlReportError()` if you want to use rich error reporting. In addition, such an object cannot be aggregated. Finally, if you remove `CComCoClass<>` as a base class you need to implement an empty category map in the class for it to compile.

The object map macros indicate various methods that should be used in ATL classes for specific tasks like object registration, category registration and class creation. You can alter these methods by using the following macros in your ATL class:

Macro Type	Description
DECLARE_REGISTRY_*xxx*	These determine the information, if any, which will be used to register the COM class.
DECLARE_CLASSFACTORY*xxx*	These determine the ATL class that will be used as the class factory.

Macro Type	Description
DECLARE_*xxx*_AGGREGATABLE	Declares whether the object is aggregatable or not, and influences the method used to create instances of the COM class.
DECLARE_OBJECT_DESCRIPTION	Provides a string description of the object.

Using these macros will change the values added to the object map for the class.

ATL has an object type called a **component registrar** that allows you to register and unregister individual components in a module. (Normally, during registration *all* classes are registered.) This object can return the description for each object so that a client (typically MTS) can choose whether to register a particular object or not. If you don't have a component registrar in your project then you won't use the DECLARE_OBJECT_DESCRIPTION() macro.

Interface Map

Every COM object must implement at least IUnknown, and to be useful at least one more interface. The interfaces of an object represent its functionality. However, your object may implement many more interfaces, which is a good idea because it reinforces interface programming where interface methods are functionally related. The purpose of QueryInterface() is to allow a client to request a particular interface on the object. This way the object can either return the requested interface or return an error code, in which case the client knows that the object does not support the specified functionality. This is known as **dynamic discovery of interfaces at runtime**.

Clearly, there must be a mechanism for the ATL class to declare which interfaces it supports, and this is carried out using the interface map. The interface map is delimited with the BEGIN_COM_MAP() and END_COM_MAP() macros and hence is often called the COM map.

The first macro adds several members to your class. In particular it adds a static array of _ATL_INTMAP_ENTRY items and a method, _GetEntries(), to return a pointer to this. It also declares a method called _InternalQueryInterface() which uses this array to implement IUnknown::QueryInterface().

END_COM_MAP() adds the last entry to the array and declares the three methods of IUnknown (QueryInterface(), AddRef(), and Release()) as *pure virtual* methods of your class. This means that your ATL class will be abstract, it will *not* have an implementation for these methods. Instances can only be created by using this class as a base class for another class that implements these methods, such as CComObject.

The other macros in the map add entries to the table, consisting of the IID of the interface, a DWORD value and a function pointer. The pointer to the vtable (vptr) of a particular interface is indicated by the DWORD value, which is an offset from the this pointer of the ATL object. It can also be obtained by calling the function given in the entry using the DWORD field as a parameter. This is a very flexible architecture.

One interesting aspect of this map is that in debug builds an extra entry is added to the beginning of it. This entry has the name of the class (a static string) cast as the DWORD value. Obviously this will not give access to an interface vptr, so it is ignored by _GetEntries(), which under debug builds will return a pointer to the second entry. This entry is used when you have compiled a class to provide interface debugging output, giving the name of the interface that is queried. There is more information about debugging interfaces in Appendix L.

The macros that you can use in the map are:

Macro	Description
COM_INTERFACE_ENTRY Parameter: x	Declares an interface x as part of the class.
COM_INTERFACE_ENTRY_IID Parameters: iid, class	Disambiguates an interface request to specify that interface with iid is implemented by the base class class.
COM_INTERFACE_ENTRY2 Parameters: x, x2	Disambiguates two branches of inheritance, interface x is implemented using x2.
COM_INTERFACE_ENTRY2_IID Parameters: iid, x, x2	A combination of the previous two macros.
COM_INTERFACE_ENTRY_AGGREGATE Parameters: iid, punk	Exposes the interface specified by iid of the aggregated punk
COM_INTERFACE_ENTRY_AGGREGATE_BLIND Parameter: punk	Forwards a QueryInterface() for any IID to the aggregated punk.
COM_INTERFACE_ENTRY_AUTOAGGREGATE Parameters: iid, punk, clsid	Automatically creates aggregate if required
COM_INTERFACE_ENTRY_AUTOAGGREGATE_BLIND Parameters: punk, clsid	A combination of the last two macros.

Macro	Description
COM_INTERFACE_ENTRY_BREAK Parameter: x	This is used for debugging interface x.
COM_INTERFACE_ENTRY_CHAIN Parameter: classname	Check the interface map in base class classname for interfaces.
COM_INTERFACE_ENTRY_FUNC Parameters: iid, dw, func	Run func to test for the interface iid.
COM_INTERFACE_ENTRY_FUNC_BLIND Parameters: dw, func	Run func for any interface.
COM_INTERFACE_ENTRY_NOINTERFACE Parameter: x	Indicates that this object does not implement this interface.
COM_INTERFACE_ENTRY_TEAR_OFF Parameters: iid, x	Used to specify that an interface is a tear-off.
COM_INTERFACE_ENTRY_CACHED_TEAR_OFF Parameters: iid, x, punk	Used to specify that an interface is a tear-off and cached in punk.
COM_INTERFACE_ENTRY_IMPL Parameter: x	Used when the class that implements interface x is not derived from the interface (Deprecated in ATL 3).
COM_INTERFACE_ENTRY_IMPL_IID Parameters: iid, class	Used when the class that implements interface x is not derived from the interface (Deprecated in ATL 3).

The parameters for these macros are:

- ❑ class is a base class used to implement an interface
- ❑ x is an interface name, which is usually a base class of the ATL object
- ❑ x2 is used to specify a base class through which an interface is obtained
- ❑ iid is the ID of the interface
- ❑ punk is a pointer to an IUnknown interface

- ❑ `clsid` used in the aggregation macros to specify the CLSID of the object to create if required

- ❑ `classname` is the C++ class to be checked for an COM map

- ❑ `func` is a function to run to test for the interface, this is a `static` member or a global function

Most often you will use the `COM_INTERFACE_ENTRY()` macro to specify an interface that the ATL class implements. The macro uses `_ATL_IIDOF()` to get the IID from the interface name which is defined either using C string preprocessing (prefixing the interface name with `IID_`) or using `__uuidof()` (depending on whether `_ATL_NO_UUIDOF` is defined or not). In addition it also calculates the offset of the interface base class object from the `this` pointer of the ATL object. If the IID cannot be obtained from the interface name (most likely because the interface is a base interface of another interface implemented by the class) then you can explicitly specify the IID with `COM_INTERFACE_ENTRY_IID()`.

The order of the entries in the map determines the order that the object's `QueryInterface()` will search for a particular interface, so if one interface is likely to be queried more often than the others then move it nearer to the top of the map. However, bear in mind that the first entry in the map will be used for the implementation of `IUnknown` (every interface ultimately derives from `IUnknown`), so do not place aggregation or tear-off macros as the first entry.

The aggregation macros are interesting. In aggregation you can decide to allow the aggregated object to provide an implementation for a specific interface, or you can expose all the interfaces that the aggregated object implements. If you have written the aggregated object you will have designed it to provide certain interfaces and you may decide to expose all of them, in this case use one of the `_BLIND` macros. However, you will rarely want to do this (do you know all the interfaces implemented by an object you aggregate?). In most cases you will only want the aggregated object to expose specific interfaces, in which case use the non-blind versions.

The difference between the `_AGGREGATE` and `_AUTOAGGREGATE` versions involves the existence of the aggregated object. For example, `COM_INTERFACE_ENTRY_AGGREGATE()` assumes that the `punk` parameter points to a valid object, so you should ensure that the *aggregated* object is created when the *aggregating* object is created. You will use this macro most often, but if you have an object that implements an interface that is rarely ever asked for then you can aggregate it with the `_AUTOAGGREGATE` macros. The first time the interface is queried the macro will create and aggregate the object exposing it and cache its pointer in the `punk` parameter. For successive queries the cached pointer will be used, just like with the `_AGGREGATE` macros.

Here is an example of aggregating objects:

```
BEGIN_COM_MAP(CMyObject)
    COM_INTERFACE_ENTRY(IMyObject)
    COM_INTERFACE_ENTRY_AGGREGATE(IOtherItf, pOther.p)
    COM_INTERFACE_ENTRY_AUTOAGGREGATE(IAnotherItf, pAnother.p, CLSID_Another)
END_COM_MAP()
```

```
CComPtr<IOtherItf> pOther;
CComPtr<IAnotherItf> pAnother;

HRESULT FinalConstruct ()          // Called on the contruction of the
{                                  // aggregating object.
    return pOther.CoCreateInstance(CLSID_Other, GetUnknown(),
        CLSCTX_INPROC_SERVER);     // pAnother does not need to be
}                                  // instantiated here.
```

You may decide to implement a hierarchy of C++ classes, to centralize code in specific base classes. If you do this then you can allow a derived class to return the vptr of the interface implementation in a base class. To do this you should use the _CHAIN macro with the name of the base class.

The _FUNC macros allow you to write your own method to find the vptr of the interface based on the IID and DWORD parameter. The function can be a part of your ATL class (if it is static) or it can be a global function. The function has this prototype:

```
HRESULT WINAPI func(void* pv, REFIID riid, LPVOID* ppv, DWORD dw);
```

This function is not called through an object instance (the interface map is implemented in a static array), however the caller of the method will pass the object's this pointer in the first parameter pv. You can use this to access the object's members if you cast it to an appropriate pointer. Additional information about the interface requested is passed in dw, typically the offset of the interface from the this pointer of the ATL object, but if you use COM_INTERFACE_ENTRY_FUNC() then your function can use dw to pass whatever data you like.

This gives you the most flexibility, because in this method you can do almost anything you want. However, remember the COM spec when you write this function. This states that once an object says that it implements an interface it must implement that interface for its entire lifetime. Also, remember that in the specific case of IUnknown (and only in this case) the *same* pointer must be returned whenever the interface is queried.

The spec says that for all interfaces other than IUnknown you can return a different interface pointer for each query. One situation where this may occur is for a **tear-off interface**. When you implement an object by deriving your ATL class from the interfaces it supports then you will get a vptr for each interface in each instance. If your object has very little state (i.e. its data members take up little memory) but has many interfaces then the interface vptrs will take up a large proportion of the memory occupied by the object. This may be a problem if you want to have many instances of this object. Furthermore, if only a few of the interfaces are regularly queried, why have the memory taken up for all interfaces?

A tear-off implements an interface in a separate heap object, which should maintain a reference count for the specific interface so that when the last reference is released the object can be destroyed. A client could query for IUnknown on the tear-off object, so to maintain its COM identity, it must forward such calls to the main object. Since tear-offs are created only when the interface they refer to is queried you can use them for interfaces that have costly initialization. In this way the expense (time or memory) will only be incurred when that particular interface is queried.

What are the disadvantages? Well, since a tear-off has a separate reference count it does mean that you have the extra 4 byte overhead. Although you save the vptr in the main object before the tear-off is created, you lose out by having a vptr *and* a reference count when it is created. Also, if the object is accessed through a proxy then only when the entire object is destroyed will the final release be passed from the proxy to the tear-off interface. This means that although you have delayed initialization the resources held by the tear-off object are held until the entire object is released. You do not have this problem with inproc objects accessed without a proxy.

A tear-off is created using the _TEAR_OFF macro. This will create a new tear-off object for *every* query for the interface. If this is not the behavior you want then you can use the _CACHED_TEAR_OFF macro, which will create the tear-off object once and cache it in an instance variable for the next time the interface is queried. The disadvantage of this is that the memory you gain from the vptr you lose with the cached pointer, but you still get delayed initialization.

The classes that implement tear-offs should derive from CComTearOffObjectBase<> with the main object class as the parameter. This class should also have an interface map with entries of the interfaces being implemented. The combination of this map and the base class allows the tear-off object to delegate calls to QueryInterface() back to the main object, while being able to manage its own reference counts.

There are occasions where you will want to debug code when a particular interface is queried. You can do this with the _BREAK macro. This macro runs the _Break() function which is inherited from CComObjectRootBase, although you can add your own implementation. The inherited version will dump the interface name to the debug stream and then call DebugBreak() to break in the debugger. The function returns a value of S_FALSE, which the code will interpret as meaning that the macro failed, but the search for the interface should continue with the next item in the map. Typically, you would place this macro just before the actual macro that mentions the interface you wish to debug, giving you the facility to examine how the query is handled.

Be wary about this macro. It will be compiled into release builds, which means a hard breakpoint exception will be thrown. My advice is to always bracket calls with conditional compilation, indeed you could use the following macro to reinforce this:

```
#ifdef _DEBUG
    #define COM_INTERFACE_ENTRY_BREAKIFDEBUG(x) COM_INTERFACE_ENTRY_BREAK(x)
#else
    #define COM_INTERFACE_ENTRY_BREAKIFDEBUG(x)
#endif // _DEBUG
```

Use it like this:

```
BEGIN_COM_MAP(CTest)
    COM_INTERFACE_ENTRY(ITest)
    COM_INTERFACE_ENTRY_BREAKIFDEBUG(ITest2)
    COM_INTERFACE_ENTRY(ITest2)
END_COM_MAP()
```

The ATL implementation of `QueryInterface()` will go through each entry in the map looking for an interface. If an entry returns `S_FALSE` then it will move on to the next entry, if the entry returns `S_OK` then the interface was found. If it returns any other value the search ends and the result is passed back to the client. If there is not an entry for the interface being queried then `E_NOINTERFACE` is returned to the client when the end of the map is reached. If the interface map is large and involves calls to other classes or complicated routines through the `_CHAIN` or `_FUNC` macros then this searching can become a performance issue.

To get around this you can use the `_NOINTERFACE` macro to specify that a particular interface is definitely *not* supported. A typical example is the `IMarshal` interface. When your object is first created COM will query for this to determine if you want to use custom marshaling. In most cases you will not, so you should use the `_NOINTERFACE` macro with `IMarshal` to specify this. The effect of this macro is a single call to the `_NoInterface()` function that returns `E_NOINTERFACE` and prevents any following entries in the macro from being called. In addition you can use this macro to prevent requests for certain interfaces going to a `_BLIND` macro.

Connection Point Map

A connectable object must implement a connection point object for every outgoing interface it supports and it must also be able to fire events on those outgoing interfaces. The connection point map, coupled with 'proxy' classes will do both.

The map starts with `BEGIN_CONNECTION_POINT_MAP()` which defines a `static` method with a `static` array of `_ATL_CONNMAP_ENTRY` items. The map ends with `END_CONNECTION_POINT_MAP()`, which inserts the last entry in the array and returns a pointer to the first item. The entries in the map are made with `CONNECTION_POINT_ENTRY()` macros, which specify the ID's of outgoing interfaces. Each entry in the array contains an offset from the `this` pointer of the base class that implements the connection point for the specified outgoing interface.

To a certain extent you do not have to worry about all this because the "Implement Connection Point" context menu item of the ClassView will do all this for you. It will:

- ❑ derive your class from `IConnectionPointContainerImpl<>`, if necessary
- ❑ add an entry for `IConnectionPointContainer` in the interface map, if necessary
- ❑ add the connection point map, if necessary
- ❑ add the outgoing interface to the connection point map
- ❑ create a 'proxy' class in a separate file for the outgoing interface
- ❑ derive your ATL class from the 'proxy' class

The 'proxy' class does two things. Firstly, it derives from `IConnectionPointImpl<>` which implements the connection point object that will be returned to the client when it attempts to connect to the object. Secondly, it provides `Fire_` methods for each of the methods in the outgoing interface. The object can call these `Fire_` methods to generate events, and the code will make sure that every object connected through this particular connection point will be sent them. This method replaces the use of the proxy generator in VC5.

An example of the connection point map is:

```
BEGIN_CONNECTION_POINT_MAP(CMyConnectableObject)
    CONNECTION_POINT_ENTRY(DIID_DSinkInterface)
END_CONNECTION_POINT_MAP()
```

Category Map

The interfaces an object supports define its behavior. To determine what an object can do you can activate it and then call `QueryInterface()`. This can be done either for specific interfaces that you are interested in or for all interfaces registered on the local system. This is obviously not the most efficient way of doing things, an object could have a tear-off interface which has some long or expensive initialization.

To prevent you from having to activate an object to determine what it can do, Microsoft came up with the idea of adding keys to an object's `CLSID` key (for example `insertable`, or `control`). However, this is not very flexible because it requires some authority to determine what a particular string means. Furthermore, even this idea is not adhered to: Excel requires the `insertable` key to be in the versioned `ProgID` entry rather than in the `CLSID` key.

To address these issues COM uses component categories. Categories are defined in the `Component Categories` key in the registry. Each one has a CATID (a GUID) and a named value containing the description of the category (the name of the value is the locale for the string).

Components belonging to categories declare this in the registry. Under their CLSID key they have a key called `Implemented Categories`, which contains keys named with the CATID of every category that the component implements. As well as this, a component that requires a container to support particular categories has a key called `Required Categories`, containing the CATIDs of all the required container categories.

Indicating the categories implemented or required by your class is clearly a registration issue. However, rather than requiring that you edit the RGS file for a control (which would be a real pain to get right) you can instead use the category map.

The map starts with `BEGIN_CATEGORY_MAP()` which declares a `static` method called `GetCategoryMap()` in your class, with a `static` array of `_ATL_CATMAP_ENTRY` items. The map ends with `END_CATEGORY_MAP()` which adds the last entry to the array and returns a pointer to the first item. The `GetCategoryMap()` method for your class is added as one of the values added with the `OBJECT_ENTRY()` macro. The macros that you add to the category map merely add entries to the array:

Macro	Description
IMPLEMENTED_CATEGORY Parameter: catid	Categories implemented by the component.
REQUIRED_CATEGORY Parameter: catid	Categories required to be implemented by the component's container.

Where:

catid is the ID of the category

When the server is registered or unregistered the GetCategoryMap() method is called to get access to the array, which is passed to AtlRegisterClassCategoriesHelper(). This loads the system supplied component category manager and gets it to register the values in the map. An example of the category map is:

```
BEGIN_CATEGORY_MAP(CProductAccess)
    IMPLEMENTED_CATEGORY(CATID_Insertable)
    IMPLEMENTED_CATEGORY(CATID_Control)
END_CATEGORY_MAP()
```

Services Map

COM services are not the same as NT services. An NT service is an executable that is started by the system and can be run under a system account. COM services are typically implemented by control containers to provide access to one or more interfaces that represent some functionality an object requires.

Controls talk to their container through the IOleClientSite interface that is passed to the control during the initial handshake period when the container creates the control. This interface is usually implemented on a site object, so to get hold of interfaces on other objects implemented in the container (like a frame object) the control cannot simply call QueryInterface() for the interface. Instead, the control should query for IServiceProvider and use its QueryService() method to ask for an interface that is part of a specific service. QueryService() is implemented like this because a service may use the functionality of more than one object, so a control will have to mention the particular interface that it requires.

If your ATL object (running inside a container) supports services then it should derive from IServiceProviderImpl<>, have this interface in the interface map, and implement the services map. The BEGIN_SERVICE_MAP() macro adds a method called InternalQueryService() to your class and the END_SERVICE_MAP() macro ends the method. Entries are added to the map with two macros:

Macro	Description
SERVICE_ENTRY Parameter: sid	Gives the service ID of a service implemented in the object.
SERVICE_ENTRY_CHAIN Parameter: x	Indicates a global or class member that will be queried for the service.

Where:

> sid is the service ID
>
> x is an instance of a class that has a service map

These macros add if statements to check for the requested interface. An example is:

```
BEGIN_SERVICE_MAP(CMyObject)
    SERVICE_ENTRY(SID_SContainer)
    SERVICE_ENTRY_CHAIN(m_pObject)
END_SERVICE_MAP()
```

This indicates that CMyObject implements a service identified by SID_SContainer. If a client calls IServiceProvider::QueryService() for *any* interface that is part of this service then CMyObject will be queried for that interface. If the object does not implement that interface then an error result is returned to the client.

> **If the interface that is specified in QueryService() is implemented on another object then you will have to aggregate that object (which is *not* the intended behavior of IServiceProvider). This is a deficiency of the ATL implementation.**

If the client queries for a service other than SID_SContainer then the map will direct the call to an embedded object, m_pObject. Note that you should only have one _CHAIN entry in a map because the macro just checks the specified object and returns. For this reason, it should be the last macro in the map.

If you have a container object that will give access to more than one object through the services architecture you have no choice other than to implement your own version of QueryService().

Property Map

Property maps are used by any object that implements one of the persistence interfaces. Your class does not have to be a control to implement these interfaces, but if it isn't, the class must have a bool data member called m_bRequiresSave that should be initially set to true. The persistence interfaces that are implemented using the property map are:

Interface	Description
IPersistStream	'Lightweight' persistence interface where data is serially persisted to a byte stream within a storage object.
IPersistStreamInit	A version of IPersistStream that also has a method to initialize the object to a default state.
IPersistStorage	The 'heavyweight' persistence interface representing the storage object from which a stream can be obtained. It also has methods to implement the protocols to handle low memory situations and incremental saves.
IPersistPropertyBag	Interface that allows data to be persisted in a random access way, to named VARIANTs.

ATL implements IPersistStream and IPersistStorage in terms of its implementation for IPersistStreamInit (but you should only expose one of IPersistStream and IPersistStreamInit). This means that low memory and incremental save support in IPersistStorage are not provided. Also, ATL does not implement InitNew() (to initialize a component to its default state) and it does not take into account that only one of InitNew() or Load() (to initialize a component to some persisted state) can be called during the lifetime of a component. If you want this functionality, you must implement these methods yourself. Furthermore, ATL does not implement IPersistStream::GetSizeMax(), which is used to return the maximum size of the byte stream. However, this is fairly easy to calculate from the map entries.

IPersistStreamInitImpl<> and IPersistPropertyBagImpl<> are implemented using entries in the property map. The map is also used by ISpecifyPropertyPagesImpl<>, which is used to specify that a component uses property pages.

The property map starts with BEGIN_PROP_MAP(), or, if the component is a control, BEGIN_PROPERTY_MAP(). The latter should not be used for simple objects because it will automatically add the size of a control to the map, which assumes that the component is a control. This macro will add a static method to your class called GetPropertyMap() that has a static array of ATL_PROPMAP_ENTRY items. In addition, this macro adds a typedef that is used by the control to generate events on the IPropertyNotifySink interface for bound properties. The _END macro (either END_PROP_MAP() or END_PROPERTY_MAP()) finishes the array and returns a pointer to the first entry.

The entries in the array describe properties and class data members that you want to be made persistent. These macros are:

Macro	Description
PROP_ENTRY Parameters: szDesc, dispid, clsid	This adds an object property to the property map, the dispid should be for a property that has both propput and propget methods.
PROP_ENTRY_EX Parameters: szDesc, dispid, clsid, iidDispatch	This is used when an object has more than one dual interface and is used to identify on which interface to look for the property.
PROP_DATA_ENTRY Parameters: szDesc, member, vt	This adds a data member to the map. This member is not a COM property, so you must give its type and name.
PROP_PAGE Parameter: clsid	This adds a property page to the map. This is not used by the persistence interfaces.

The parameters to the macros are:

❑ szDesc is a string describing the property, do not use spaces

❑ dispid is the DISPID of the COM property

❑ iidDispatch is a dual interface to use to find a property (otherwise IDispatch is used)

❑ member is the C++ variable that you want to persist

❑ vt is the type of the C++ variable

❑ clsid is the CLSID of a property page

Note that you do not have to worry about using the _T() macro on szDesc because ATL will do this for you. You can use whatever name you choose for this value — it is only used by IPersistPropertyBagImpl<> — but it is advisable to give it the same name as the COM property that is being persisted (or a suitable alternative for data member persistence). Spaces must *not* be used in this name.

If the item that you are persisting is a COM property then ATL will query the owning object for its type and size. From this it can determine how many bytes will be written to a stream (for IPersistStreamInitImpl<> and IPersistStorageImpl<>).

If the item is a raw data member of the ATL class (and *not* a COM property) then you have to provide this information. This is the reason for the vt member of the PROP_DATA_ENTRY() macro, which specifies the type of the item. The size of the data is determined by the macro with a simple call to sizeof(), which restricts the data types that you can persist. This means that you cannot persist the data through a pointer, for example.

It is best to restrict yourself to simple integer types, because
`IPersistPropertyBagImpl<>` has a further restriction with raw data items. This
implementation must read and write the data through a container interface using a
`VARIANT`, so it must convert between raw data and a `VARIANT`. Currently, the
implementation only converts the following types:

vt value	C++ Type
VT_UI1	unsigned char
VT_I1	signed char
VT_BOOL	VARIANT_BOOL
VT_UI2	unsigned short
VT_UI4	unsigned long
VT_INT	signed int
VT_UINT	unsigned int

Notice that floating point types, `struct`s and strings are not supported.

> If you want to persist raw data of types other than the specified integer
> types you have to override the `Save()` and `Load()` methods of the ATL
> implementations. "Professional ATL COM Programming" explains how
> to do this.

Note that this restriction on raw data members only applies if your object implements
`IPersistPropertyBag`. If you are using the property map for the other persistence
interfaces then the only restriction (so long as the stream is created and used on the
same CPU type) is that you cannot use pointers.

It is generally not a good idea to have more than one dual interface on an object,
because scripting clients will only be able to access the default interface. If you really
insist on doing this then you must let ATL know how to find information about a
COM property. By default it will use the `IDispatch` interface on the object, and if you
have two dual interfaces then one will be nominated to be the implementation of this
interface using the `COM_INTERFACE_ENTRY2()` macro in the interface map. Thus,
ATL will only be able to get information about the properties on this nominated dual
interface. If you want to persist properties on another dual interface then you must
provide its ID in the property map. ATL can then query for the specified dual and use
it to obtain information about the property.

Clients can access COM properties through their `propput` and `propget` methods.
However, you may decide that treating a property as a raw value is inappropriate (for
example you may have a `BSTR` property called `Color` and thus a value of "Chisel" is
invalid). Or you may decide that several properties are related and hence it makes
sense to change one in conjunction with the others (for example the properties
`CountryCode`, `AreaCode` and `PhoneNumber`). To do this you use a property page,
which is essentially a page of a tabbed dialog that a client can load to allow a user to
alter the properties.

For your component to use a property page three things are necessary:

- ❑ there must be a suitable property page
- ❑ your class needs to implement ISpecifyPropertyPages (hence you need to derive your class from ISpecifyPropertyPagesImpl<> and add the interface to the interface map)
- ❑ you need to add the CLSID of each page to the property map

Property pages are used to view or change specific properties; the object that implements a page will be passed the IUnknown pointer to your object and be capable of reading and modifying those properties. Since the property page needs to know about the properties that are part of the object it means that generally a page is specific to a particular object. However, there are some generic property pages provided with Windows:

Name	CLSID	Property
MS Stock Font Property Page Object	CLSID_StockFontPage	IFont*
MS Stock Color Property Page Object	CLSID_StockColorPage	OLE_COLOR
MS Stock Picture Property Page Object	CLSID_StockPicturePage	IPicture*

These work by reading the type information of the object that is using the page to look for properties of the particular type that it is designed for. For example, if you have several color properties, each of type OLE_COLOR you can manipulate these with the Color Property Page. When this page is shown it will query your object (through its type information) to find all the OLE_COLOR properties and present these on the page. You can then select a property and view or change its value. These three pages are implemented in msstkprp.dll, which is provided as part of Windows.

More often you will want to implement your own property page, which you can do using the ATL Object Wizard property page type (for a discussion see Chapter 6).

Message Map

Controls typically have some visual element, which will be part of some window. The window will either be the control's own window - 'windowed' - or it will be part of a window maintained by the container - 'windowless' (see Chapter 6). The control's window will be sent messages by the system during its construction or when the user interacts with it, and it will receive notifications about the system changing. In addition, if the control has child windows these will pass notifications to the main window. To be able to respond to all of these messages there must always be some message handling routine.

ATL supplied control code checks to see if the control has created its own window, and if so registers a Windows procedure that handles messages. If the container creates the window (the control is 'windowless') then the container will call the control through its `IOleInPlaceObjectWindowless::OnWindowMessage()` method to pass messages intended for this portion of the container owned window. Both of these methods (`OnWindowMessage()` and the 'windowed' Windows procedure) pass the message to a method in your class called `ProcessWindowMessage()`. This method is part of the abstract base class `CMessageMap` (which all classes that handle messages should derive from) and is implemented by the message map.

The message map starts with `BEGIN_MSG_MAP()`, which declares `ProcessWindowMessage()`, adds a `switch` statement based on the message map ID passed, and starts the `case` for the first message map (an ID of 0). The `END_MSG_MAP()` ends the `switch` with a `default` statement that will return FALSE from `ProcessWindowMessage()`, indicating that the message has not been handled so a default Windows procedure should be called instead.

The entries in the message map do one of two things. Either they declare an alternative message map, adding a new `case` statement to the `switch`, or they use an `if` statement to check for a particular message or range of messages and call a handler method passing the message parameters.

If your control has child windows you can manage these using a data member which is an instance of `CContainedWindow`. This is initialized with a pointer to your ATL class and a unique ID, meaning that the object can forward messages to your main object's message map. To identify the source of the message the child window passes its assigned ID, which your class uses to identify an alternative message map in its own message map. So your message map can handle the same message from the control's window and any child windows, giving you the choice of using the same handler code or not

Note that although I have mentioned 'control' in the above description the same is true for any window class derived from `CWindowImpl<>`: a class does not have to be a COM class to have a message map. This means that you can use the ATL windowing classes to write Win32 window code using ATL without using COM at all.

There are many macros that you can use, and I have divided them up into related groups. In most cases, you can handle a single message or a range of messages with a single handler function. In the first case you can add the handler to your map using the ClassView message handler wizard, otherwise you need to do the editing by hand. Note that the macros do not 'crack' the message parameters like MFC, you have to interpret them yourself.

Message Handlers

These handle messages sent by the system in response to some user action (eg. a mouse button click) or window event (like window creation). The macros give the name of a function that will handle the message. This is usually a method of your class, but it could be a method inherited from a base class, a global function, a `static` method of a named class, or a public method of an object that is a member of your class. The function must have this prototype:

```
LRESULT MessageHandler(UINT uMsg, WPARAM wParam, LPARAM lParam,
                                                BOOL& bHandled);
```

The message map will pass the message, its parameters and a reference to a BOOL parameter to this method. You use the BOOL parameter to indicate if handling of this method should continue after the method returns, by default it will have a value of TRUE which means that message handling stops after this method returns.

Macro	Description
MESSAGE_HANDLER Parameters: msg, func	Gives the function that will handle a message.
MESSAGE_RANGE_HANDLER Parameters: msgFirst, msgLast, func	Gives the range of messages and the single function that will handle them.

The parameters to the macros are:

- ❑ msg is the message to handle
- ❑ msgFirst is the first in a range of messages
- ❑ msgLast is the last in a range of messages
- ❑ func is the handler function

Here is an example:

```
BEGIN_MSG_MAP(CMyCtrl)
    MESSAGE_HANDLER(WM_LBUTTONDOWN, LButtonHandler)
    CHAIN_MSG_MAP(CComControl<CMyCtrl>)
END_MSG_MAP()

LRESULT LButtonHandler(UINT uMsg, WPARAM wParam, LPARAM lParam,
                                                BOOL& bHandled)
{
    ATLTRACE("Left button click\n");
    return 0;
}
```

The CHAIN_MSG_MAP() macro used here is covered later. If you want to handle a range of messages (for example to centralize all mouse messages) then you can use MESSAGE_RANGE_HANDLER() passing the start and end of the range.

Command Handlers

Command messages are sent when a contained window sends a notification to its parent, using the WM_COMMAND message. The Platform SDK lists the possible command messages for the predefined Windows classes like edit boxes and list boxes. Command handler functions have this prototype:

```
LRESULT CommandHandler(WORD wNotifyCode, WORD wID, HWND hwndCtl,
                                               BOOL& bHandled);
```

The parameters for these functions are calculated from the message parameters by the map macro. The notification code wNotifyCode is obtained by taking the high WORD of the message's wParam. The contained (child) window ID wID comes from the low WORD of wParam and hwndCtl contains the HWND of the child, obtained from lParam.

The relevant message map entries are:

Macro	Description
COMMAND_HANDLER Parameters: id, code, func	Gives the function that will handle a WM_COMMAND message from a particular window.
COMMAND_CODE_HANDLER Parameters: code, func	Gives the function that will handle a notification message sent via WM_COMMAND.
COMMAND_ID_HANDLER Parameters: id, func	Gives the single function that will handle all the command messages for a window.
COMMAND_RANGE_HANDLER Parameters: idFirst, idLast, func	Gives the single function that will handle all command messages for a range of child windows.

The parameters to the macros are:

- ❑ id is the child window ID
- ❑ idFirst is the first in a range of child window IDs
- ❑ idLast is the last in a range of child window IDs
- ❑ code is the notification code
- ❑ func is the handler function

The first is the most specific, handling a notification message from a specific child window. You can use the COMMAND_ID_HANDLER() macro to specify that a function should handle all notifications from a particular child window. The COMMAND_CODE_HANDLER() macro can be used to specify that a particular notification from any window will be handled by a single function. The most generic macro is the last one in the table, which specifies that a single function will handle all notifications for a range of child windows.

Here is an example; CMyCtrl is a composite control with two edit boxes, a button and a list box:

```
BEGIN_MSG_MAP(CMyCtrl)
    COMMAND_CODE_HANDLER(EN_CHANGE, OnCheckText)
    COMMAND_HANDLER(IDC_BUTTON1, BN_CLICKED, OnClickButton1)
    COMMAND_ID_HANDLER(IDC_LISTBOX1, OnListBox1Messages)
    CHAIN_MSG_MAP(CComCompositeControl<CMyCtrl>)
END_MSG_MAP()
```

When the user changes text in either of the edit boxes (resulting in the EN_CHANGE notification message) OnCheckText() is called. No check on the child window ID is made here. The second macro does check this, so only clicks on IDC_BUTTON1 will be handled by OnClickButton1(). Finally, all messages for the list box will be handled by OnListBox1Messages(), you will have to check the message type in that routine to determine how you handle it. The CHAIN_MSG_MAP() macro is covered in the 'Chained Message Maps' section of this Appendix.

Notification Handlers

One thing that may have seemed strange to you about the WM_COMMAND message is that lParam and wParam are taken up entirely with the notification message, the control ID and the HWND of that child control; there is no space for any parameters of the notification. Therefore, if your control window gets the EN_CHANGE message to indicate that the text in an edit control has changed, your control must interrogate the child edit control to determine what the text has changed to.

The Windows 95/NT 4.0 common controls remedy this by sending the parent window the WM_NOTIFY message to notify the parent. In this case lParam holds the child control's ID, but wParam holds a pointer to a NMHDR structure. If you look at this structure, you'll find that all it holds is the ID of the control that generated the notification, its HWND and a notification code. This is just the same information that was encoded in the message parameters of the WM_COMMAND message, so what have you gained?

In fact, what is pointed to is actually a control specific structure, the first item of which is an NMHDR structure (HDR stands for *header*). For example a Tree View control sends a pointer to an NMTREEVIEW structure. It is perfectly legal to cast the NMHDR pointer to a LPNMHDR. The reason why the notification message works like this is that the Windows API is a C API, but WM_NOTIFY must be able to work with many different controls that will pass different notification structures. Casting to LPNMHDR is the nearest you'll get in C to overloading.

Notification messages are handled like command messages, the macros you can use are:

Macro	Description
NOTIFY_HANDLER Parameters: id, code, func	Gives the function that will handle the notification from a particular control.

Macro	Description
NOTIFY_CODE_HANDLER Parameters: code, func	Gives the function that will handle a particular notification code.
NOTIFY_ID_HANDLER Parameters: id, func	Gives the single function that will handle all notifications from a particular control.
NOTIFY_RANGE_HANDLER Parameters: idFirst, idLast, func	Gives the single function that will handle all notification messages from the controls in a particular range.

The parameters to the macros are:

- ❑ id is the child window ID
- ❑ idFirst is the first in a range of child window IDs
- ❑ idLast is the last in a range of child window IDs
- ❑ func is the handler function
- ❑ code is the notification code

Handler functions should have this prototype:

```
LRESULT NotifyHandler(int idCtrl, LPNMHDR pnmh, BOOL& bHandled);
```

The macros cast the wParam to a pointer to the NMHDR structure, but to get control specific information you need to re-cast it to a pointer to the notification structure filled by the child control. For example, if your control has a Tree View control then you can handle a user click on an item with:

```
BEGIN_MSG_MAP(CMyCtrl)
    NOTIFY_HANDLER(IDC_TREE, TVN_SELCHANGED, OnSelChangedTree)
    CHAIN_MSG_MAP(CComCompositeControl<CMyCtrl>)
END_MSG_MAP()

LRESULT OnSelChangedTree(int idCtrl, LPNMHDR pnmh, BOOL& bHandled)
{
    LPNMTREEVIEW pnmtv = static_cast<LPNMTREEVIEW>(pnmh);
    MessageBox(pnmtv->itemNew->pszText, _T("You selected"));
    return 0;
}
```

To get the text of the item you need to cast the pnmh parameter to a LPNMTREEVIEW pointer.

Alternative Message Maps

When you create a control class you will get a window, either created by your class (your control is 'windowed'), or part of a container created window (your control is 'windowless'). In addition, you can create child windows, which can handle their own messages and notify the parent by sending WM_COMMAND or WM_NOTIFY messages.

Another thing you can do is to create child windows as part of your control, typically using CContainedWindow. The child window you create will then be sent messages by the system like any other window. As its name suggests, this ATL class does not have a message map, and instead it redirects the messages it receives to the message map of the window that contains it. To identify where the message originated the contained window specifies that the message should be handled by a particular **alternative message map**. This has two advantages. Firstly, you can use an instance of CContainedWindow in your class without having to create a new class, and secondly you can have all the message handling code in one place.

The most likely situation where you will use an alternative message map is when you use the Object Wizard to base a control on a Win32 or Common Control. In this case your control will have a window, but the window that the user will see is sub-classed from the selected Windows class. In order that you can handle its messages they are redirected to an alternative message map in your control.

You declare the alternative message map with the following macro, and then all entries that follow it will be in that map until you declare another alternative message map:

Macro	Description
ALT_MSG_MAP	Declares an alternative message map.
Parameter: dwMsgMapID	

The parameter to the macro is:

dwMsgMapID is the ID for the alternative map

For example, if you have two child windows on your control, say a button and an edit control, then you can have a message map like this:

```
CContainedWindow m_ctlEdit;
CContainedWindow m_ctlButton;

CMyCtrl() : m_ctlEdit(_T("Edit"), this, 1),
            m_ctlButton(_T("Button"), this, 2)
{
    m_bWindowed = TRUE;
}

BEGIN_MSG_MAP(CMyCtrl)
    CHAIN_MSG_MAP(CComControl<CMyCtrl>)
    MESSAGE_HANDLER(WM_CREATE, OnCreate) // create the child windows
    MESSAGE_HANDLER(WM_LBUTTONDOWN, OnCtrlClick)
ALT_MSG_MAP(1)
    MESSAGE_HANDLER(WM_LBUTTONDOWN, OnEditClick)
ALT_MSG_MAP(2)
    MESSAGE_HANDLER(WM_LBUTTONDOWN, OnButtonClick).
END_MSG_MAP()
```

Here, you create the C++ objects in the constructor specifying the Windows class that will be used, a pointer to the class with the message map, and the alternative message map ID. The actual window is created when the control's window is created, hence you should make the control 'windowed' so that you will be sent, and have to handle, the WM_CREATE message. In this handler you should create the windows (Chapter 6 and Appendix J) and position them on the control's window.

The message map has three handlers for a left mouse click, depending on where the user has clicked, all three handler functions are members of the same class.

Chained Message Maps

Your C++ design of a control may use more than one class. For example you may have a base class to provide generic message handling of certain messages and then in a derived class provide control specific handling of messages. Alternatively you could create a member of your class that is an object that can handle messages. In these situations you can chain the message map to the base class or member object.

The macros you can use are:

Macro	Description
CHAIN_MSG_MAP Parameter: theChainClass	Routes messages to the default message map of a base class
CHAIN_MSG_MAP_ALT Parameters: theChainClass, msgMapID	Routes messages to the alternative message map of a base class
CHAIN_MSG_MAP_MEMBER Parameter: theChainMember	Routes messages to the default message map of data member derived from CMessageMap
CHAIN_MSG_MAP_ALT_MEMBER Parameters: theChainMember, msgMapID	Routes messages to the alternative message map of data member derived from CMessageMap
CHAIN_MSG_MAP_DYNAMIC Parameter: dynaChainID	Routes messages to the default message map determined at runtime

The parameters to the macros are:

❑ theChainClass is the class which should be used

❑ theChainMember is the data member possessing the message map to use

❑ msgMapID is an alternative message map ID

❑ dynaChainID is the ID of the object to be used

The first two are designed to pass the message to the message map of a base class. Of these the first is used to pass messages to the default message map, whereas the second passes the message to a specified alternative message map. The next two will pass the message to the message map of an object member of the class, again either the default or an alternative message map. That object must be an instance of a class derived from CMessageMap and must implement a message map, but it does not have to be a control class, or be derived from any of the ATL window classes.

The final macro, CHAIN_MSG_MAP_DYNAMIC(), is interesting because it allows you to determine at runtime the objects that will handle messages. You cannot do this with the _MEMBER macros because they take a parameter which is an instance not a pointer, so you cannot use polymorphism. The _DYNAMIC macro does not use polymorphism either, it uses the methods of a base class to determine what object (if any) to use to handle messages. The control, or the code that has access to the control's C++ object, can change the objects that are registered with this base class at runtime, adding or removing objects *dynamically*.

It works like this: your control class should derive from CDynamicChain, which has public members to add and remove objects from the array it uses to handle messages. Since your class publicly derives from this class any code that has access to your control's C++ object can add items into this array. These objects should derive from CMessageMap and have a message map. You add an object by calling SetChainEntry() and passing three values: a pointer to the object, the alternative message map ID (which can be omitted if the default message map is to be used) and a chain ID.

The chain ID is referenced in the CHAIN_MSG_MAP_DYNAMIC() macro and indicates that a particular object should handle messages. If you call SetChainEntry() with a chain ID that has already been used then the existing entry will be replaced with the new one. If you want to remove an entry you can call RemoveChainEntry() with a chain ID.

Reflected Messages

Controls talk to their container using events; Windows controls communicate by sending Windows messages Certain messages sent by a control are meant only to notify its container and are handled within the sending object. The container responds to such messages by 'reflecting' them. The reflected message consists of the original message plus the constant OCM_BASE. When the control gets these messages it can identify them as being reflected from the container and handle them by sending an event.

The macros you can use to implement this are:

Macro	Description
DEFAULT_REFLECTION_HANDLER	Default windows handler for reflected messages.
REFLECT_NOTIFICATIONS	Will reflect the message to the child code specified in the message.

Sink Map

The general way to generate an event is for a client to implement an event interface and register this with the object that will generate the event. You will typically do this using connection points in the connectable object (see the section on the connection point map). Objects that generate events will use dispinterface outgoing interfaces (if scripting clients are supported), so a client accepting the event should implement IDispatch and use its Invoke() method to check the passed DISPID and invoke the appropriate handler method.

One way to do this in ATL is to implement a dual interface in the client with methods that have the same DISPIDs as the sink dispinterface and then use the COM_INTERFACE_ENTRY_IID() macro to associate the dispinterface with the dual. The client can then pass a pointer to this interface to the connectable object when advising (making) the connection. Since the object will want a pointer to IDispatch this is not a problem, because a dual interface implements this interface. However, this is far from the ideal solution, because the client sink object will have vptr for the custom part of the dual as well as the IDispatch part — duplicating code.

Another solution is to implement the dispinterface in the client sink object by implementing just IDispatch. This implementation should test the DISPIDs passed in Invoke() and dispatch the method request to a member function (you don't have to implement GetIDsOfNames() because the connectable object will not call this method). The implementation of IDispatch is the purpose of the sink map and associated templates. Sink maps are typically used by composite controls to handle events generated by child ActiveX controls, but you can use them yourself if you want to connect to another object.

There are two classes used to implement sink dispinterfaces: IDispEventImpl<> and its base class IDispEventSimpleImpl<>. When an event is sent to an object it needs to call the appropriate handler. To do this the Invoke() methods in these classes will call an API method called DispCallFunc(). They do this because they are generic (and obviously do not know the name, parameters and return value of your handlers), so DispCallFunc() must be passed a description of the method (its call type and parameters) so that it can construct the correct stack frame to call the handler. The difference between the two event handler classes is where they get this information from. IDispEventImpl<> will get the method description from the type library that describes the dispinterface, hence when you use this template you *must* give the LIBID and version of this library. IDispEventSimpleImpl<>, on the other hand, will look in the sink map for the description.

There are three steps to using a sink map. Firstly your class should derive from `IDispEventImpl<>` (or `IDispEventSimpleImpl<>`) for each `dispinterface` that you implement. `IDispEventImpl<>` has seven parameters, the first three it has in common with `IDispEventSimpleImpl<>`. The first parameter is a unique ID that is used to identify the `dispinterface` in the sink map and the second is your ATL class. The third parameter is a pointer to the IID of the `dispinterface`, which is important if the connectable object has more than one outgoing interface (because it allows you to identify which one to connect to). The fourth parameter is a pointer to the LIBID of the type library that describes the `dispinterface` (which `IDispEventImpl<>` uses in its implementation). This is followed by two parameters that give the version of the type library, which is managed by the class specified in the final parameter.

Of these seven parameters, the last four have default values, but if you use it yourself you should only use the default value for the final parameter. In particular, the default values used for the version give a version number of `0.0`, which will result in the class failing to load the type library, therefore you *must* supply values.

The second thing that you need to do is add the sink map, which has members associating `dispinterface` DISPIDs with methods in your class. If you derive from `IDispEventSimpleImpl<>` then you must use `SINK_ENTRY_INFO()` and pass the pointer of a `static` member that describes the handler function (described later) otherwise you can use any of the macros in the table below.

The final thing you need to do, of course, is to implement the handler methods in your class. Each of these methods should have the same signature as the method in the `dispinterface` that it is handling, and must use the `__stdcall` calling convention.

The sink map is declared using `BEGIN_SINK_MAP()` which adds a `static` method called `_GetSinkMap()` that has a static array of `_ATL_EVENT_ENTRY<>` items. The `END_SINK_MAP()` macro ends the function by returning a pointer to the first item in the array. The macros shown below add items into this array:

Macro	Description
`SINK_ENTRY` Parameters: `id, dispid, fn`	Specifies that the event with the DISPID of `dispid` on the interface identified by `id` is handled by `fn`. This can only be used by `IDispEventImpl<>`.
`SINK_ENTRY_EX` Parameters: `id, iid, dispid, fn`	The same as the previous macro, but it also gives the sink interface's IID. This can only be used by `IDispEventImpl<>`.
`SINK_ENTRY_INFO` Parameters: `id, iid, dispid, fn, info`	The same as the previous macro, but it also describes the function.

The parameters to the macros are:

- ❑ id is the ID that identifies the sink interface

- ❑ dispid is the DISPID of the method

- ❑ fn is the function to handle the event

- ❑ iid is the ID of the sink interface

- ❑ info is a struct that describes the function

For example, if an object has this outgoing interface defined in its IDL file:

```
dispinterface _DNotifications
{
   properties:
   methods:
      [id(1)] HRESULT OnItemProcessed([in] long lItem);
      [id(2)] void OnError([in] BSTR bstrDesc);
};
```

Then an object that connects to it can derive from

```
IDispEventImpl<1, CMyObject, &DIID__DNotifications, &LIBID_ObjLib, 1, 0>
```

(Notice that the version is specified). The sink map will look like this:

```
BEGIN_SINK_MAP(CMyObject)
   SINK_ENTRY(1, 1, OnItemProcessed)
   SINK_ENTRY(1, 2, OnError)
END_SINK_MAP()

HRESULT __stdcall OnItemProcessed(long lItem)
{
   ATLTRACE(_T("Item %ld processed\n"), lItem);
   return S_OK;
}
VOID __stdcall OnError(BSTR bstrDesc)
{
   ATLTRACE(_T("failure: %S\n"), bstrDesc);
}
```

The object that CMyObject connects to has only one outgoing interface, so in this example you do not need to specify the dispinterface in the map. Also, although IDispEventImpl<> needs a description of the method to call your handler, you do not need to specify it because the class will get it from the type library specified in the template.

This provides an implementation of the sink interface, but you still need to make the connection to the object that has _DNotifications as an outgoing interface, and at some point break the connection. You do this by calling the inherited DispEventAdvise() and DispEventUnadvise() methods, passing the IUnknown pointer to the object that you are trying to connect to.

Since IDispEventImpl<> uses a type library you have to ensure that it is registered on the client machine. If this is not the case then you can use IDispEventSimpleImpl<> as long as you provide a description of the handler methods.

For example, using the previous example, you can derive your sink class from:

```
IDispEventSimplImpl<1, CMyObject, &DIID__DNotifications>
```

The sink map would look like this:

```
static _ATL_FUNC_INFO ItemProcInfo;
static _ATL_FUNC_INFO ErrorInfo;

BEGIN_SINK_MAP(CMyObject)
    SINK_ENTRY_INFO(1, 1, OnItemProcessed, &ItemProcInfo)
    SINK_ENTRY_INFO(1, 2, OnError, &ErrorInfo)
END_SINK_MAP()
```

The static members are initialized like this:

```
_ATL_FUNC_INFO CMyObject::ItemProcInfo
    = {CC_STDCALL, VT_HRESULT, 1, VT_I4, 0, 0, 0, 0, 0, 0, 0};
_ATL_FUNC_INFO CMyObject::ErrorInfo
    = {CC_STDCALL, VT_EMPTY, 1, VT_BSTR, 0, 0, 0, 0, 0, 0, 0};
```

The first parameter is the method call type (which must be CC_STDCALL) and the second is its return type (with VT_EMPTY for a return type of void). This is followed by the number of parameters and the types of those parameters. You can create handlers which have up to 8 parameters, (in this case I have filled the empty values with zero), but if your handlers need more than this you can define _ATL_MAX_VARTYPES to the maximum number of parameters before including atlcom.h.

B

Registration

Introduction

Registration is important because it allows COM to find the code that implements a particular object. By default ATL adds registration scripts to your project as resources, and it registers the information in these scripts using the ATL registrar. However, there are several other ways that you can register your object. In this appendix, I'll outline the various registration macros and how to use them.

Registration

First, a little explanation about registration — if you are a seasoned COM programmer you can skip this section.

COM uses the registry as a persistent store to hold information about objects, servers and interfaces. This information is held in keys in the HKEY_CLASSES_ROOT hive, which is also mapped to the HKEY_LOCAL_MACHINE\Software\Classes key.

On a server machine three keys are important:
AppID, CLSID and Interface.

AppID

Holds information about object servers. In particular, it states whether the server is an NT service, or if it's a DLL and should be run in a surrogate process. It also holds security information about:

- ❑ Who can launch the server (on NT).

- ❑ Who can access the server (both NT and Windows 9x).

- ❑ Which account it will run under (obviously only appropriate for NT machines).

These values are configured with DCOMCnfg. They also require a value in each CLSID key of the coclasses implemented in the specified server to map the CLSID to the AppID.

> Note that there is a bug in DCOMCnfg that causes it to show the first class of the server rather than a server description string. Because of this, it appears that when you administer the security settings you are changing the settings for a single coclass, you are *not*, you are changing the security settings for a *server*.

CLSID

Holds information about the coclasses that are implemented in the servers installed on the machine. The purpose is to give information to COM about the file system path to the code that implements the object. This path *must* be to a local drive, because the system component that loads the server (the COM Service Control Manager (SCM) — don't confuse this with the NT Service Control manager which is a separate system component!) does not have access to the network. In addition, objects that are implemented in DLLs also have a key to indicate the threading model the object is designed to use. Of course, there's also a value that gives the AppID of the server that implements the object.

Interface

Contains information about the interfaces that objects implement. In particular this is used to give the CLSID of the proxy and stub objects (they have the same CLSID) that is used to marshal the interface. For standard marshaling, proxy objects are required on the client end of a connection and stub objects are required on the server side. These CLSIDs refer to an entry in the CLSID key for an inproc object. If the interface is type library marshaled then the CLSID refers to the Universal Marshaler (implemented in OleAut32.dll). To give this generic object information about the interface there should be a key called TypeLib that gives the LIBID of a registered type library.

These three keys are required on the server machine, but there are two other keys usually registered for an object:

ProgID

This is a human-readable string generally used by scripting clients to create objects. The actual name of the coclass is the CLSID, the ProgID key maps the ProgID to the CLSID and a client can call CLSIDFromProgID() to get this mapping.

TypeLib

This holds information about registered type libraries. ATL will usually create one type library for your server and bind it as a resource. The TypeLib entry associates a LIBID with the path to the type library (.tlb or .olb) or code (.exe, .dll or .ocx) file that contains the type library. Type libraries contain textual information about objects and interfaces and so they are locale dependant, so registration of a type library requires the locale that is appropriate to the library. Note that objects that will be used with Visual Basic must have a type library for integration with the Visual Basic IDE.

Client

On the client machine, the required keys are those for the interfaces that an object uses. These are required, as once a client has a reference to an object it must be able to marshal the interface methods. So, on the client machine the COM runtime must be able to load the proxy object for that interface. Often, this means registering a proxy-stub DLL on the client machine. If the interface uses type library marshaling then the proxy object will be the Universal Marshaler, so the interface must be registered to use a particular (registered) type library.

The CLSID entry is not required for an object client because it is used to give the path to the code that implements the object on the local machine. For a remote client it is inappropriate to specify the remote server name when using CoCreateInstanceEx(). However, if the client does not use this API (if, for example, it uses CoCreateInstance() or it's a Visual Basic 5 client) then you need to have a CLSID entry to indicate the AppID that will have the remote server name. The AppID will have a RemoteServerName value that contains the IP address or machine name of the server that has the object server.

ATL takes care of the server-side registration, and if the client and server are the same machine then will provide all the information for both. If they are separate machines then you will need to write a script or some other installation program to make the client-side registration. A command line utility is available from the WorldOfATL web site (**www.WorldOfATL.com** or see **www.wrox.com**) that will make registration entries based on an RGS script; you can use this within your installation script.

The Registrar

Servers should support both registration and unregistration so that you can safely clean up the machine when you uninstall a server. Adding entries to the registry using the registry API is a bit of a pain: it's OK for a few values, but can be very tedious for adding (or removing) multiple entries. To get round this problem ATL provides an object called the registrar. This can be used as a COM object or a C++ object.

Why is it implemented as both? If you have several ATL servers on a single machine it makes sense to centralize the code in one module, which ATL does in ATL.DLL. One major advantage of COM is that it provides management for dynamically loading DLLs, so the registrar is provided as a COM object.

This can give rise to the case where you install your object on another machine without knowing whether that machine has ATL.DLL registered. You have two options here. The first is that you can distribute ATL.DLL with your object server and install both servers on the new machine. However, this will bloat the size of your CAB file because ATL.DLL contains code other than the registrar (see Appendix E). It would be better to distribute just the code that your server needs to use. To do this you can take the second option, which is to use the C++ object version of the registrar and *statically link* it to your server. This has the disadvantage of increasing the size of your server (but not as much as the combined size of both your server and ATL.DLL), but it makes no assumption about what objects are registered on the target machine.

When you create an ATL project the AppWizard will give you two release build options: MinSize and MinDependency. MinSize will use the registrar as a COM object (and will use the other methods exported from ATL.DLL — see Appendix C); MinDependency will use the C++ object version of the registrar.

Note that ATL.DLL is supplied in two flavors, a Unicode version and an ANSI version. The ANSI version will work on both Windows9x machines and NT machines since they use ANSI string functions. (LPOLESTR strings, which are used by most ATL methods and by all of the methods of the registrar are converted to ANSI strings before they are processed.) However, NT uses Unicode, making it more efficient to have a server that calls the Unicode version of functions that use strings. If the ANSI DLL were used, Unicode strings would be converted to ANSI, which the system will just convert back to Unicode. Obviously, you need to know which version to distribute to your target machines, in this situation the ANSI version is the safest choice (although there will be a performance hit on NT machines). You may be able to use your installer to choose the correct DLL.

Registration Scripts

The information that the registrar will use to change the registry is supplied in registration scripts that you can either bind into your server as resources or generate dynamically. The ATL AppWizard will add a registration script to register the AppID of the server if it is an EXE server. It will *not* do this for a DLL server, which is a problem if you want the DLL to be used in a surrogate. When you add an ATL class to your server using the ATL Object Wizard you will get an additional registration script for each class that you add, containing registration information for the object's CLSID and ProgID. By default, ATL adds these as resources to your server and adds code to pass the script to the registrar.

RGS Format

The format of the registration scripts is quite straightforward. They are made up of named blocks delimited with braces ({}) just like code blocks in C++. The name of the block represents a registry key, which you can optionally give a default value. The name of a block can be modified by one of the following:

Modifier	Description
ForceRemove	If it exists, this key and all entries within it will be removed before registration. It will be recreated during registration. This key and all entries within it should be removed during unregistration
NoRemove	Do not remove this key during unregistration
Delete	Remove this key during registration

For example, here is an excerpt from an RGS script:

```
NoRemove CLSID
{
    ForceRemove {A41F2F0D-5644-11D2-99E9-00104BDC361E} = s 'MyObject Class'
    {
        val AppID = s '{A41F2F01-5644-11D2-99E9-00104BDC361E}'
    }
}
```

This is saying that whatever the script is being used for it should *never* remove the
CLSID key. (If this key was removed then you would not be able to use any COM
object and your Windows machine would probably stop working.) During
registration, this script indicates that if an entry for the MyObject Class already
exists it should be refreshed. This involves removing the MyObject Class key, along
with any subkeys and values it may possess, and then adding it again. If the key does
not already exist it is merely added. During unregistration the key is removed, as
NoRemove is not specified.

Notice that the key has a default value, added by using the = sign. The script indicates
that this is a string by prefixing the value with s. You can specify that the value is a
string, a DWORD or a binary value using the following codes:

Type Specifier	Type	Example
S	String	s 'Test String'
D	DWORD	d 99
B	Binary	b '5465737420537472696E6700'

There are two things to notice here. The first is that you should specify the DWORD
values as decimal not hex. The second is that if you want to add a binary value you
should do so by converting the bytes to hex and presenting this value as a string. In the
example in the table above the registrar will add the string "Test String" as a binary
value.

You can also add named values to a key by prefixing the name with the string val (see
the AppID example above). If this is omitted the registrar treats the entry as a key. The
string you use for the named value (and this applies to keys too) can have spaces, if
this is the case then enclose the name in single quotes:

```
val 'Number of Objects' = d 4
```

If you are accessing a key you should give the key name. If you are accessing one of
the standard hives you should give the hive name (as shown in RegEdit) or one of the
following abbreviations:

String	Hive
HKCR	HKEY_CLASSES_ROOT
HKCU	HKEY_CURRENT_USER

String	Hive
HKLM	HKEY_LOCAL_MACHINE
HKU	HKEY_USERS
HKPD	HKEY_PERFORMANCE_DATA
HKDD	HKEY_DYN_DATA
HKCC	HKEY_CURRENT_CONFIG

One further point is that you can add values dynamically into a script. One example of this is the %MODULE% place holder, for example:

```
LocalServer32 = s '%MODULE%'
```

This indicates that at runtime the code will provide a string that will be inserted in place of the %MODULE% place holder by calling the registrar method IRegistrar::AddReplacement(). In this case %MODULE% is replaced with the file location obtained by GetModuleFileName(). You can use this technique yourself. For example, if you want to add a key with the date that an object is registered you could change the object's .rgs file and add the following:

```
HKLM
{
    NoRemove Software
    {
        NoRemove Wrox
        {
            ForceRemove MyObject = s 'MyObject Class'
            {
                InstallDate = s '%Date%'
            }
        }
    }
}
```

To provide a value for the custom %Date% place holder, you will need to write the UpdateRegistry() method, as will be explained later.

This is essentially all there is to registration scripts. If you would like to experiment with them then I recommend that you download the *RegRgs32 RGS File Registration Utility* from the download page of the WorldOfATL site (**www.WorldOfATL.com** or click through **www.wrox.com**). This command line utility takes a registration script as a command line parameter and will use the registrar COM object to either register or unregister the script. This utility is also useful if you want to install registry values on a target machine, for example if you want to add the AppID and RemoteServerName (and the associated CLSID keys) for a client that cannot use CoCreateInstanceEx().

Registrar Methods

The IRegistrar interface is declared in atliface.idl, which can be found in VC98\atl\include. The methods it possesses are:

Method	Description
AddReplacement	Gives the value for a place holder in the script, the actual replacement is carried out when the registration/unregistration occurs.
ClearReplacements	Clears any values set by AddReplacement().
ResourceRegisterSz	Indicates that a registration script is a resource in a file. The method parameters are the filename, the resource name as a string and the type of the resource (which should be REGISTRY).
ResourceUnregisterSz	Unregisters a script held as a resource in a file.
FileRegister	This takes the name of a text file that contains the registration script. The method will load the file and register its contents.
FileUnregister	This method unregisters a text file that is passed as a parameter to the method.
StringRegister	You can use this to pass a string that contains a registration script, the registrar will register the values.
StringUnregister	You can use this to pass a string that contains a registration script, the registrar will unregister the values.
ResourceRegister	Indicates that a registration script is a resource in a file. The method parameters are the filename, the resource ID (a number) and the type of the resource (which should be REGISTRY).
ResourceUnregister	Unregisters a script held as a resource in a file.

The difference between the ResourceRegister() and ResourceRegisterSz() (and the corresponding unregistration versions) is that the RGS resource is specified with a string resource name in the Sz versions (for example OLESTR("MyRegScript")) and with a resource ID for the other versions (for example IDR_MYREGSCRIPT — a number).

As you can see, you can provide a registration script either as a resource in a code module (referenced using a resource name or an ID), in a text file by itself, or in a string. This last option allows you to dynamically create a resource script.

Registration Macros

Before I explain the registration macros, I must first introduce the _ATL_STATIC_REGISTRY symbol. This symbol is automatically defined if the project is set to **Release MinDependency**. If you define this symbol (using the project settings, or by defining it in stdafx.h before any ATL header is included) your object will use the C++ registrar (implemented in CRegObject) rather than the COM version. This adds the registrar code, *statically linked*, to your project. I find this useful if I want to debug the registration of a server because it allows me to step into the registrar code to see exactly what it is doing.

Macro	Description
DECLARE_NO_REGISTRY	Used for classes that do not need registration, for example those that are not externally creatable
DECLARE_REGISTRY Parameters: class, pid, vpid, nid, flags	This allows you to register a class *without* using a script
DECLARE_REGISTRY_RESOURCE Parameter: str	Gives the name of a resource that contains the registration script
DECLARE_REGISTRY_RESOURCEID Parameter: id	Gives the ID of a resource that contains the registration script

The parameters for these macros are:

- ❑ class is the name of the ATL class
- ❑ pid is the ProgID of the coclass
- ❑ vpid is the version independent ProgID for the coclass
- ❑ nid is the resource ID of a string that describes the coclass
- ❑ flags determines the apartment model and remote automation access
- ❑ str is the string name of the resource
- ❑ id is the symbol for the resource

The various DECLARE_ macros add a method called UpdateRegistry() to your ATL class. By default the Object Wizard will also add an RGS script to your projects as a REGISTRY resource, and the DECLARE_REGISTRY_RESOURCEID() macro to your class. If, by personal preference, you want to rename this resource to a string then you can use the DECLARE_REGISTRY_RESOURCE() macro, for example:

```
DECLARE_REGISTRY_RESOURCE(MyObject)
```

here MyObject is the string name of the resource (you don't need quotes, or the _T() macro):

```
// REGISTRY
MyObject    REGISTRY DISCARDABLE    "MyObject.rgs"
```

Custom registration

If the object is not externally creatable and you have no object-specific values that should be made persistent then there is no point in adding registration information to the class, hence you can use the _NO_REGISTRY macro. You can use the _REGISTRY macro to register a coclass for an inproc object *without* using a registration script. In this case you need to specify the ProgID, version independent ProgID and string resource that describes the class. You also need to indicate the threading model that the coclass is designed for. You do not need to pass the CLSID because ATL will get this from the ATL class. The flags parameter used by this macro can be one of:

Symbol	Description
THREADFLAGS_APARTMENT	Sets the ThreadingModel value to Apartment.
THREADFLAGS_BOTH	Sets the ThreadingModel value to Both
AUTPRXFLAG	Indicates that the object will be accessed through remote automation.

If you decide that you need to add additional entries when registering a particular coclass you can write your own version of UpdateRegistry() (and hence remove the registry macro that Object Wizard gave you). You can also do this to provide values for place holders. For example, if you have a place holder called %Date% (as shown earlier), you can give it a value by adding the following method to your class:

```
static HRESULT WINAPI UpdateRegistry(BOOL bRegister)
{
    USES_CONVERSION;
    TCHAR strDate[20];
    SYSTEMTIME st;
    GctLocalTime(&st);
    wsprintf(strDate, _T("%02d-%02d-%04d %02d:%02d:%02d"),
        st.wDay, st.wMonth, st.wYear, st.wHour, st.wMinute, st.wSecond);

    static _ATL_REGMAP_ENTRY MapEntries[2];
    size_t t = sizeof(MapEntries);
    memset(MapEntries, 0, sizeof(MapEntries));
    MapEntries[0].szKey - OLESTR("Date");
    MapEntries[0].szData = T2OLE(strDate);
    return _Module.UpdateRegistryFromResource(IDR_MYOBJECT,
        bRegister, MapEntries);
}
```

So that this code can compile both under ANSI and UNICODE builds the ATL string conversion macros are used (T2OLE()), so USES_CONVERSION is added — more information on this is given in Appendix M.

Here I create a string, holding the current date and time, and a `static` array of `_ATL_REGMAP_ENTRY` members. This array has to be one greater than the number of place holders it will hold because the last member is cleared to zero to indicate the end of the array. The `_ATL_REGMAP_ENTRY` `struct` has two fields `szKey` and `szData`, both `LPOLESTR` values. The first indicates the name of the place holder and the second is the value that it will be replaced with. A pointer to the first entry in the array is passed as the last parameter of `UpdateRegistryFromResource()`. You can see that I also pass the resource ID of the registry script.

In fact, there is no method `UpdateRegistryFromResource()` in `CComModule`, instead there are two methods that have this name with the suffix `D` and the suffix `S`. The `D` version uses the COM object version of the registrar (`D` for dynamic linking) and the `S` version uses the C++ object version of the registrar (`S` for static linking). The `UpdateRegistryFromResource()` is `#defined` to one of these using the `_ATL_STATIC_REGISTRY` symbol.

Registering Type Libraries

By default ATL will bind the project's type library into the project's EXE or DLL and register it when the server is registered. Before you read any further you should decide if this is what you want. A type library can add several kilobytes to the server (which may be important if you intend to download the server across the Internet). In addition, if you intend to use a proxy-stub DLL to marshal your object's interfaces then you will *not* want the type library registered. This is because, at the time of writing, there is a bug in `regsvr32` that will cause it not to unregister an interface's registry entry if there is a `TypeLib` entry in that key.

Why would you want to register the type library? You need to do this if your interfaces will use type library marshaling. Both dual and custom interfaces can use type library marshaling, but if you have custom interfaces you must edit the ATL-generated IDL by hand to add the `oleautomation` attribute. You may also want to use a type library if you intend to use the object in VB. The VB IDE uses a type library to get information about the object and the interfaces that it supports. If there is no registered type library for the object then you will not be able to use the statement completion facilities of the IDE. Furthermore, since VB will not know about the interfaces the object supports you will not be able to access any interface on the object other than `IDispatch`, which restricts you to late binding to the object. (VB's method of calling `QueryInterface()` is to use `Set` with an object 'typed' to the interface type and this type information is held in the type library.)

Automatic ATL Typelib Registration

Now you know the pros and cons of registering the type library, let's look at how ATL does it. The ATL AppWizard generated code for both EXE and DLL projects will call `CComModule::RegisterServer()` (inherited by the global `_Module` object) in the registration handling code. Similarly `CComModule::UnregisterServer()` is called in the unregistration code. The `RegisterServer()` method will register all the classes that have an entry in the object map (by calling their `UpdateRegistry()` method added by the `_REGISTRY` macros), and it will register the type library as long as the first parameter is `TRUE` (which it assumes is the first `TYPELIB` resource in the module).

Preventing Type Library Registration

You can achieve this by following the procedure below:

- ❑ Change the calls to `RegisterServer()` and `UnregisterServer()` in `_tWinMain()` (for an EXE project), or `DllRegisterServer()` and `DllUnregisterServer()` (for a DLL project) to have a first parameter with a value of `FALSE`

- ❑ Remove the type library from the resources by selecting **Resource Includes** from the **View** menu and remove the `TYPELIB` entry from the **Compile-time directives**

- ❑ Remove the `TypeLib` line from the `CLSID` entry in the registration script generated for each `coclass` in your project

Additional Type Libraries

What about if you want to register an additional type library? For example, you may have specified that your object uses an interface described in a type library other than your project's, through the ClassView **Implement Interface** wizard. If the object will be distributed and installed separately to the project that originally described the interface it makes sense to add the additional type library to your project and register it.

To do this you can call `CComModule::RegisterTypeLib()` inherited by the global `_Module` object. This overloaded method has a form that takes a parameter that indicates the `TYPELIB` resource to register. By default, it will register the first resource with an ID of 1. If you add another resource then it should have a ID other than 1, and you should pass a string with this ID preceded by a backslash. For example, to register the second type library in a module, use the following in your registration code:

```
nRet = _Module.RegisterTypeLib(_T("\\2"));
```

Make a similar call to the `CComModule::UnRegisterTypeLib()` in the unregistration code.

Registry Manipulation

There are times when you will want to manipulate registry keys and values in your code, which you can do using the `CRegKey` class. This class is a thin wrapper around the Win32 registry API, and its main use is to maintain a registry key handle.

Its methods and its single operator are shown in the following table:

Method	Description
operator HKEY	Conversion operator to convert a CRegKey to a HKEY
Detach	Returns the HKEY value and sets the data member to NULL
Attach	Assigns the CRegKey a HKEY
Create	Creates (and opens) a specified key
Open	Opens an existing key
Close	Closes the key (the destructor will call this)
SetValue	Overloaded method that sets a value in the currently open key to a DWORD or a string (for the default key value use NULL for the value name)
SetKeyValue	Creates a key and sets a string value in one action (for the default key value use NULL for the value name)
QueryValue	Overloaded method that reads a DWORD or string value from a named value (use NULL for the default)
DeleteSubKey	Delete a sub key (this key must not contain sub keys)
RecurseDeleteKey	Deletes a sub key and all keys it contains
DeleteValue	Delete a named value

Thus, when you call Create() or Open() on an instance of CRegKey it will cache the HKEY handle of that key. This handle is released when you either call Close() explicitly, or if the object is destroyed. This means that you can write code like this:

```
LONG CMyObject::SetInstallerName(LPCTSTR strName)
{
    CRegKey hKey;
    LONG lRet;
    lRet = hKey.Open(HKEY_LOCAL_MACHINE,
        _T("Software\\Wrox\\ATLProgRef"));
    if (lRet == ERROR_SUCCESS)
        lRet = hKey.SetValue(strName, _T("Installed By"));
    return lRet;
}
```

Notice that you don't see the HKEY of the key that is opened in Open() or explicitly release it, this is done in the destructor of the object.

> Note the error handling: Open() has a third parameter that is used to
> pass the access type that you want on the key, the default value is
> KEY_ALL_ACCESS. If the account calling this method does not have the
> correct privileges (for example writing to HKEY_CLASSES_ROOT on NT
> with a non-Administrator account) then the actions will fail.

CRegKey can't do everything that is possible with the registry API: it allows you to
read and write values, create and destroy values and keys and recursively delete keys.
What it does not allow you to do is enumerate keys and values or query values for
their types and the size of data they hold. To do this you need to call the Win32
registry API directly. To help you here CRegKey has a conversion operator to convert
the object to an HKEY. This means that you can write code like this:

```
CRegKey hKey;
hKey.Open(HKEY_LOCAL_MACHINE, _T("Software"));
DWORD dwIndex = 0;
TCHAR strName[MAX_PATH + 1];
while (ERROR_SUCCESS == RegEnumKey(hKey, dwIndex, strName,
                                   MAX_PATH + 1))
{
    dwIndex++;
    ATLTRACE(_T("%s\n"), strName);
}
```

This will print the names of all of the keys in the HKLM\Software key to the output
stream. It works because the conversion operator is called to return the HKEY
encapsulated in the hKey object.

If you have an HKEY returned from another function call you can call
CRegKey::Attach() to get an CRegKey object to maintain it for you.

There is no operator PHKEY() so if you want to initialize a key from an out parameter
then you will have to directly access the public m_hKey, for example:

```
CRegKey hKey;
RegConnectRegistry(_T("MyMachine"), HKEY_LOCAL_MACHINE, &hKey.m_hKey);
```

C

ATL.DLL

Static and Dynamic Linking

When you install Visual C++ on your development machine ATL.DLL will be copied to your system directory (**System32** for NT, **System** for Windows9x) and registered. This file is used for two purposes. The first is that it is the server code for the registrar COM object (see Appendix B), used by the ATL registration code to register keys and values specified in a registration script. Because the registrar is a COM object, you must register ATL.DLL with regsvr32 on any machine that will use this component. Failing to do this is the most common cause of a server failing to register. If you decide that you don't want to use this component, then you can statically link the C++ equivalent, details of which are given in Appendix B.

The other purpose of ATL.DLL is to provide code for some of the methods used by ATL objects. Providing a dynamically linked version of these methods is useful if you intend to install several ATL servers on a single machine. If you statically link the methods (which is the default) then each server will have a copy of them. If you dynamically link to these methods then all the servers will use the shared version of them. This will result in a reduction in the disk space needed to store the servers and the total memory taken up by the servers when they are loaded in memory.

Your choice of whether you dynamically or statically link to these methods should be based on both your dependency on them and whether you want to distribute ATL.DLL. For example, if your server only implements simple objects it will be better to statically link to these methods (use the MinDependency build), because you won't need the windowing and control methods that are also exported from ATL.DLL. If you have controls in your server and you know that ATL.DLL is used on the target system then it is prudent to dynamically link (use the MinSize build).

The methods that are implemented in `ATL.DLL` are shown in the following tables.

Controls and Windows Functions

If your server contains controls then you will use at least one of these methods. In addition, you will also use them if you have an object that uses rich error reporting or connection points (see Chapter 4).

Method	Description
`AtlAdvise`	Set up a connection to a connectable object
`AtlAxAttachControl`	Attaches an existing control to the class window, used by `CAxWindow`, which is used by composite and HTML controls
`AtlAxCreateControl`	Creates a control and Initializes it from a stream, used by `CAxWindow`
`AtlAxCreateControlEx`	Creates a control, initializes it from a stream and connects to it, used by `CAxWindow`
`AtlAxCreateDialog`	Creates a modal dialog that can host ActiveX controls, (there are ANSI and UNICODE versions). This is used by `CAxDialogImpl`, which is used by composite controls or if you create a dialog through the Object Wizard
`AtlAxDialogBox`	Creates a modeless dialog that can host ActiveX controls, (there are ANSI and UNICODE versions), used by `CAxDialogImpl`
`AtlAxGetControl`	Obtains a child control hosted by your control, used by `CAxWindow`, composite controls and `CWindow` if you have hosting enabled
`AtlAxGetHost`	Obtains the `IUnknown` of the host control, used by `CAxWindow`
`AtlAxWinInit`	Registers a Windows class for a hosted window
`AtlCreateTargetDC`	Creates a device context, used by all controls
`AtlDevModeW2A`	Converts `DEVMODEW` to `DEVMODEA`, not used by any ATL templates

Method	Description
AtlGetObjectSourceInterface	Method used to get the IID of the default outgoing interface of an object, used by composite controls
AtlHiMetricToPixel	Converts HIMETRIC units to pixels, used by all controls and CAxHostWindow (for HTML controls)
AtlModuleAddCreateWndData	Adds information about a window to a temporary store, used by all classes that register a Windows class
AtlModuleExtractCreateWndData	Extracts the window information from the temporary store, used by all classes that registers a Windows class
AtlPixelToHiMetric	Converts pixels to HIMETRIC units, used by controls
AtlSetErrorInfo	Sets the error object for the current thread, used by all objects that use rich error information
AtlUnadvise	Break the connection to another object

Note that AtlAdvise() and AtlUnadvise() have few lines of C++ code, but use smart pointers (see Appendix K), which will be the main source of code bloat because a smart pointer class will be generated for both IConnectionPoint and IConnectionPointContainer. If you want to statically link these methods to save space then it's simple to rewrite them using interface pointers:

```
ATLINLINE ATLAPI MyAdvise(IUnknown* pUnkCP, IUnknown* pUnk, const IID& iid,
                          LPDWORD pdw)
{
    IConnectionPointContainer* pCPC;
    IConnectionPoint* pCP;
    HRESULT hRes = pUnkCP->QueryInterface(IID_IConnectionPointContainer,
                                reinterpret_cast<void**>(&pCPC));
    if (SUCCEEDED(hRes))
    {
        hRes = pCPC->FindConnectionPoint(iid, &pCP);
        if (SUCCEEDED(hRes))
        {
            hRes = pCP->Advise(pUnk, pdw);
            pCP->Release();
        }
        pCPC->Release();
    }
    return hRes;
}

ATLINLINE ATLAPI MyUnadvise(IUnknown* pUnkCP, const IID& iid, DWORD dw)
{
```

```
IConnectionPointContainer* pCPC;
IConnectionPoint* pCP;
HRESULT hRes = pUnkCP->QueryInterface(IID_IConnectionPointContainer,
                              reinterpret_cast<void**>(&pCPC));
if (SUCCEEDED(hRes))
{
   hRes = pCPC->FindConnectionPoint(iid, &pCP);
   if (SUCCEEDED(hRes))
   {
      hRes = pCP->Unadvise(dw);
      pCP->Release();
   }
   pCPC->Release();
}
return hRes;
}
```

My tests have indicated that in a release build doing this will save you around 4K, but make sure that you don't use any methods that use `AtlAdvise()` (for example `CAxHostWindow::CreateControlEx()` or `IDispEventSimpleImpl<>::DispEventAdvise()`).

Interface Pointer Functions

The marshaling methods (`AtlMarshalPtrInProc()`, `AtlUnmarshalPtr()` and `AtlFreeMarshalStream()`) are not used by any of the ATL templates, but you can use them at your convenience. The other methods in this table are used throughout ATL. Any project that implements objects or accesses them with smart pointers will use these methods, and therefore be dependent on them.

Method	Description
AtlComPtrAssign	Copies an interface pointer, used by CComPtr<>, CComQIPtr<> and CComDispatchDriver (used, for example, by all controls)
AtlComQIPtrAssign	Copies an interface pointer and queries for a specified interface, used by CComQIPtr<>
AtlFreeMarshalStream	Frees a stream that holds a marshaled interface pointer, not used by any ATL templates
AtlUnmarshalPtr	Unmarshals an interface pointer from a stream, not used by any ATL templates
AtlInternalQueryInterface	Implementation of QueryInterface(), used by all objects that have an interface map
AtlMarshalPtrInProc	Marshals an interface into a stream, not used by any ATL templates

Module Functions

As the name suggests these are methods used by all ATL modules. You can reduce your dependency on these functions by removing type library registration (if your interfaces do not use type library marshaling).

Method	Description
AtlModuleAddTermFunc	Adds a termination function to an internally held array, used if your objects use IDispatchImpl<> or if you register a termination function with AddTermFunc() through _Module
AtlModuleLoadTypeLib	Loads a type library, called if your module registers or unregisters a type library.
AtlModuleRegisterClassObjects	For an EXE server this registers all the class factory objects
AtlModuleRegisterServer	Registers all the externally creatable coclasses mentioned in the object map
AtlModuleRegisterTypeLib	Registers a type library
AtlModuleRegisterWndClassInfo	Registers the Windows class, (there are ANSI and UNICODE versions)
AtlModuleRevokeClassObjects	For an EXE server this revokes the class factory objects before the server shuts down
AtlRegisterClassCategoriesHelper	Registers the categories the objects use or implement
AtlModuleGetClassObject	Returns the class factory object for a specified coclass
AtlModuleInit	Initializes the _Module data members and calls the ObjectMain() for each ATL class
AtlModuleTerm	Cleans up the _Module data members and calls all the termination functions added by AtlModuleAddTermFunc()

Method	Description
`AtlModuleUnRegisterTypeLib`	Unregisters a type library
`AtlModuleUnregisterServer`	Unregisters all the externally creatable `coclasses` mentioned in the object map, but not the type library
`AtlModuleUnregisterServerEx`	Unregisters all the externally creatable `coclasses` mentioned in the object map
`AtlModuleUpdateRegistryFromResourceD`	Loads a registry script from resources and registers it
`DllCanUnloadNow`	Returns whether a DLL server can be unloaded from memory
`DLLGetClassObject`	Returns a class factory object for an `inproc` server
`DLLRegisterServer`	Registers a DLL server
`DLLUnregisterServer`	Unregisters a DLL server

Notice that `ATL.DLL` has default implementations of the DLL server entry points (but not `DllMain()`, which is odd). If you want to customize any of these then you will (obviously) have to use your version! The most frequent situation is if you do not want the module's type library to be registered.

Interface Method Implementations

These methods are implementations of the save and load persistence methods of `IPersistPropertyBag` and `IPersistStreamInit`. If you want to provide persistence support for other data types (these methods will persist COM properties and integer 'raw' data) then you will have to override these. Even so, you will want to call the base class implementation, which does not preclude you from using the version in `ATL.DLL`.

Method
AtlIPersistPropertyBag_Load
AtlIPersistPropertyBag_Save
AtlIPersistStreamInit_Load
AtlIPersistStreamInit_Save

Others

Of these, AtlWaitWithMessageLoop() is only used if you have a thread pool server, in which case your server will be an EXE so dynamically linking to ATL.DLL is not much of an issue.

Method	Description
AtlGetVersion	Returns the ATL version, not used by any ATL templates
AtlWaitWithMessageLoop	Returns when the specified object has become signaled while pumping the message queue

Using the Methods in ATL.DLL

By default, the methods given above will be statically linked into your project if you have a debug build or a **MinDependency** release build. To dynamically link to these methods you need to define the symbol _ATL_DLL as a preprocessor symbol, which is done for you if you select one of the **MinSize** release builds.

When this symbol is defined the following line is added to atlbase.h:

```
#pragma comment(lib, "atl.lib")
```

which means that your project will link to the import library for ATL.DLL. ATLAPI is defined to be modified by __declspec(dllimport), so the methods with this symbol will be dynamically linked from ATL.DLL. Depending on which methods you call in your server this will reduce the size of your module by about 4K.

ATL Wizards

There are essentially five wizards provided for you, three of which are accessed through ClassView. In this appendix, I will outline the options that each of these wizards give you.

ATL Wizards

The two wizards not accessed through ClassView are: AppWizard, Object Wizard.

AppWizard

The ATL COM AppWizard is accessed through the File, New menu item from the Projects tab. This will create a new project for you with the specified name and give you the following options:

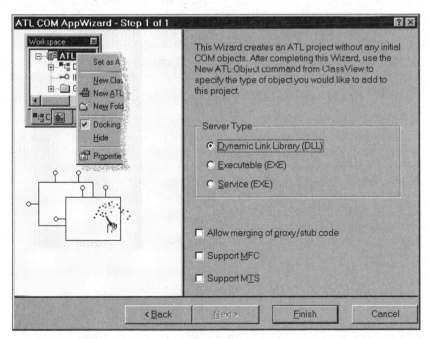

Server Type

This determines the type of module that will be created. The three options are:

❏ **Dynamic Linked Library.** This creates an `inproc` server. This is used for servers that will house controls and MTS objects. Typically, you will also use this for objects that should be run in the client's memory space under its security settings. Access to these objects is very quick, but lacks the isolation of EXE servers.

❏ **Executable.** This creates a 'local' server. The advantage of this type is that you can isolate the object's code from the client, meaning that you can change the security settings and that the object has its own protected memory. You can also use this type of server to share data between clients. EXE servers are slower to load and access to objects is slower due to the need for inter-process communication.

❏ **Service.** This makes your server an NT service. It should be used if you want your COM server started with the system, making it permanently available. Another reason to use this option is if you need to have your code run under the NT `SYSTEM` account.

Obviously, you should only use the **Service** type if the server will be run on NT. If you want to create an object to be run on a machine other than the client then you will typically select **Executable**. You can run a DLL-based object on a remote machine, but this requires that you use a surrogate (such as `DllHost.exe` or MTS).

Allow Merging of proxy/stub code

This option is only enabled for DLL servers. It will add the stub code needed for standard marshaling into your project. Before you select it you need to question whether you really do need to use it. The advantage is that you'll only have to distribute one DLL to the server machine (both the server and stub code are in the same DLL), so you only have to register one DLL. Since only one DLL is used this also speeds up the load time of your code. This makes this option useful if you want to use the server in MTS, or any other surrogate.

The disadvantage is that your server is also the stub DLL for the interfaces used in the DLL. If you have another object, implemented in a different server, that also uses these interfaces, then your DLL will be loaded as the stub code. In addition, your DLL will be registered as containing the proxy object for the interface, so any client that uses these interface (whether using your object or another object that implements these interfaces) will load your DLL. This will waste memory in that other server (or client) because it'll be loading code that it won't use.

If your clients run on a machine remote to the server then you will also have to build and distribute the proxy-stub DLL so that they'll have the proxy object for the interface.

One final consideration is whether you will actually use the code. If you use `dual` interfaces, or mark your custom interfaces with the `oleautomation` attribute, then type library marshaling will be used. In this case custom proxy/stub objects will not be needed for marshaling and the merged code will not be used. There is a possibility of type library marshaling some interfaces and using merged stub code for others. However, unless you are willing to edit the MIDL generated code you will link to the proxy and stub code for *all* the interfaces, whether they are type library marshaled or not.

Generally, if you want to merge the stub code then you need to turn off type library marshaling, requiring these additional steps:

❑ Make sure that your interfaces are custom and do not have the `oleautomation` attribute

❑ The `dlldatax.c` is added to the project, but not to the build, so add it by right clicking on the file in FileView, and then selecting **S**ettings…. Make sure that you select **All Configurations** in the **Settings for** box and then in the **General** tab uncheck **Exclude file from build**.

❑ For this file move to the **C/C++** tab, choose **Precompiled Headers** as the category, and select **Not using precompiled headers**.

❑ Now select the project, choose the **Preprocessor** category and add the `_MERGE_PROXYSTUB` symbol for the project.

❑ Edit the registration code to make sure that the type library is not registered — that is, make sure that the parameter to the calls to `_Module.RegisterServer()` and `_Module.UnregisterServer()` is `FALSE`.

❑ From the **View** menu select **Resource Includes** and remove the reference to the type library from the **Compile time directives** box.

❑ Right click on the IDL file in FileView and select **Settings**, and then remove the type library name from the **Output file name** box.

❑ Open the RGS file for each of the objects and remove the line that mentions the TypeLib from the `CLSID` section

These last three steps are used to remove the type library from your module.

Support MFC

This option is only enabled for DLL servers. You will use this option if you have legacy code written in MFC that you want to use in your ATL server. There is also the possibility that if you have developers that are new to ATL, moving over from MFC, they will want the comfort of MFC facilities. *Resist this urge!* Other than legacy MFC code *there should be no other reason to use MFC in an ATL project.* You cannot use the AppWizard to add MFC support to an **Executable** project, but it is possible to add MFC support by hand. The steps required are listed in the Microsoft MSDN 'Knowledge Base' article Q173974.

What are the excuses that people make when they say that they need MFC? Well, one is the convenience of CString. A better solution is to use the standard library's std::basic_string<> template, although the STL implementation of this is such that certain Windows-specific functionality (like initializing a string from a module string resource) is not supported. If you decide that you don't want to learn how to use the C++ standard library (for some obscure reason) then you can download Alex Stockton's "NotMFC::CString" (www.WorldofATL.com or click through www.wrox.com). This has the same methods as CString but is implemented using the C++ standard library, so it has no dependence on MFC. If you need to load strings from module string tables then you will have to write the required code yourself, which would be fairly trivial.

Other situations include deciding that you need the MFC ODBC classes. In this case you should really consider using ADO or the ATL OLE DB consumer classes instead. Similarly, if you want a list or map class use the STL container classes or ATL's CSimpleArray<> or CSimpleMap<> templates (see Appendix F). In addition, if you statically link to MFC, your components are likely to be large (but note that if you use many different templated classes, using STL, your code is likely to be large too). If you dynamically link to the MFC runtime DLL then you'll have to check to see if the correct version exists during installation (or component download). If it isn't, you'll have to install it.

Support MTS

Microsoft Transaction Server is a surrogate process used to run inproc objects. However, this description does not do it justice, because MTS:

- ❑ will handle object activation and concurrency

- ❑ allows you to take part in distributed transactions with ACID properties (atomicity, consistency, isolation and durability)

- ❑ has a simplified, role based security model

- ❑ is inextricably linked with the future of COM and COM+

Today, MTS is installed as a separate system component, but, starting with Windows 2000, it will be part of the operating system, and therefore all inproc servers will be able to run under its influence.

However, for an object to be able to use MTS's context object (through which you can control the object's transaction and create other objects to run under the same transaction) you must link your DLL with mtx.lib. The Support MTS option does this, and will also link your DLL to mtxguid.lib (to give you the MTS GUIDs) and delayimp.lib.

In addition, this option adds a reminder in the registration build step to run mtxrereg.exe *before using the component in MTS. It does not run this process.*

`delayimp.lib` is used to allow your project to **delay load** the `mtxex.dll` file. Delay loading is a new feature of Visual C++ 6 that allows you to specify a list of DLLs (using the `/delayload` linker option) that will only be loaded when their exported functions are actually called.

Object Wizard

The Object Wizard is used to add new ATL classes to your project. This is a large topic, so the whole of Appendix E is devoted to it.

ClassView Wizards

To use these wizards you need to select a class in ClassView and the wizard from the right-click context menu.

Implement Interface

This wizard is enabled for all classes that have an interface map, and serves two functions. The first is if you want to add a totally new interface to your object and the second is when you want to add an interface that has been defined in another project. In both cases you need a compiled type library that describes the interface. This dependence on a type library gives rise to this wizard's main problem: type libraries can only describe interfaces with certain data types and parameter attributes.

The attributes that you can use are:

Attribute	Description
`[in]`	The parameter is used to pass data from the client to the object
`[out]`	The parameter is used to pass data from the object to the client
`[in, out]`	The parameter passes data from the client to the object and then data from the object to the client
`[lcid]`	The parameter is the local ID of the client
`[retval]`	The `[out]` parameter is used as the return value of the method
`[optional]`	The parameter is optional
`[default]`	The parameter has a default value
`[custom]`	Used to add custom attributes to methods

The data types that you can use are those that you can put in a `VARIANT`. In addition, objects used on Windows98 and NT4 (with service pack 4 applied) can also have methods that pass structures (Visual Basic User Defined Types).

To add support for a new interface to a class, this wizard needs to do three things:

❑ Derive your ATL class from the interface

❑ Add the interface to the interface map

❑ Create empty implementations for the interface's methods in your class

If the object that you are adding is a dual interface the wizard will derive your ATL class from a specialization of IDispatchImpl<> to implement IDispatch. If your object already has a dual interface you can use COM_INTERFACE_ENTRY2() to specify which dual interface will implement IDispatch. For example:

```
BEGIN_COM_MAP(CMyObject)
    COM_INTERFACE_ENTRY(IMyObject)
    COM_INTERFACE_ENTRY2(IDispatch, IMyObject)
    COM_INTERFACE_ENTRY(IAddedInterface)
END_COM_MAP()
```

The wizard does not do anything else, and, as you can see, you can perform each of these actions by hand.

When you run the wizard it will check to see if your project's type library has been compiled (by default it assumes that you will add a new interface). However, you have the choice of using a different type library, in which case the wizard will first show you a dialog with the libraries registered on the local system. You can also browse to use an unregistered type library.

Once you have chosen a type library you will be shown all the dual and custom interfaces mentioned in the library (that is, the interfaces that were mentioned in the source IDL's library block). You cannot add dispinterfaces because ATL will only implement dual interfaces.

Adding a New Interface

I would not recommend that you do this with the wizard, it requires just as much work as doing it by hand. However, for completeness I will mention the steps.

❑ Edit your project's IDL file to add the new interface

❑ Compile the IDL file to create the type library

❑ Run the Implement Interface Wizard through ClassView

❑ Use the ClassView Add Method and Add Property wizards to add entries to the interface and to your class

If you decide to add an interface by hand then you need to replace the middle two steps with the three steps to add an interface as mentioned in the previous section.

Adding an Already Defined Interface

Again, there are two options, in the first case you may decide to add an interface to your object that another object in your project has already defined. You can use your project's type library for this. Alternatively, you might want to use an interface defined by another project. As I have outlined above, this wizard does not do much work for you. The main reason why you would want to use it is because the wizard will read all the methods in the interface and create implementation-less methods for each one in your class. These methods are not totally empty, they will check that out parameters are valid pointers and also return E_NOTIMPL.

You cannot add standard COM interfaces (like IOleContainer) because there is no type library that describes them. The reason for this is that most standard interfaces use data types and attributes that prevent them from being described in a type library (as explained earlier).

Implement Connection Point

Normally, to add support for connection points to a class you need to use the **Support Connection Points** option in the Object Wizard. Alternatively, you can use the connection point wizard. To add support for connection points a wizard (the Object Wizard or the connection point wizard) needs to do this:

- ❑ derive the class from IConnectionPointContainerImpl<>
- ❑ add IConnectionPointContainer to the interface map
- ❑ add a connection point map (see Appendix A)

In addition, the connection point wizard will allow you to select a dispinterface (or a custom interface, but *not* a dual) that's been marked as the outgoing interface of an object. The Object Wizard will add an outgoing dispinterface for your coclass by:

creating a dispinterface with the name _*interface*Events where *interface* is the name of your object's default interface

add the interface as the outgoing interface by marking it with [default, source] in the object's coclass in the library section of the IDL

When you run the connection point wizard it will look in your project's type library for all dispinterfaces and custom interfaces marked with [source]. You can specify a registered type library to use for this, or you can load one explicitly. Once you have selected an appropriate outgoing interface the wizard will:

- ❑ generate a 'proxy' class that is used to fire events
- ❑ derive your class from the 'proxy' class
- ❑ add the outgoing interface to the connection point map

The connection point wizard is, unfortunately, not perfect. In particular, you can't select an interface that has not been specifically marked as the outgoing interface of the `coclass`, you need to edit the IDL to allow for this.

In addition, you should also consider deriving your ATL class from `IProvideClassInfo2Impl<>` and adding `IProvideClassInfo2` to the interface map so that the object can tell clients what its default outgoing interface is. This interface is required if you want to handle events from a control placed in a form in Visual Basic. It is also useful for other objects, because there is a performance gain in not having to search the object's type library for its outgoing interface.

Message and Event Handler Wizard

There are two parts to this wizard, I will tackle them one at a time.

Message Handler Wizard

Any class that has a message map can be manipulated with the message handler wizard. This is not a universal panacea for message handlers, because it will only allow you to add handlers for the messages that have been chosen by the author of the wizard. Also, it only provides handlers for single messages, it does not give you the option of using the macros for ranges of messages, or all messages for a particular control. To do this you need to edit the message map by hand (see Appendix A).

You run the wizard by selecting the **Add Windows Message Handler** context menu item from ClassView. The Wizard looks like this:

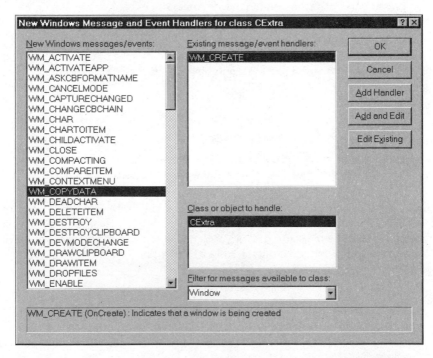

The class is shown in the list box labeled Class or object to handle. The messages that can be sent to the window are listed in the left hand list box. Since this list is quite long you can use the Filter box to filter out messages you are not interested in. The values you can use for this are:

Filter	Description
Not a Window	Filter out all Windows messages
Child Window	List Windows messages relevant to child windows
MDI Child Frame	List Windows messages relevant to MDI child windows
Topmost Frame	List Windows messages relevant to frame windows
Window	List all relevant Windows messages (don't filter)
Dialog	List Windows messages relevant to dialogs

When you select a message, the wizard will add an appropriate macro for the message to the message map and create a method to handle it. If the message is a `WM_` message then a `MESSAGE_HANDLER()` macro will be used, otherwise a `COMMAND_HANDLER()` or `NOTIFY_HANDLER()` is used, depending on the type of message. Note that the messages are not 'cracked', that is, your handler will have to interpret the parameters passed to it according to the type of message that is being handled.

Event Handler Wizard

This uses the same dialog as the message handler wizard. Indeed, you will only be able to use this wizard if your class has a message map, because the wizard is really designed to be used with ATL composite controls, which have message maps. The wizard will look in the class for an anonymous `enum` that has a value for the symbol `IDD`, which is used as the ID of a dialog template resource. The wizard will parse this resource and list all the IDs of the controls that it can find in the list box labeled Class or object to handle.

Since dialog templates also contain the types of the controls that they use, the wizard can list the relevant Windows messages that a selected control can send to your window (command and notification messages). If the control is an ActiveX control the wizard can use the control's type information to list the events that it can generate.

When you add an event handler, the wizard will do these things:

- ❑ Add a sink map if one does not exist
- ❑ Derive your class from a specialization of `IDispEventImpl<>` for the control ID
- ❑ Add an entry for the event into the sink map
- ❑ Add an event handler method
- ❑ Add an `#import` line to import the interface definition into the class header

Sink maps are covered in Appendix A.

Editing Interfaces

ClassView will list all the interfaces defined in the project's IDL. Since your project has created these interfaces you can add methods and properties to them. ClassView also shows all the classes in the project, along with the interfaces they implement. It will not list standard interfaces or interfaces defined in other projects. Thus if your IDL has interfaces that are implemented on objects in your project you will find that the interface is shown twice in ClassView:

Logically then, an interface's entry in the top level of the ClassView tree (for example, IProducts) should allow you to edit the definition of an interface, and the interface's entry within a class (for example, below CProducts) should allow you to change its implementation. However, ClassView does not work like this, you can edit the interface from wherever it's displayed.

You can edit an interface by right clicking on its entry in ClassView and then selecting **Add Method** or **Add Property** from the context menu. In the next two sections I will list the options that each of these wizards give you.

Add Method

When you select this you will see the following dialog box:

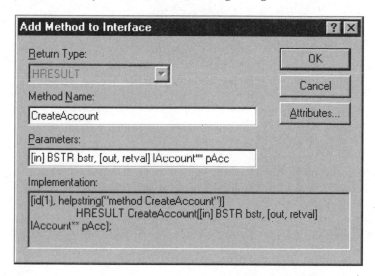

The top box gives the return type of the method. If the interface is a custom or dual the return type has to be HRESULT so that the marshaling layer can return an error value if there is a marshaling error. In this case you will not be allowed to change this field, so it will be grayed out.

If the interface is a dispinterface then you can choose the return type of a method. The reason is that dispinterface methods are actually sent to the object via a call to IDispatch::Invoke(), so the return value of Invoke() can be used to return any marshaling errors. The return type you can use for a dispinterface method is one of:

HRESULT	void	OLE_XPOS_HIMETRIC
short	short*	OLE_YPOS_HIMETRIC
long	long*	OLE_XSIZE_HIMETRIC
float	float*	OLE_YSIZE_HIMETRIC
double	double*	OLE_XPOS_PIXELS
CURRENCY	CURRENCY*	OLE_YPOS_PIXELS
CY	CY*	OLE_XSIZE_PIXELS
DATE	DATE*	OLE_YSIZE_PIXELS
BSTR	BSTR*	OLE_HANDLE

SCODE	SCODE*	OLE_TRISTATE
BOOL	BOOL*	OLE_OPTEXCLUSIVE
VARIANT	VARIANT*	LPFONTDISP
LPDISPATCH	LPDISPATCH*	LPPICTUREDISP
IDispatch*	IDispatch**	
LPUNKNOWN	LPUNKNOWN*	
IUnknown*	IUnknown**	
OLE_COLOR	OLE_COLOR*	

In the parameters box you should list all the parameters of the method. Each parameter must have a type, and you should precede each one with its attributes. At the very least you should specify whether the parameter is:

[in] (sent from client to object)

[out] (sent from object to client)

[in, out] (sent in both directions)

If a parameter is [out] or [in, out] then it *must* be a pointer type.

For non-dispinterface methods you can mark the last parameter with [out, retval]. This indicates in the typelib (used by #import, scripting languages, etc.) that the parameter should be treated as the return value of the method. In the screenshot above a Visual Basic client will treat the CreateAccount method as taking a String parameter and returning an IAccount object (Visual Basic is peculiar in how it treats interfaces).

There are many more attributes that you can apply to method parameters, you can find them all listed in the MIDL reference in the MSDN Library. For example, a method could be declared as:

```
HRESULT CreateAccount([in] BSTR bstr, [in] REFIID iid, [out, iid_is(iid),
retval] void** ppAcc)
```

to allow a client to pass the IID of the account type that it's interested in and be returned a pointer to that account object. However, iid_is() is not one of the attributes that can be placed in a type library, so this interface wouldn't be oleautomation-compatible, and hence couldn't be type library marshaled or used by scripting languages or environments like Visual Basic.

Indeed, if the interface is dual, or custom and oleautomation compatible, then you are restricted to the parameter attributes shown in the 'Implement Interface' section

Methods themselves can have attributes, which you can modify by clicking on the Attributes button, the attributes that you can use are:

Attribute	Description	Parameter
[call_as()]	For a [local] function, this indicates the remote version	The local method
[helpcontext()]	Defines a help file context ID	The ID
[helpstring()]	Describes the method	A descriptive string
[hidden]	The method is hidden from object browsers	—
[id()]	The DISPID for the method	Positive or 0
[local]	Indicates that the function cannot be called through a proxy	—
[restricted]	Prevents macro languages from calling the method	—
[source]	Indicates that the method returns an object that is the source of events	—
[vararg]	Indicates that the method takes a variable number of parameters	—

> The wizard will also list the [callback] attribute. This is a present bug, this attribute can only be used with RPC interfaces and not COM interfaces.

[call_as()] and [local] are used to indicate that a method is marshaled with different parameters than those that a client will pass or an object will implement. You have to use these in pairs giving the signature of the method that a client will call and the proxy will marshal. It requires that you write marshaling code to convert the parameters in the [local] method to those marshaled by the [call_as()] method. This is an advanced topic that I will not cover in this book.

Note that in VC++ 6.0 this dialog has the annoying restriction that you cannot change the [id()] to a negative number nor use a symbol. If you want your object to have a stock property, then you need to edit the IDL by hand.

The [source] attribute is used to indicate that a method will return an object that will generate events; it is rarely used. Finally, [vararg] is used to indicate that the method has a variable number of arguments, much like the ellipsis in C. The method must have a final parameter that is of the type SAFEARRAY(VARIANT) so that the client can indicate how many extra parameters there are and pass their values.

Add Property

This uses the following dialog:

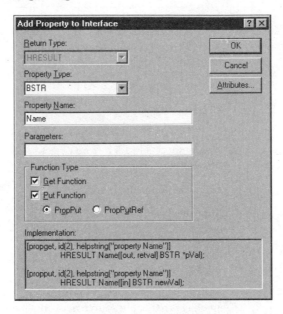

Properties on dual or custom interfaces are implemented using methods. A read-only property will only have a [propget] method, and a write only property will only have a [propput] method; a read/write property will have both. [propputref] methods are used for object properties and indicate that they will be used with the Set keyword in Visual Basic.

As for methods, the return type is HRESULT for properties on custom and dual interfaces, or one of the method return types given in the previous section for dispinterface properties. Even though you can use a return type, it's a good idea to make this void because it's *not* the type of the property. That's given in the next box. Note that for dispinterfaces you can only select one of the types in the dropdown list box (the same types that can be used for dispinterface method return types). For dual and custom interfaces it can be any type you like, allowing you to have properties that are interface pointers, pointers to structs or typedefed types.

The **Parameters** box is used to specify extra parameters when getting or setting the property. Typically you will avoid this edit box. However, if you're implementing a property that behaves like an array, you would specify the parameter(s) used to subscript that array here. An example is the Item property used on collections.

Properties can also have attributes, added through the Attributes button. The attributes you can add are:

Attribute	Description	Parameter
[bindable]	The property supports data binding with IPropertyNotifySink	—
[call_as()]	Indicates the method that is called when a [local] property is remoted	The name of the [local] property
[defaultbind]	A bindable property that is the default property for the interface	—
[defaultcollelem]	An optimization used on collections for Visual Basic, it allows collection members accessed through the ! syntax to be treated as properties of the object that implements the collection	—
[displaybind]	Indicates to object browsers that a property is bindable	—
[helpcontext()]	Gives a help file context ID	The context ID
[helpstring()]	Associates a descriptive string with the property	The string
[hidden]	The property is hidden in object browsers	—
[id()]	The DISPID of the property	Positive or zero
[immediatebind]	Indicates that when the property changes, the value is sent to the binding container	—
[local]	Indicates that the property is not marshaled	—
[nonbrowseable]	Indicates that the property can appear in an *object* browser (like the Visual Basic Object Browser), but not in a *property* browser (like the Visual Basic property box)	—
[requestedit]	The property is bound via IPropertyNotifySink::OnRequestEdit()	—

Attribute	Description	Parameter
[restricted]	Prevents macro langues from accessing the property	—
[source]	The property represents an object that generates events and indicates that high level languages should read the type information for this object to determine what these events are	—
[vararg]	Indicates that the property's method takes a variable number of parameters	—

Some of these attributes allow you to specify that the property is bound. To bind an object's property, the client must implement the IPropertyNotifySink sink interface and the object must implement a connection point for this interface (i.e. it must support IConnectionPointContainer). When the property changes, it must use the object's connection point mechanism to inform the client that the property is about to change ([requestedit]) or has changed. In the former case, the client has the option of canceling the change, causing properties with [requestedit] to discard the new value.

Object Wizard

Introduction

The Object Wizard can be used to add a new ATL class to any ATL or MFC project. When you select **New ATL Object** from the **Insert** menu, the Object Wizard will perform the following checks to see if the project is suitable:

- ❏   It checks to see if the project is a Win32 DLL or application (it will fail for a Console project)

- ❏   It checks to see if there is an object map in the .cpp file with the same name as the project

- ❏   It checks that there is an IDL file, with the same name as the project, that also has a library block

So long as these criteria are met, it's possible for you to fake an ATL project by creating a Win32 EXE or DLL project and adding the required files. Why would you want to do this? Well, there are some Object Wizard items that you may want to use in other projects (for example, the OLE DB consumer classes and the ATL dialog classes).

If the project is MFC and it does not contain ATL code then the Object Wizard will adapt the project to allow it to be a server for ATL objects by adding:

- ❏   A method InitATL() (and a BOOL data member to indicate that it has been called) to the application (CWinApp-derived) class

- ❏   ATL headers to stdafx.h - which defines a CComModule-derived module class and adds the ATL registry headers to stdafx.cpp

- ❏   The implementation of InitATL() to the application .cpp file and a call to it in InitInstance(). If the project is an EXE it will add code to revoke class factories in ExitInstance()

- ❏   An object map to the application .cpp file, which declares the module class members and declares a global instance of the module class

❑ An IDL file to the project if there isn't one present

❑ The appropriate RGS files to the project as REGISTRY resources

These steps ensure that the project satisfies the criteria given above, that the correct ATL files are included and that the library is initialized.

The Object Wizard looks like this:

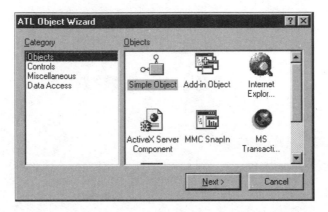

The object types it can add to your project are divided into four categories: Objects, Controls, Miscellaneous and Data Access, which are explained in the following sections.

> Note that some object types should only be inserted into DLL servers. The Object Wizard performs no check on server type, so you have to check this yourself before you insert an object.

Objects

This page has varied types of objects, which are listed in the following table:

Object Type	Description	Server Type
Simple Object	Minimal COM Object	All server types
Add-in Object	Visual C++ Add-in object	DLL server only
Internet Explorer Object	IE object without a user interface	DLL server only
ActiveX Server Component	An object that can be used by Active Server Pages	All server types

Object Type	Description	Server Type
MMC Snap-in	Microsoft Management Console snap-in object	DLL server only
MS Transaction Server Component	A non-aggregatable object with the MTS headers	DLL server only
Component Registrar Object	Object that implements `IComponentRegistrar`	DLL server only

Simple & IE

The most flexible type is **Simple Object**. By default, it only implements `IUnknown` and a `dual` or custom interface declared for your `coclass`. (You can also have connection point and error object support, as you'll see in a moment.) It's up to you to add any other interface that your object requires. The **Internet Explorer Object** type is just a **Simple Object** that implements `IObjectWithSite`.

MTS Component

The **MS Transaction Server Component** includes `mtx.h` (so that you can access the context object) and gives you the option of implementing `IObjectControl`.

Registrar

The component registrar is used *with* MTS to allow you to register particular classes in a server.

Controls

Controls should only be added to DLL servers. You can add a control to EXE servers, but if you do so you'll not be able to create it. This is because a control *must* be a DLL, and so a container will attempt to create it using `CLSCTX_INPROC_SERVER`. The control types are listed in the following table:

Control Type	Description
Full Control	Supports control interfaces used by all control containers
Lite Control	Lite version of the Full Control
Composite Control	Control that hosts other ActiveX controls
Lite Composite Control	Lite version of the Composite Control
HTML Control	DHTML control
Lite HTML Control	Lite version of the HTML Control
Property Page	Property page

There are two versions of all the control types: a normal version and a 'lite' version. The normal versions are 'heavy' in that they support the full range of interfaces required for the control, typically including interfaces that many containers do not use. The lite versions omit some of the more esoteric interfaces, which makes their code smaller (Appendix J contains a full description of the difference between the two).

Be careful about choosing a lite version, because some containers will only accept full controls, so check your intended container before you write the control. In general, the full versions are used to support OLE embedding, which is why they are required by Office applications. The lite versions are used by newer containers like IE.

> Wordpad is one such example — it requires a control to implement `IPersistStorage`. You can do this either by implementing a full control, or by adding support for this interface to a lite control.

Miscellaneous

This page has only one entry:

Entry	Description
Dialog	A dialog object

The Dialog type is ATL in that it uses the ATL windowing classes, but it does not implement COM objects. This type can be used to create a simple, lightweight, modal or modeless dialog class. Note that, by default, the class will be derived from `CAxDialogImpl` to allow you to use ActiveX controls. If you don't want this support then you can derive the class from `CDialogImpl`.

Data Access

These two types use the ATL OLE DB classes, the two types are:

Entry	Description
Consumer	An OLE DB consumer
Provider	An OLE DB provider

You use the Consumer type to create wrapper classes to give you simple access to an OLE DB data source. Since there are OLE DB drivers for ODBC data sources you will have access to virtually all relational databases. In addition, other data sources are provided with OLE DB drivers (for instance, the Active Directory) so these classes allow you access to a diverse collection of data. Furthermore, if the correct drivers exist then you will be able to do joins between heterogeneous data sources.

The Object Wizard is useful for the **Consumer** type because it will read the database and table properties and generate classes based on them. If you knew the database schema you could do this by hand, but using the Wizard is far quicker. Chapter 5 shows this in action — although the Object Wizard is used to create the initial classes, they are extensively edited to suit our needs.

The **Provider** type is used to create a new OLE DB data source. The Object Wizard will generate classes to implement the data source as well as table, command and rowset objects. It will give these default properties in property maps. You can alter these tables and classes to change how your data source is used, and even define your own parsing language to implement executed commands. However, coding OLE DB Providers is beyond the scope of this book.

Object Wizard Pages

Once you've selected an Object Wizard type, you'll be presented with a property sheet dialog. This dialog contains various property pages, which allow you to customize your objects. In the following sections I'll list the various pages and explain how they're used.

Names

The Names tab is used to provide basic names for your object and looks like this:

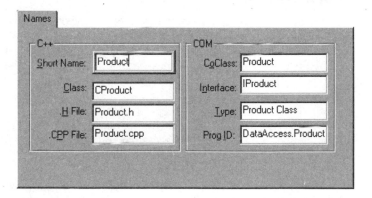

This is used by all object types except the data access objects, but some object types will disable some of these boxes. The page will generate names for all the boxes based on the name you type in the **Short Name** box, but you are free to change the values in the other enabled boxes.

Attributes

The Attributes tab is used to allow you to change various object specific settings. It looks like this:

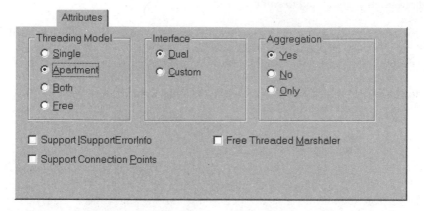

This box is used by the Simple Object, Internet Explorer Object, ActiveX Server Component from the Object category and all the types on the Controls page. The options are:

Threading Model

This radio button group specifies the type of apartment in which the object will be run. It ensures that the correct synchronization is used for the instance state and any global data that the object may use. If you have an EXE server then the object will be run in an STA or an MTA. In the first case, you should use the Apartment type and in the second you can use either of the last two types. You shouldn't use the Single type for EXE servers.

It is important for DLL servers to select the right threading model. If the object is to be run in a client that will only ever have a single thread, then you can use the Single type. This is unlikely, so if the object is to run in an STA (absolving you of all responsibility for making the object methods reentrant and protecting data members from multithreaded access) you should select the Apartment type. Note that even in this case you *still* have to protect global resources from multithreaded access (because there may be several STA threads running in the process).

If the DLL object can be run in a MTA then you should choose Free or Both. These protect the data members that are used by the ATL classes from multithreaded access, and provide methods to allow you to protect your data members (note that the onus is on you). The choice between Free and Both depends on how the object is to be used and its relationship with other threads in its process.

If the object is likely to be created by an STA client then it can be used with no marshaling if the object is marked as Both. Similarly, the same object can be used in an MTA with no marshaling. Free is useful if the object creates MTA worker threads because you ensure that the object and its workers are in the same apartment and so no marshaling occurs. However, you should be wary about creating worker threads from an inproc object, and take particular care to make sure that worker threads are terminated before the DLL is allowed to unload.

For an inproc (DLL) object, this option will change the registration of the object to add a `ThreadingModel` value in the `CLSID` key of the `coclass`. When a client asks COM to create an object, it will use this setting to see if the object can be created in the apartment where the call originated. If this is not the case, then COM will create an appropriate apartment and marshal all access to it.

Interface

You can choose whether the interface will be custom (derived directly from `IUnknown` and not `oleautomation` compatible) or `dual` (derived from `IDispatch` and implicitly `oleautomation` compatible). You should consider carefully which interface type to use. The criteria that you need to take into account are:

❑ Do you want to use type library marshaling? If so, you can use either type but you need to manually add the `oleautomation` attribute to the IDL for a custom interface.

❑ Will the interface be used by a scripting client? If so, then you must use a `dual` interface.

❑ Do you want to affect the variance and conformance of arrays passed as parameters? If so, then you must use a custom interface. Variance and conformance are facilities that you have to apply explicitly to your parameters.

The Object Wizard will add an appropriate interface to the project's IDL. Use the names in the Names tab to add a `coclass` and mark the interface as the `[default]` interface for this `coclass`. It will also derive the ATL class it creates from this interface (or `IDispatchImpl<>` for `dual` interfaces) and add the interface to the interface map.

Aggregation

You use these options to determine whether the object will be used as the inner object in aggregation. The settings affect how the object is created by the class factory.

Rich Error Information and Connection Points

Support ISupportErrorInfo is used to add the `ISupportErrorInfo` interface to the object so that it can use COM error objects. Creating an error object in a COM object is equivalent to generating exceptions in C++. They are used to convey information about errors (including the object and interface GUID and a description of the error) to the client. If you select this option then you can use the `Error()` methods inherited through the `CComCoClass<>` base class to generate an error object.

The `ISupportErrorInfo` interface is used to indicate which interfaces in the object can create error objects, so you have to make sure that you update the code generated by the Object Wizard accordingly, whenever you add another interface. (See Chapter 4).

If the object is connectable (can generate events) then you should select **Support Connection Points**. This adds support for `IConnectionPointContainer` and a connection point map. It also creates an outgoing `dispinterface` that you use to generate events. However, you still need to run the connection point ClassView wizard to add the `dispinterface` to the connection point map and generate a proxy class. Make sure that you do this *after* you have defined the events in the outgoing interface, and recompiled the type library.

Free Threaded Marshaler

The **Free Threaded Marshaler** option is used to make your object apartment neutral. You should select this option if you have a process that has an MTA and one or more STAs. STAs each have a single thread and the MTA has one or more threads. Any object that runs in an MTA must protect its state from multithreaded access. Objects in one apartment are protected from code in another apartment by requiring interfaces to be marshaled between apartments, so you'll have a proxy object in the client apartment. Proxies are typically used to marshal interfaces between processes and between machines so it may seem like overkill to use them for inter-apartment calls in a single process. After all, if an object in an STA has an interface pointer to an object in an MTA it will be designed for multithreaded access. In this case, a proxy is not needed because the MTA object will synchronize calls.

This is why the FTM was developed. Its purpose is to check when an interface is being marshaled to see if it is out-of-process or cross apartment in-process. If the interface is out-of-process then the FTM uses standard marshaling through a proxy object, otherwise the marshaling packet is filled with the raw interface pointer and hence interface access is direct. When you select the FTM option, the Object Wizard will aggregate the FTM into your object and calls to `QueryInterface()` for `IMarshal` are delegated to the FTM. This means that you cannot implement this interface yourself, so you won't be able to use custom marshaling or marshal by value.

The FTM can make access to objects much quicker, but there are pitfalls. The main problem is that if your object holds on to interface pointers for objects implemented in another apartment then those objects must also use the FTM, otherwise any access to them will fail. There are ways round this problem, but they are beyond the scope of this discussion. Marshaling works fine *without* the FTM ...use with caution.

DevStudio Add-in

This is only used by the DevStudio Add-in object and it allows you to specify which facilities the add-in will provide or use. The tab looks like this:

If you don't select the Provide Toolbar checkbox, you'll only add a command. Otherwise, a toolbar is added with the single button that you specify using Command Name and Method Name. The former is the command that will be added to the Visual Studio object model, while the latter refers to the method that the Wizard will add to your object to perform the command.

The Add-in Features allow you to provide support for sinking events from the Visual C++ IDE or from the debugger. If one (or both) of these options is selected, the Wizard will add the appropriate interface to your objects (IApplicationEvents or IDebuggerEvents), along with stub methods. You can use these to handle events such as those arising from the creation of new documents or windows, opening and closing workspaces, or building projects.

ASP

This tab is only available for ActiveX Server Components:

This object type is essentially a simple object that holds interface pointers for the objects mentioned in the right hand pane. These pointers are initialized in the OnStartPage() event handler which is generated when a page is first loaded. Hence, if you were to uncheck the box on the left hand side you'd get the same class that you would have got if you'd selected a Simple Object. The Object Wizard implements the OnEndPage() handler to release the object pointers.

MMC Snap-in

This object type allows you to implement a snap-in for the Microsoft Management Console. This is the new tool that will replace the Windows control panel in Windows 2000. It is also available for earlier versions of Windows through the NT 4 option pack. MMC has a treeview, called the scope pane, that presents the various items you can configure. The configuration is carried out using a COM object called a **snap-in**. Snap-ins are responsible for integrating themselves within the scope pane, adding more nodes if necessary, and providing a user interface. This UI is called the result pane and generally (though not exclusively) it uses a ListView. You can also provide context menus, property sheets and command bars.

The tab (as shown below) allows you to specify which facilities you will implement:

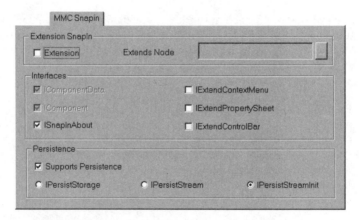

Extension

When you implement a snap-in you can either create your own branch in the scopepane of the console, or you can extend an existing one. The first option allows you to specify whether your snap-in is an extension, and if so which node it extends (nodes are registered in the system registry, so the Object Wizard will list all the nodes registered on the local machine).

Interfaces

The Interfaces section allows you to specify the features of the snap-in's user interface. You should implement:

❑   ISnapInAbout should be implemented because this allows the console to list a description of your snap-in for a user who wants to use it.

❑   IExtendContextMenu allows you to manipulate the snap-in items using a right-click context menu.

❑   IExtendPropertySheet provides property pages for the context menu properties item.

❑   IExtendControlBar enables you to put controls (for example, buttons and combo boxes) on the control bar.

Persistence

The Persistence options determine how the snap-in is made persistent. You can load one or more snap-ins into a window of the console, the combination of which is called a **tool**. When you've finished using the console you'll be given the option of saving the tool so that in a future session you can reload the same settings. If you want to support this you should make sure that you select Supports Persistence and choose one of the options.

MTS

When you add a MS Transaction Server Component to your project, `mtx.h` will be included in your class header so that you can call the MTS methods and interfaces. In addition, you will see this dialog:

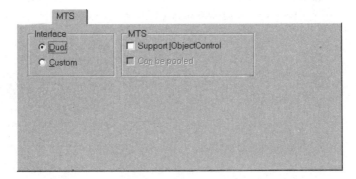

The important item here is the Support IObjectControl option. If you leave this clear, the Wizard will just create a simple object. However, if you check this box the object will implement `IObjectControl` and Can be pooled will be ungrayed. This interface is used to provide code when an object is activated or deactivated.

> Note that MTS servers must be linked with `mtx.lib`, so you must have selected Support M**T**S in the AppWizard.

Miscellaneous

This tab allows you to define the properties and appearance of both lite and full controls:

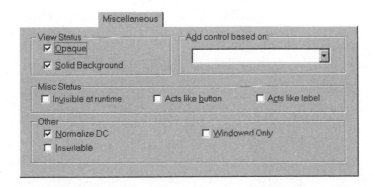

View Status

The View Status options determine the values returned by the control's
`IViewObjectEx::GetViewStatus()` method, which the control container calls to
ask the control about how it will draw itself. This helps the container to optimize its
interaction with the control, but note that you still have to make sure that the control
has the specified functionality. If you uncheck Solid Background then the container
simply won't optimize certain calls. It's up to you to give the control a transparent
background.

Add Control Based On

Add Control Based On allows you to superclass a Windows class. This means that your
control can use the functionality of the window, with the added option of intercepting
and handling its messages before it does. You can either type the Windows class name
in the edit box, or you can use the drop down list to get the names of some of the more
useful standard Windows classes. The Object Wizard will:

- ❑ Initialize the Common Control DLL if necessary
- ❑ Make your control 'windowed' (it will create its own window rather than using a portion of a container-created window)
- ❑ Add a `CContainedWindow` data member for the superclassed window
- ❑ Add a handler for `WM_CREATE` to create and superclass the window
- ❑ Add methods to handle key presses and the resizing of the control
- ❑ Add an alternative message map for the window

Misc Status

The options in the Misc Status group affect the control's `MiscStatus` key in the
registry. This is read by the control's implementation of
`IOleObject::GetMiscStatus()`, which is called by a container to determine the
status of the object. The options given by the Object Wizard are explained in the
following table:

Option	Description
Invisible at Runtime	This indicates that the control does not have a runtime window, but should have one at design time
Acts like a button	Surprisingly enough, the control acts like a button
Acts like a label	The control acts as a label, so that it activates the next control in the tab order when its mnemonic is pressed

Other

Finally, the Other options affect how the control is drawn and also how it is registered. When you select **Windowed Only**, you specify that the control should create its own window. If you leave this box clear then the control will be windowless *only if this is supported by the container*. A windowless control will still have a window, but rather than creating its own window the container will pass part of a window that it maintains to the control.

Windowless controls are an optimization technique that prevents many windows being created with the corresponding hit on resources and performance. This optimization is not supported by all containers — if the control determines that the container does not have this functionality it will create its own window.

The **Normalize DC** box is checked by default. This specifies that the device context passed to the drawing code will be normalized so that the device units will be pixels and the origin of the drawing area will be (0,0) — the top left corner. If this box is not checked, then the device context will not be normalized, so you will have to determine the drawing units, the direction of the co-ordinate system and the position of the origin. If you are happy to do this then you may gain a little performance for windowed controls.

The **Insertable** option indicates that a control can be inserted into a container. This merely means that the `Insertable` key will be added to the control's `CLSID key`. When a container uses the standard OLE 'insert object' dialog, only objects with this key will be included.

Stock Properties

This allows you to add stock properties to a control and is available for all control types:

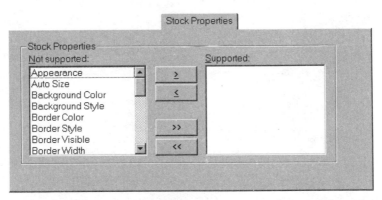

The list box on the left contains the stock properties that a control can support, and the list box on the right shows those that you have selected. The Object Wizard will take this information and add the properties to your `coclass`'s default interface. It will derive your class from `CStockPropImpl<>`, which implements the `get_` and `put_` methods for all stock properties. The wizard will also add an appropriate data member for each stock property selected, to be accessed by the `get_` and `put_` methods and will adjust the definition of your class's default interface to support these properties.

Strings

This tab is shown when you add a Property Page using Object Wizard. It allows you to specify the various strings that the property page will use.

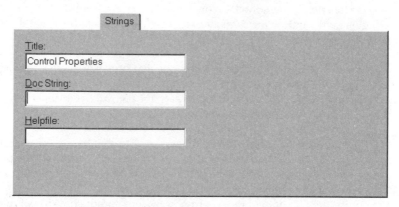

The Title is used for the tab when the property page is shown.

The Doc String is an additional string that some property sheets can show in a status bar or tool tip, which describes the purpose of the page.

Helpfile specifies the name of the file that will be called if the user clicks on the property sheet's Help button.

OLEDB Provider

This tab is essentially an extended version of the names page:

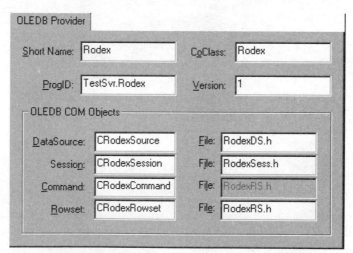

The Object Wizard will fill the boxes based on the string you type in the Short Name box, and, as in the Names page, you can change any of these strings.

OLEDB Consumer

Again, this is essentially an extended form of the Names dialog. The following screenshot shows the tab you see when you first select this object type:

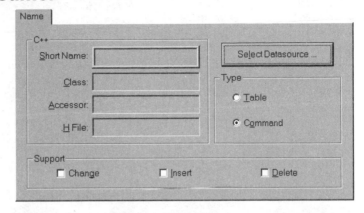

You cannot type a Short Name, the reason being that you first need to click on the Select Datasource button to select an OLE DB data source for which the Object Wizard will create wrapper accessor classes. Once you have selected a data source (a table, query or stored procedure) the Object Wizard will generate a Short Name for you and enable the edit boxes, allowing you to change their contents.

After that you can choose whether you want the generated class to give you table access (that is, access to all fields in the table) or run a query. Furthermore, you can specify whether you want to have the facility to insert or delete rows in the table, or to change (update) existing values.

When you click on the Select Datasource button, the wizard will check your system for all the registered OLE DB data sources and present them on following tab in the Data Link Properties dialog:

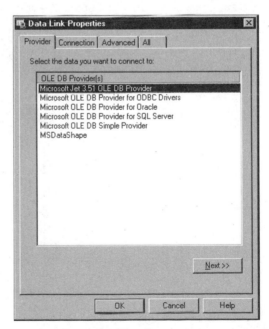

Your dialog may have different entries. When you click on the Next>> button, you'll be taken to the Connection tab. The contents of this tab will depend on the OLE DB provider you selected. If you selected the Jet provider you will get this:

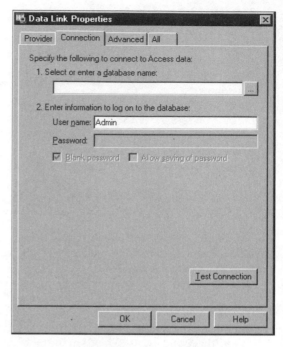

You can use the first edit box to specify the path to the MDB file that holds the database and use the other edit boxes to give a username and password. You can use the Test Connection button to test that the username and password work.

The other tabs on this dialog allow you to alter the properties that you will use (OLE DB properties are described in Appendix I). Properties are used to specify the facilities that the provider supports, and can be used to indicate which facilities you want to use.

Once you click on OK, the Object Wizard will access the data source and read the names of the tables, queries and stored procedures that are in the database. For example:

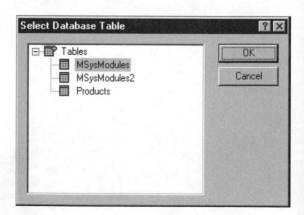

This database has a single table called Products (the other two tables are system tables). You should select the table (or stored procedure) that you're interested in — you'll then be sent back to the OLE DB Consumer Name tab.

Enumerators and Collections

Introduction

Collections are generally an automation concept. They are objects that contain collections of other objects. An analogy from the exciting world of stationery is that a pocket folder can hold multiple paper pages, and so the folder is a collection of pages. Like your pocket folder, you can add or remove items from an automation collection and you can access the items individually (take a page out and read it) or several at a time (like taking a handful of pages out of the folder and then reading them one at a time).

Adding and removing items is carried out with methods called Add() and Remove(). Reading several items at a time is carried out with an enumerator. Collections that support this use will have a read-only property called _NewEnum that returns an object with an enumerator interface. Clients that use the collection can call methods on the enumerator object to get access to the items in the array. The most noticeable use of such an enumerator is when you access a collection using the Visual Basic For Each statement.

Enumerators are not used exclusively with collections, they are used by many parts of COM (for example IEnumSTATSTG is returned by the IStorage interface to give information about the child storage and streams objects it contains). This appendix will start by explaining enumeration interfaces, then move on to how ATL implements these and finish off by discussing how ATL implements collections.

Enumeration Interfaces

An enumerator is an object that gives access to one or more items of a particular type in a particular order. Enumerators must implement an enumeration interface, because different types of data will be returned. One single interface will not do, so instead, enumeration interfaces have methods that follow a particular convention.

COM defines a few such enumerator interfaces for common object types, for example IEnumVARIANT and IEnumString, but you are free to define your own. You must guarantee though, that the clients using the enumerator know about the interface. If you are going to use a scripting or Visual Basic client then this restricts you to using IEnumVARIANT.

Enumerators interfaces should look like this:

```
interface IEnumType : public IUnknown
{
    HRESULT Next([in] ULONG celt,
                 [out, size_is(celt), length_is(*pCeltFetched)] Type* rgVar,
                 [out] ULONG *pCeltFetched);
    HRESULT Skip([in] ULONG celt);
    HRESULT Reset();
    HRESULT Clone([out] IEnumType** ppEnum);
};
```

Here Type is the type of the objects that will be returned.
The most important method is Next() which a client calls to get the next batch of items. It does this by passing the pointer to a client allocated array in rgVar and the number of required items in celt. The enumerator should attempt to fill the array with the required number of items and return the actual number via the pointer pCeltFetched.

This last point is important because the client may not know how many items there are in the enumeration and so will often ask for more items than are available. pCeltFetched enables the client to understand how many of the items in the array are valid, and also allows the marshaling layer to optimize how it transmits the data if the call to Next() is across an apartment boundary. Next() will return a value of S_OK if it returns celt items, S_FALSE if less than celt items are returned and some other value if there is an error. There is a slight oddity in the COM spec. that says that if a client passes a value of 1 in celt then it can pass a value of NULL for pCeltFetched and hence use the return value of Next() to determine if the single requested item has been returned. The ATL enumerator templates have been coded to take this into account.

Next() Skip() Reset()

Since an enumerator will most likely be returning more than one item through Next() it is likely that the data will be in some ordered list, or array. The enumerator will keep hold of the current position and update this whenever Next() is called. If a client decides to move this current position without reading values it can call Skip() passing the number of items to skip. To start the enumeration again, a client can call Reset() which resets the current position to the first item.

Clone()

The final method is interesting. Imagine you have an enumerator that contains product items that fit some criteria at a particular point of time, for example products from a particular supplier. In this case, each product item has a product name and a product ID, and a client can use the contents of the enumerator to populate a list box. As the user scrolls the list box, the enumerator is consulted to obtain the product names, which are then put into the list box. Now imagine that you want a second list box to use the same information but list, say, product IDs. If you used the same enumerator object then you will have the same index in the enumerator object, so scrolling in one list box will affect the items returned when you next scroll in the other list box. However, you cannot ask for another enumerator because the original data that was used to populate the enumerator may have changed (e.g. your supplier may suddenly supply more items), so the two enumerators will be based on different data. Instead, you need an exact copy of the enumerator: a *clone*.

The `Clone()` method will return a pointer to a new enumerator object that has access to the same data as the creating enumerator even to the point of initializing the current position pointer to point to the equivalent position as its creator. This means that you can use `Clone()` to create a 'bookmark', which is especially useful if the enumerator does not own the data.

Enumerations and Data

When you implement an enumeration object you have two choices about the data that will be used. The first is a 'snap-shot' implementation, and the second is a dynamic implementation. Which type of data you use depends on how the enumeration object will be implemented.

Snap-shot of Data

In this situation the enumeration holds 'static' data, that is, once the enumerator object has been initialized the data will not change.

Consider this example: imagine you have a database table that holds information about product items including the current stock level of each item. If you want to perform an audit of all the items at a particular point in time you will want to take a 'snap-shot' (a copy) of the contents of the database table. You can then peruse those values at your leisure, safe in the knowledge that since you have made a copy of the data you don't have to worry about any changes made to the table after the snap-shot was taken. To do this, the code that creates the enumerator should copy the data and use this to initializes the enumerator. The enumerator is said to *own* the data, and hence has the responsibility to clean it up when it's destroyed.

Dynamic Data

In this case the enumerator will give access to data that can change dynamically, and the enumerator should reflect these changes as best it can.

For example, imagine that within the products database previously mentioned, you want to implement an object to allow you to purchase items. You will want to have up-to-date information about the products, and stock level, to determine if the purchase can succeed. It follows, that the information the object uses should reflect the actual data. This means that if a new item is added to the table, then the enumerator will reflect this when the client iterates past the item's position in the enumeration. However, if the data is ordered so that the new item occupies a position *before* the current position in the iteration, then the change may not be picked up until the enumerator is reset (with a call to `Reset()`).

In this case the enumerator does not own the data. For each call to `Next()` it will attempt to access the data from its original source ensuring that it's totally up-to-date. This is sometimes known as lazy evaluation. Note that since the data is dynamic, your object should not really have a method to return the number of items in the enumeration. If it does (for example if the object is a collection), the client should only use this value as a guideline.

ATL Enumeration Templates

As shown, enumerator interfaces are effectively the same except for the type that is enumerated, making them prime candidates for being implemented with a template. There are two ATL classes for implementing enumerator objects:
CComEnum<> and CComEnumOnSTL<>
If you trawl through atlcom.h you will find two other templates for enumerators:
CComEnumImpl<> and IEnumOnSTLImpl<>

The Impl templates are used to add an enumerator interface to your object, the non Impl templates are used to create individual enumerator objects using CComObject<> (or similar).

Finally, you will notice the term OnSTL. These are templates that assume that the data being enumerated is implemented in an STL container, the other classes assume that the data will be contained in a contiguous array in memory.

Copy Classes

Before covering the enumeration templates in detail, the issue of copying data should be covered. The enumeration templates need to be initialized with data, either by caching pointers to dynamic data or by copying the data and caching the copied values. Furthermore, when Next() is called a copy of the data must be made to pass back to the client. Since the type of the data is passed as a parameter to the enumerator template it could be any type you choose, so you must inform the template about how to copy the data. This is done by using an appropriate Copy class:

```
class CopyClassName
{
public:
    static HRESULT copy(T* p1, T* p2);
    static void init(T*);
    static void destroy(T*);
};
```

Notice that all three methods are static. The only reason a class is used is to provide a namespace for those methods. You can give the class whatever name is appropriate, but it must have the three methods copy(), init() and destroy(), with parameters appropriate to the data type. The enumerator will call init() when it creates the data item, passing a pointer; this allows you to initialize the item to an empty state. Next, the enumerator will call copy() passing a pointer to the object that will receive the data (the out parameter p1) and a pointer to the data (the in parameter p2). In this example, they have the same type, but this is not required, it depends on the other parameters of the enumeration template, as you'll see later. When the enumerator dies (and if it owns the data) it will iterate through all the data items and call destroy(), passing a pointer to the item to destroy.

ATL provides the following _Copy classes, but it's easy to write your own.

Class	Description
`template <class T>` `class _Copy`	Generic copy class that does not initialize or destroy the items, and copies them with `memcpy()`.
`template<>` `class _Copy<VARIANT>`	Copies, initializes and destroys `VARIANT`s, use with `IEnumVARIANT`.
`template<>` `class _Copy<LPOLESTR>`	Copies, initializes and destroys `LPOLESTR`s, use with `IEnumString`.
`template<>` `class _Copy<OLEVERB>`	Copies, initializes and destroys `OLEVERB`s using the task memory allocator, use this to implement `IOleObject::EnumVerbs`.
`template<>` `class _Copy<CONNECTDATA>`	Copies and destroys `CONNECTDATA` items, which hold information about connected clients, including their sink interface - use this to implement `IEnumConnections`.
`template <class T>` `class _CopyInterface`	Generic class to enumerate interfaces of type T. It copies and destroys *references* on the specified interface, that is `copy()` calls `AddRef()` and `destroy()` calls `Release()`.

CComEnum<> and CComEnumImpl<>

`CComEnum<>` has the following parameters:

Template Parameter	Description
`class Base`	Enumeration interface that the object will use
`const IID* piid`	IID of the enumeration interface
`class T`	Type of the data to be enumerated
`class Copy`	Class used to initialize, copy and destroy data of type T
`class ThreadModel`	Threading model of the enumeration object

The final parameter has a default value which is the default threading model of the server set by defining an appropriate _THREADED symbol (see Appendix H). `CComEnumImpl<>` uses the same parameters except for the last one (because it comes from the `CComObjectRootEx<>` base class). With these templates, the type T determines the type of the items enumerated by the interface Base and the type of the array that will be used to initialize the enumerator.

CComEnum<> members

CComEnum<> is used to create objects, so it needs an interface map. The bulk of its enumeration code is implemented by deriving from CComEnumImpl<>. In addition to the enumeration methods this template has the following public members:

Member	Description

HRESULT Init(T* begin, T* end,
    IUnknown* pUnk,
    CComEnumFlags flags)
	Used to initialize the enumerator with the data it will enumerate. flags is used to determine if the enumerator has a copy of the data.

CComPtr<IUnknown> m_spUnk;	Used when cloning an object, this is the IUnknown on the object cloned.
T* m_begin;	Points to the first item in an array that holds the data.
T* m_end;	Pointer to the memory position *after* the last item in an array that holds the data.
T* m_iter;	Points to the current position in the array of data.
DWORD m_dwFlags;	Holds the flags passed in Init().

The Init() method is passed the data that the enumerator will use. This data *must* be in an array of T items (not pointers to T). You pass a pointer to the first item in begin and a pointer to the item *after* the last item in end. The flags parameter indicates whether the enumerator owns the data or not, it can have one of the following values:

ATL Flags

Flag	Description
AtlFlagNoCopy	Don't copy the data
AtlFlagTakeOwnership	Don't copy the data, but take ownership of it
AtlFlagCopy	Copy the data

These have values that are combinations of the values in CComEnumImpl::FlagBits, shown below:

Flag	Description
BitCopy	Copy data
BitOwn	Own the data

Thus `AtlFlagCopy` implies ownership and has a value of `BitCopy | BitOwn`.

The default is `AtlFlagNoCopy`, so the data is owned by another object, which has the responsibility of releasing the data when it's no longer needed. The data between the pointers `begin` and `end` must be held in a contiguous array, which means that you may need to create a new array and copy the raw data. If you pass this array to `Init()` with the `AtlFlagCopy` flag then the array is copied *again*. To prevent this you can use `AtlFlagTakeOwnership`, which indicates that `Init()` should *not* copy the data, and puts the responsibility of releasing the data on the enumerator.

Efficient data control with enumerators – AtlFlagTakeOwnership

Consider this code fragment:

```
//pEnum is created somewhere
LONG pArray = new LONG[m_iNoItemsm_pNoItems];
for (int i = 0; i < m_iNoItems; i++)
    pArray[i] = factorial(i);
pEnum->Init(pArray, pArray + m_iNoItems, NULL, AtlFlagCopy);
delete [] pArray;
```

Here the enumerator gives access to the factorials up to some limit set by `m_iNoItems`. Since these are calculated values you have to create an array to contain them and pass this to `Init()`, which makes a copy of the array using repeated calls to the appropriate `copy()` method. Finally, the original array is deleted. The problem with this code is that *two* arrays are created dynamically, `pArray` and the array held by `pEnum`.

Now look at this code:

```
//pEnum is created somewhere
LONG pArray = new LONG[m_iNoItems];
for (int i = 0; i < m_iNoItems; i++)
    pArray[i] = factorial(i);
pEnum->Init(pArray, pArray + m_iNoItems, NULL,
    AtlFlagTakeOwnership);
```

The enumerator takes the ownership, so you do not have to delete `pArray`, and no new copy is made. Note that to use `AtlFlagTakeOwnership` you must:

- ❏ Create the array on the heap
- ❏ Create the items in such a way that their resources can be released by calling `Copy::destroy()`

If the enumerator object is initialized with `AtlFlagNoCopy` then it means that it will merely copy the pointers passed in `Init()`. In this situation you must ensure that the data will be as long lived as the enumerator object (remember this is a COM object so it manages its own lifetime). If the data is held as a data member of some other COM object then you must pass the `IUnknown` pointer of that object in the `pUnk` parameter of `Init()`. The enumerator will increment this object's reference count and will only release it when it's destroyed, ensuring that the external object is longer lived than the enumerator.

One case where this will happen is if a user calls `Clone()`, where a copy is made of the enumerator. The clone should use the same data as its creator object, so `Clone()` initializes the new enumerator with the same data using `AtlFlagNoCopy`. Now, if the creator object owns the data then it must live as long as the clone, since if it dies it will delete the data and invalidate the clone's pointers to it. Thus, its `IUnknown` pointer is passed to the clone's `Init()`, which caches it and hence keeps a reference on its creator.

In a similar way, if you create the enumerator in an object method (for example `get__NewEnum()` in a collection) and the object owns the data (you call `Init()` with `AtlFlagNoCopy`) you must pass the creator object's `this` pointer to `Init()`.

> There is an anomaly in ATL 3.0, `CComEnumImpl::Clone()` does not check for ownership. Instead it checks to see if the creator *copied* the data, and if so passes its own `this` pointer to the clone, otherwise it passes the cached m_spUnk. If you use **AtlFlagTakeOwnership** this check will fail, so m_spUnk is passed. The check should be made for *ownership*, so the corrected code should be:
>
> ```
> // If the data is a copy then we need to keep "this" object around
> hRes = p->Init(m_begin, m_end, (m_dwFlags & BitOwn) ? this : m_spUnk);
> ```

Note that the array of data that the enumerator uses through `AtlFlagNoCopy` could be held as a global resource, in which case `NULL` could be used as the `pUnk` parameter to `Init()`. This presents a threading problem, because in a multithreaded server (with an MTA or more than one STA) one thread could change the data in the global resource while another thread accesses the code through the enumerator. A solution will be shown later in this appendix.

Creating an Enumerator

`CComEnum<>` has an interface map, so you can create it using `CComObject<>` (or equivalent). For example:

```
STDMETHODIMP CMathSeries::get__NewEnum(LPUNKNOWN *pVal)
{
    typedef CComObject<CComEnum<IEnumVARIANT, &IID_IEnumVARIANT, VARIANT,
        _Copy<VARIANT> > > EnumVar;
    EnumVar* pEnum = new EnumVar;
    LPVARIANT pVar = new VARIANT[m_iNoItems];
    for (int i = 0; i < m_iNoItems; i++)
    {
        VariantInit(&pVar[i]);
        pVar[i].vt = VT_I4;
        pVar[i].lVal = factorial(i);
    }
    pEnum->Init(pVar, &pVar[m_iNoItems], NULL, AtlFlagTakeOwnership);
    return pEnum->QueryInterface(&pVal);
}
```

Here I am creating an enumerator object that implements `IEnumVARIANT`, which is created on the heap as a C++ object. Since the values are calculated it creates a dynamic array and passes this using `AtlFlagTakeOwnership` to `Init()`. At this point the heap C++ object does not have a reference count, and since a COM object *must* have a reference count of at least 1 the code calls `QueryInterface()` for `IUnknown` (this code will use `__uuidof()` to get the IID of the passed interface pointer).

To get this enumerator you would use code like this in Visual Basic:

```
Dim Math as New MathSeries
Dim v As Variant
Math.NoItems = 10
For Each v In Math
   Debug.Print v
Next
```

Adding Enumeration Interfaces to an Object

The last section showed how to create a separate object to enumerate data.
What happens if you have an object that contains data and you want to give external clients access to that data through an enumerator interface?
To do this your ATL code needs to:

- ❑ Derive from `CComEnumImpl<>`

- ❑ Add the enumerator interface to the interface map

- ❑ Initialize the base class with the data in the constructor (or `FinalConstruct()`)

Note that you will be able to use this object with a C++ client, but not with a Visual Basic client. The reason is that to use `For Each` your object must have a read-only property called `_NewEnum` with a DISPID of `DISPID_NEWENUM`.
Once you have created a class derived from this class you can use it for the object returned by the `_NewEnum` property on another object.

> Out of interest, when Visual Basic 6 has an enumerator and iterates through the items with `For Each`, it will only ask for a single item each time (i.e. `celt == 1`). This is OK for inproc enumerators, but presents a performance problem for local and remote enumerators. To overcome this problem you could create a smart proxy: that is an inproc object that will call the out of process object to obtain many items and then cache them. The proxy should implement `IEnumVARIANT` so that when Visual Basic asks for individual items they are taken from the inproc cache. The proxy is 'smart' because when Visual Basic asks for items beyond the end of the cached buffer the proxy can get additional items from the out of process enumerator. This is beyond the scope of this book, but anyone experimenting in this area is welcome to post code to the Wrox website.

For example, imagine you have a database table that contains the colors that a set of products can have. You can give access to this via an enumerator object:

```
class ATL_NO_VTABLE CColors :
    public CComObjectRootEx<CComSingleThreadModel>,
    public CComEnumImpl<IEnumVARIANT, &IID_IEnumVARIANT, VARIANT,
        _Copy<VARIANT> >
{
public:
    CColors()
    {
        CColorsTable db;
        db.Open();
        CSimpleArray<CComVariant> varArray;
        while (db.MoveNext() == S_OK)
            varArray.Add(CComVariant(db.mColor));
        Init(varArray.m_aT, varArray.m_aT + varArray.m_nSize, NULL);
    }
```

```
BEGIN_COM_MAP(CSeries2)
    COM_INTERFACE_ENTRY(IEnumVARIANT)
END_COM_MAP()
};
```

Here, CColorsTable is an OLE DB consumer class (see Appendix I) giving access to the database table that contains the colors. The code reads these values and adds them to a CSimpleArray<> object, which holds the data in a contiguous memory block. CSimpleArray<> is an ATL container template that is explained more fully later in this appendix.

The CColors object is then used to provide an enumerator object for another object that has a _NewEnum property:

```
STDMETHODIMP CProductColors::get__NewEnum(LPUNKNOWN *pVal)
{
    CComObject<CColors>* pObj;
    CComObject<CColors>::CreateInstance(&pObj);
    return pObj->QueryInterface(pVal);
}
```

Problems with CComEnumImpl<>

CComEnumImpl<> is fine for a general purpose enumerator class and in most cases it will do most of the things that you need, however, there are problems…or is that challenges ?

When you initialize the enumerator with a call to Init() you specify the data that the enumerator will use. The class is not really designed to allow you to change the data dynamically. m_begin, m_end and m_iter (pointers to the first item, the item after the last one, and the current position) are public, so your code can use them and change the data they point to. However, when the enumerator accesses the data it uses these pointers without any locking code, so if you use one thread to try and change the data, how can you guarantee that another thread is not accessing the data through the enumerator?

Data Protection

Well, you can protect access to the actual data by writing your own Copy class. The Copy::copy() method is called by the enumerator to get access to the data, so you can place some locking around this, for example if the enumerator provides access to longs:

```
CComAutoCriticalSection g_Lock;

class _CopyLongThreadSafe
{
public:
    static HRESULT copy(long* p1, long* p2)
    {
        g_lock.Lock();
        *p1 = *p2;
        g_lock.Unlock();
        return S_OK;
    }
    static void init(long*) {}
    static void destroy(long*) {}
};
```

Data Updates

If you have an object that derives from `CComEnumImpl<>`, you can change the data used by the enumerator with:

```
STDMETHODIMP CMyObject::ChangeItem(long lIndex, long lVal)
{
    g_lock.Lock();
    this->m_begin[lIndex] = lVal;
    g_lock.Unlock();
    return S_OK;
}
```

This is fine for changing values, but what about adding or inserting new items?

Data Create

If you decide to insert an item with one thread and another thread calls `Next()` then there is a possibility that the data returned will be out of date, but only for that call to `Next()`. However, what you should not do is delete items; if you do this by reallocating the memory pointed to by `m_begin`, `m_end` and `m_iter` there is no way to lock the enumerator methods to prevent other threads accessing these pointers while this process is occurring.

To get round this you need to derive your own enumerator class:

```
template <class Base, const IID* piid, class T, class Copy>
class ATL_NO_VTABLE CSafeEnum : public CComEnumImpl<Base, piid, T, Copy>
{
    typedef CComEnumImpl<Base, piid, T, Copy> _base;
public:
    STDMETHOD(Next)(ULONG celt, T* rgelt, ULONG* pceltFetched)
    {
        g_lock.Lock();
        HRESULT hr = _base::Next(celt, rgelt, pceltFetched);
        g_lock.Unlock();
        return hr;
    }
    STDMETHOD(Skip)(ULONG celt)
    {
        g_lock.Lock();
        HRESULT hr = _base::Skip(celt);
        g_lock.Unlock();
        return hr;
    }
    STDMETHOD(Reset)(void)
    {
        g_lock.Lock();
        HRESULT hr = _base::Reset();
        g_lock.Unlock();
        return hr;
    }
    STDMETHOD(Clone)(Base** ppEnum)
    {
        g_lock.Lock();
        HRESULT hr = _base::Clone(ppEnum);
        g_lock.Unlock();
        return hr;
    }
};
```

Now you can change the underlying data that the enumerator uses as long as that code uses the global lock object `g_lock`. This is true whichever copy flag you use in the initial call to `Init()`.

CComEnumOnSTL<> & IEnumOnSTLImpl<>

It's obvious from the previous discussion, that, if your ATL class has data items that it needs to expose through an enumerator interface, it'll most likely hold those items in some container. For example, the CColors example used a CSimpleArray<>, another implementation may use a fixed size C++ array, but the most likely situation is to use an STL container.

STL Containers

The Standard Template Library has containers designed to give optimal access to data while providing methods to allow you to add and remove items. ATL allows you to base your enumerator on any of the STL containers (the requirements are that the STL container must have an iterator and support begin() and end()). IEnumOnSTLImpl<> implements the bulk of this code and is used to add an enumerator interface to your class. CComEnumOnSTL<> is a template with an interface map, so you can create objects from it. The parameters of these templates are effectively the same as CComEnum<> (and CComEnumImpl<>) except that there is an additional parameter used to indicate the STL container that will be used:

Template Parameter	Description
class Base	Enumeration interface that the object will use
const IID* piid	IID of the enumeration interface
class T	Type of the data to be enumerated
class Copy	Class used to initialize, copy and destroy data of type T
class CollType	The STL class that will hold the data
class ThreadModel	Threading model of the enumeration object

IEnumOnSTLImpl<> does not have the final parameter.

Example 1

To use these classes you pass a reference rather than pointers to the STL container to Init(), and hence by definition the enumerator does *not* own the data. Because of this you must also pass the IUnknown of the object that does own the data to Init(). For example:

```
private:
    std::list<CComVariant> m_data;
public:
    MyObject()
    {
        m_data.push_back(CComVariant(L"Red"));
        m_data.push_back(CComVariant(L"Green"));
        m_data.push_back(CComVariant(L"Blue"));
    }
    STDMETHOD(get__NewEnum)(LPUNKNOWN *pVal)
    {
```

```
typedef CComEnumOnSTL<IEnumVARIANT, &IID_IEnumVARIANT, VARIANT,
    _Copy<VARIANT>, std::list<CComVariant>> EnumVar;
EnumVar* pEnum = new EnumVar;
pEnum->Init(this, m_data);
return pEnum->QueryInterface(&pVal);
}
```

If you use a `std::map<>` then you will have to write your own version of `Copy`. This is because a `std::map<>` holds a key-value pair; when you add a value you must also add a key to access that data. In STL this pair of values is added to the container as an `std::pair<>` item (to hold the key and the value. The `iterator` for the `std::map<>` returns `std::pair<>` and not merely the value. The implementation of `Next()` calls the `copy()` method, passing the address of a `std::pair<>`, but expects the copy to be made to the type that is returned by the enumerator interface, thus the two parameters of `copy()` will not be the same.

Example 2

To see this in action, consider the example, of a `std::map<>` that has `LONG` values and `CComBSTR` keys: `std::map<CComBSTR, LONG>` and an enumerator that will return `VARIANT`s using `IEnumVARIANT`. In this case the `std::map<>` iterator will return `std::pair<const CComBSTR, LONG>` but `Next()` will expect to copy this into a `VARIANT`. So your `copy()` method should look like this:

```
class CopyMap
{
public:
    static HRESULT copy(VARIANT* pVar, std::pair<const CComBSTR, LONG>* it)
    {
        pVar->vt = VT_I4;
        pVar->iVal = it->second;
        return S_OK;
    }
    static void init(VARIANT* pVar){VariantInit(pVar);}
    static void destroy(VARIANT* pVar){VariantClear(pVar);}
};
```

Thus the `get__Enum()` method would create the enumerator like this:

```
typedef CComObject<CComEnumOnSTL<IEnumVARIANT, &IID_IEnumVARIANT, VARIANT,
    CopyMap, std::map<CComBSTR, LONG> > > EnumVar;
EnumVar* pEnum = new EnumVar;
// m_data is a map<CComBSTR, LONG> class data member
pEnum->Init(this, m_data);
return pEnum->QueryInterface(pVal);
```

Remember that the version of STL supplied with Visual C++ is not thread safe, and if multiple threads have access to the enumerator those threads should only ever read its data. However, if you try to change the data dynamically through one of the threads you will need to apply locking code. The only solution is to use the heavy-handed approach I showed earlier.

ATL Collection Templates

Doesn't work!
needs Add method!

Collections are a VBA construct that give access to objects through an enumerator. A collection must, at the very least, have a read-only property called _NewEnum with a DISPID of DISPID_NEWENUM; this allows Visual Basic to use the For Each syntax. A collection object can also implement :

- ❑ A read-only Count property to return the number of items in the collection.

- ❑ The read-only Item property (or Item() method) with a DISPID of DISPID_VALUE, to give access to a named (or indexed) member of the collection.

- ❑ An Add() method to allow users to add items, and Remove() to remove them.

ATL provides a single template called ICollectionOnSTLImpl<>. As the name suggests, this assumes that the data for the collection will be held in an STL container, and adds collection code to an existing class (there is no equivalent to CComEnumOnSTL<>). This class does not implement Add() or Remove() methods, but it does provide _NewEnum, Count and Item, implemented through IEnumOnSTLImpl<>.

You use this template like this:

- ❑ Ensure that your object implements IDispatch, i.e. it has a dual interface

- ❑ Add the read-only property _NewEnum to your class through ClassView, with a return type of LPUNKNOWN

- ❑ Add the read-only property Count to your class through ClassView, with a return type of long

- ❑ Add the read-only property Item to your class through ClassView, with the type of ItemType (see below) and an [in] parameter of type long

- ❑ Edit the IDL so that _NewEnum and Item have DISPIDs of DISPID_NEWENUM and DISPID_VALUE respectively

- ❑ Delete the code that ClassView adds to your .cpp and .h files for these properties (leave the IDL definitions)

- ❑ Derive from an IDispatchImpl<> specialization using ICollectionOnSTLImpl<> according to the instructions given below

- ❑ In the constructor, initialize the enumerator by adding the data to the inherited m_coll data member

ICollectionOnSTLImpl<> parameters

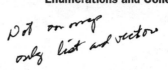

Parameter	Description
class T	The collection interface implemented by your class
class CollType	The STL container used to hold the data
class ItemType	The type of data returned by the Next() method of _NewEnum and Item
class CopyItem	Class used to copy, initialize and destroy ItemTypes
class EnumType	The specialization of CComEnumOnSTL<> used to implement _NewEnum

Example 1

The class generated by ICollectionOnSTLImpl<> will derive from your collection interface (it needs to, because it will implement the _NewEnum, Count and Item properties of the interface). The interface must be dual (the automation spec requires this), so your class should derive from IDispatchImpl<>. If it has an interface called IDocs, you will derive it like this (I have used typedefs to make the code more readable):

```
#include <list>

typedef std::list<CComVariant> VarList;
typedef CComEnumOnSTL<IEnumVARIANT, &IID_IEnumVARIANT, VARIANT,
                      _Copy<VARIANT>, VarList> VarEnum;
typedef ICollectionOnSTLImpl<IDocs, VarList, VARIANT, _Copy<VARIANT>,
                             VarEnum> CollImpl;

class ATL_NO_VTABLE CDocs :
    public CComObjectRootEx<CComSingleThreadModel>,
    public CComCoClass<CDocs, &CLSID_Docs>,
    public IDispatchImpl<CollImpl, &IID_IDocs, &LIBID_MYOBJECTLib>
```

This will mean that your class will inherit a std::list<CComVariant> data member called m_coll, so you will be able to add items to this during construction:

```
CDocs()
{
    m_coll.push_back(L"doc1.doc");
    m_coll.push_back(L"doc2.doc");
    m_coll.push_back(L"doc3.doc");
}
```

This implementation is fine for data that does not change, but what if you want to add data and remove items from the collection, i.e. implement Add() and Remove()? The problem here is yet again one of synchronization.

Example 2

Microsoft STL collections are not thread safe, so you should not attempt to use a collection from more than one thread. If you delete an item in the underlying container with one thread while another thread calls Next() on the enumerator, then the reading thread could receive false data concerning how many items there are in the container. To solve this problem you would have to derive from IEnumOnSTLImpl<> and make it thread safe, as well as deriving a class from ICollectionOnSTLImpl<> and making that thread safe. Here's a code fragment that illustrates this in action:

```
template <class T, class CollType, class ItemType, class CopyItem,
                                          class EnumType>
class ATL_NO_VTABLE ISafeCollectionImpl :
    public ICollectionOnSTLImpl<T, CollType, ItemType, CopyItem,
                                          EnumType>
{
public:
    STDMETHOD(Remove)(ItemType var)
    {
        HRESULT hr = S_OK;
        g_Lock.Lock();
        CollType::iterator iter;
        iter = std::find(m_coll.begin(), m_coll.end(), var);
        if (iter == m_coll.end())
            hr = E_INVALIDARG;
        else
            m_coll.erase(iter);
        g_Lock.Unlock();
        return hr;
    }
    STDMETHOD(Add)(ItemType var)
    {
        HRESULT hr = S_OK;
        g_Lock.Lock();
        CollType::iterator iter;
        iter = std::find(m_coll.begin(), m_coll.end(), var);
        if (iter == m_coll.end())
            m_coll.insert(iter, var);
        else
            hr = E_INVALIDARG;
        g_Lock.Unlock();
        return hr;
    }
    // other members of the class missed out
};
```

Again, this uses a global locking variable (g_Lock) that is used by other code that accesses the container. The other problem with ICollectionOnSTLImpl<> is that it assumes that Item() is indexed with a long value, that is, it is used with Visual Basic code like this:

```
Dim docs As New Docs
For x = 1 to Docs.Count
    Debug.Print Docs.Item(x)
Next x
```

However, collections can also be used like this:

```
'Cars is a collection of Car objects indexed by registration number
Dim Car1 As Car
Dim Car2 As Car
Set Car1 = Cars.Item("R111 XYZ")
Debug.Print Car1.Owner
Set Car2 = Cars.Item("F999 ABC")
Debug.Print Car2.Owner
```

(Indeed, since Item is DISPID_VALUE, you can omit it and use the syntax Cars("R111 XYZ").)

Anyway, the point is that to support this usage the property parameter to Item should be a VARIANT, in which case the code in get_Item() can test it to see if it's a number (and use the value as an index), or a string (and use it as a key). Obviously this will only work for STL associative types (like std::map<>), so it is not possible to write a generic version. If you want to do this you should override this method in your ATL class.

> *"Beginning ATL COM Programming"* shows how to write an implementation for Item, for a collection that is not implemented with ICollectionOnSTLImpl<>, but the basic algorithm is the same.

ATL Container Classes

This appendix has talked a lot about STL containers, so it's pertinent to mention the container templates provided by ATL. As the names suggest they provide a simple implementation and do not have the facilities (or the code size) of the STL equivalents.

CSimpleArray<>

This template implements a contiguous array of items, the type of which is passed as a parameter to the template. It has a single default constructor that initializes the data members to zeros, so initially it has no data. It has these methods:

Method	Description
BOOL Add(T& t)	Adds a copy of the item t to the end of the array, dynamically increasing the array if necessary
BOOL Remove(T& t)	Removes the first item with a particular value of t
BOOL RemoveAt(int nIndex)	Removes the item at index nIndex in the array
void RemoveAll()	Removes all items, freeing any memory used by the array. This is called by the destructor
T& operator[] (int nIndex) const	Gives you read/write access to existing items in the array; the index is zero based
void SetAtIndex (int nIndex, T& t)	Sets a particular existing item to t

Method	Description
int Find(T& t) const	Returns the index of the first item with a value of t
int GetSize() const	Returns the number of items in the array.
T* GetData() const	Returns a pointer to the first item in the array

You can add items using the Add() method. This will make a copy of the item (calling the copy constructor if one exists) and put it in the array at the last uninitialized position. If necessary, the array will be reallocated by doubling its size. The initial size is set to zero, in which case the class will allocate space for one item when the first item is added.

Of course this doubling can be a problem. Performance issues arise when allocating space for a small number of items. For example, to get space for 512 items you need to make 10 reallocations. There is also the problem of wasted memory when you allocate space for many items, for example if you want 4097 items you will get space for 8192 items.

You can set the initial size to another value by allocating the array yourself with malloc() and placing the pointer in the public member m_aT. In this case you also need to initialize the public member m_nAllocSize with the size of the array (in numbers of items). For example to use an array of at least 10 longs:

```
CSimpleArray<long> arr;
arr.m_nAllocSize = 10;
arr.m_aT = static_cast<long*>(malloc(arr.m_nAllocSize
                                      * sizeof(long)));
for (long lVal = 10; lVal < 20; lVal++)
    arr.Add(lVal);
```

Note that I add items using a variable not a value (Add(10) will not compile, see the next section for a solution), this is because items are being added, so Add() takes a reference. You can find the index of a particular value using Find(), using the previous example Find(lVal) where lVal has a value of 10 will return 0, the first item in the array.

RemoveAt() will remove the item with a particular index, so RemoveAt(1) in the previous example will remove the item with the value of 11. Remove() removes the first item with the specified value. Both of these methods will move data, if necessary, to fill the gap left by the removed item, but no reallocation will occur. To change the value of an existing item you can use array syntax (using operator[]()) or SetAtIndex().

CSimpleArray<> is useful if you want a lightweight container that holds data in contiguous memory.

CSimpleValArray<>

CSimpleArray<> is designed to take objects, and so the Add(), Remove() and Find() methods take references and operator[]() returns a reference. As you have seen in the example in the last section, if you want to use primitive data types you cannot pass a literal value. To get round this ATL provides a class derived from CSimpleArray<> called CSimpleValArray<>, which doesn't use references, so you can use it with primitive data types. For example:

```
CSimpleVarArray<long> arr;
arr.Add(10);
arr.Add(20);
arr.Add(30);      // arr holds 10, 20, 30
arr.Remove(20);   // arr holds 10, 30
arr.RemoveAt(0);  // arr holds 30
```

CSimpleMap<>

This is effectively two arrays, one with keys and the other with values (the data types of these are passed as parameters to the template). You can add (key, value) pairs; change the value of an item with a particular key and search the map for items with a particular key or value. The methods are:

Method	Description
BOOL Add(TKey key, TVal val)	Adds a value val with the key key
BOOL SetAt(TKey key, TVal val)	Changes the value of an existing item, key, to val
void SetAtIndex(int nIndex, TKey& key, TVal& val)	Changes the item at index nIndex have a key of key and a value of val
BOOL Remove(TKey key)	Removes the item that has a key of key
void RemoveAll()	Removes all items in the map
TVal Lookup(TKey key) const	Returns the first value with a key of key
TKey ReverseLookup(TVal val) const	Returns the first item with a value of val
int FindKey(TKey& key) const	Returns the index of the first item with a key of key (-1 if the find fails)

Method	Description
`int FindVal(TVal& val) const`	Returns the index of the first item with the value of `val` (-1 if the find fails)
`Tkey& GetKeyAt(int nIndex) const`	Returns the key of the item at index `nIndex`
`TVal& GetValueAt(` `    int nIndex) const`	Returns the value of the item at index `nIndex`
`int GetSize() const`	Returns the number of items in the map

For example:

```
CSimpleMap<CComBSTR, double> salary;
CComBSTR bstr;
double dSal;

bstr = L"Dave";
dSal = 150000;
salary.Add(bstr, dSal);
bstr = L"John";
dSal = 100000;
salary.Add(bstr, dSal);
bstr = L"Chris";
dSal = 10000; // I think Chris deserves a raise!
salary.Add(bstr, dSal);

for (int i = 0; i < salary.GetSize(); i++)
    _tprintf(_T("%S earns $%.2lf\n"),
        salary.GetKeyAt(i), salary.GetValueAt(i));
```

This gives the following results:

```
Dave earns $150000.00
John earns $100000.00
Chris earns $10000.00
```

Although there are several ways to get values and keys from the map, there is the distinct absence of `operator[]()`, the map is after all, a simple implementation.

Unlike `CSimpleArray<>` this template does not pre-allocate memory for the data. Every time you call `Add()` the buffers for the keys and values will be reallocated, which can be a performance problem. Indeed, if you are likely to add lots of items to the map, and you know beforehand how many items there will be, you will be better off creating two `CSimpleArray<>` objects and pre-allocating the necessary memory as explained earlier.

Similarly, when you remove an item from a map the other items will be moved, if necessary, to fill the gap left behind in the buffers for the keys and values, and then the memory will be reallocated. For this reason you should avoid making many removals from the map.

CVirtualBuffer<>

CSimpleArray<> allocates memory using realloc(), which ultimately leads to a call to HeapAlloc() using the CRT allocated heap. The CRT heap is created with a size of 4K, but is marked as growable so that if large allocations are made the heap size is increased. However, the memory allocated is *committed*, so resources are used even if you are no likely to use them. This means that if you take a pessimistic approach and allocate a huge buffer, then decide to use only a small portion of it, you will, of course, have wasted memory. Your process's working set will be unnecessarily large, but, on the other hand, you will have gained performance by not having to reallocate memory several times.

CVirtualBuffer<> is designed for huge numbers of items, and rather than using HeapAlloc() it uses the Win32 VirtualAlloc(). The advantage of this method is that you can specify the amount of virtual memory that you are likely to use up front, but the actual memory is not allocated until you commit pages. However, be very careful using this template, it has some serious bugs that may lock up your application.

You pass the number of items that you need to the constructor, which will reserve enough memory for all the requested items, but only enough for a single item (or a page of memory, whichever is the larger) will be committed and refer to actual memory. When you attempt to use a memory location in a page that has not been committed Windows will know that it's reserved and will throw a Win32 EXCEPTION_ACCESS_VIOLATION exception. CVirtualBuffer<> uses structured exception handling to catch this exception and handles it by committing the page that caused the access violation and then re-executing the code that caused it.

> The exception handler, Except() behaves in a strange way. Instead of committing just the page that caused the exception, it calculates the bytes between the beginning of the buffer and the end of the last written item and then commits the addition of the number of pages required to fit this memory. I think this is an anomaly, because you are likely to commit far more pages than you need. In addition, if memory is zero, which is the case if you have not written any items, then no pages will be committed, causing the exception to be repeatedly thrown.

The net effect of all this is that your instance of CVirtualBuffer<> will only use the memory that it needs (rounded up to a page size, of course, which is 4K on an x86 machine).

CVirtualBuffer<> maintains a current position, so that you can add items consecutively, or at particular positions in the buffer. Similarly, you can return items at the current position or at a particular position. The methods you can use are:

Method	Description
`void Write(const T& Element)`	Writes an item after the last item in the buffer
`void SetAt(int nElement,` `    const T& Element)`	Writes an item into the buffer at a specified index
`template <class Q>` `    void WriteBulk(Q& helper)`	Allows you to provide a method to write many items in one go
`void Seek(int nElement)`	Resets the current position
`T& Read()`	Reads the item at the current position
`const T& operator[](` `    int nElement) const`	Reads the item at a particular index
`operator BSTR()`	Returns all the bytes from the start of the buffer to the end of the last item set in a BSTR
`operator T*()`	Returns the start of the buffer
`int Except` `    (LPEXCEPTION_POINTERS lpEP)`	Exception handler that will commit pages when a access violation occurs

Using BSTR

The operator BSTR is interesting, and you should be wary of it. It will copy all the bytes from the start of the buffer to the end of the last item that was written into a BSTR. These bytes may contain uninitialized (and uncommitted) memory, which may represent a huge range.

Also, be aware that the exception handling in this conversion operator is incorrect:

```
BSTR bstrTemp;
__try
{
   bstrTemp = SysAllocStringByteLen((char*) m_pBase,
      (UINT) ((BYTE*)m_pTop - (BYTE*)m_pBase));
}
__except(Except(GetExceptionInformation()))
{
}
```

m_pTop is the end of the last item in the buffer and m_pBase is the start of the buffer. If this results in an amount of memory larger than SysAllocStringByteLen() can handle, then an exception will be thrown, which will be handled by Except(). This tries to commit a page in the virtual memory buffer and then re-executes the statement. Because the failure was in SysAllocStringByteLen(), and not due to accessing memory in the virtual memory buffer, this will result in another exception being thrown. The net effect of this is that your code will go into an everlasting loop.

WriteBulk()

If you want to fill the buffer with many items at one time you can use the
WriteBulk() method, which uses a class that has an operator() that will be
passed the address of the array. You can use this to initialize the buffer and then return
the address of the last item. ATL provides a sample class called CVBufHelper<> that
does not copy any items, but which you can use as a guide. For example, if I have a
buffer that holds BYTEs then I can initialize the first few kilobytes with the following
code:

```
class CByteInitializer
{
    int m_count;
public:
    CByteInitializer(int count) : m_count(count) {}
    BYTE* operator()(BYTE* pCurrent)
    {
        for (int x = 0; x < m_count; x++)
        {
            *pCurrent - 0,
            pCurrent++;
        }
        return pCurrent;
    }
};
```

This is used like this:

```
CVirtualBuffer<BYTE> byteArray(1024 * 1024);
CByteInitializer init(10 * 1024);
byteArray.WriteBulk(init);
```

WriteBulk() will call CByteInitializer::operator()() within a exception
guarded block, so if it accesses memory that is not committed, then the appropriate
page will be committed and the access re-executed. Before you try this code read my
warning about how pages are committed earlier on. This code will go into an
everlasting loop because no data has been written to the buffer. To prevent this from
happening place the line:

```
byteArray.Write(0);
```

before the call to WriteBulk().

Class Factories and Aggregation

Introduction

Class factories are used to create instances of objects (components). ATL provides several versions that should meet your needs and even allows you to write your own. Class factories promote code reuse, because if you have a component with a particular functionality you can load and use the component wherever the functionality is needed. Code reuse, such as this, is fairly coarse-grained — your code gets the complete functionality of the object.

Imagine that you're writing an object and have implemented most of its interfaces, but you discover that the remaining interfaces provide functionality that is also provided by an existing object. COM provides a mechanism which allows your object to utilize the interfaces of the existing object — it's called aggregation. During aggregation you create this additional object with your object and pass client requests for these interfaces to it. The interface pointers from the aggregated object are returned to the client, so that the client thinks that your object implements those interfaces.

There is more to aggregation than this, of course. In particular, when the client obtains an interface on the aggregated object and then queries for IUnknown it should get the IUnknown on the aggregating object to preserve COM's identity rules. Consequently, the aggregated object should have an interface pointer to the IUnknown of the aggregating object and implement a version of QueryInterface() that will return it when required.

So why am I talking about aggregation here? The reason is that when an aggregated object is created it must be passed the IUnknown of the aggregating object. Because class factories are used to create objects this means that aggregation support and class factories in ATL are intimately related.

Class Factories

There are five class factory macros, which are used by including them in a `public` section of your ATL class. If your class is externally creatable (that is, it derives from `CComCoClass<>` and has an entry in the object map) it will, by default, use `DECLARE_CLASSFACTORY()`, which is the class factory implemented by `CComClassFactory`. The full set of macros are:

Macro	Description
DECLARE_CLASSFACTORY No parameters	Specifies that the object class factory is implemented through `CComClassFactory`
DECLARE_CLASSFACTORY2 Parameter: `lic`	Specifies that the object uses runtime and design time licenses, and that the class factory is implemented through `CComClassFactory2`
DECLARE_CLASSFACTORY_EX Parameter: `cf`	Allows you to specify the ATL class that will be used for the class factory
DECLARE_CLASSFACTORY_AUTO_THREAD No parameters	Indicates that the object will be created in a thread pool
DECLARE_CLASSFACTORY_SINGLETON Parameter: `obj`	Indicates that there will only ever be one instance of your object

The parameters for these macros are:

- ❑ `lic` is the name of a class to provide licensing support used by `CComClassFactory2`
- ❑ `cf` is the name of the ATL class that implements `CreateInstance()`
- ❑ `obj` is the name of your ATL class

The COM API functions `CoCreateInstance()`, `CoCreateInstanceEx()` and functions that use them (like `CreateObject()` or `New()` in Visual Basic) assume that the object will be created through a class factory that implements `IClassFactory`, or its derivative `IClassFactory2`. Therefore, in most cases, you will use `DECLARE_CLASSFACTORY()` or `DECLARE_CLASSFACTORY2()`. If you want an inproc object to be created through MTS and have the benefit of the MTS-created context object, your object must be created through a class factory that implements `IClassFactory`. Hence, you must use `DECLARE_CLASSFACTORY()`.

Licensed Objects

Licensing means that your object distinguishes between two situations: when it's used in a development tool whilst designing an application, and when it's actually used on execution of the finished application. Because of its nature, licensing is mainly used on ActiveX controls, but you can use it on other types of objects.

Design Time Licenses

The design time tool will query for `IClassFactory2` and then call `GetLicInfo()` to determine if the object is licensed for design time use and whether the class factory can generate a key for a runtime license. This information is returned in a `LICINFO` structure:

```
typedef struct  tagLICINFO
{
    ULONG cbLicInfo;
    BOOL fRuntimeKeyAvail;
    BOOL fLicVerified;
} LICINFO;
```

If a valid license exists then the design time tool can call `IClassFactory::CreateInstance()` to create the object.

If the class factory indicates that a runtime license is available, the design time tool can query for this by calling `RequestLicKey()` on the class factory object, caching this key into the final application. When this application initializes it will call `IClassFactory2::CreateInstanceLic()` and pass this key to the class factory, which creates the object. Note that in general if the runtime application calls `IClassFactory::CreateInstance()` the call will fail, because this method requires a design time license.

Runtime Licenses and License Validation

Clearly, there must be some code that will generate runtime licenses and check that runtime and design time licenses are valid. `CComClassFactory2` will do most, but not all, of the work for you. When you write a licensed object you should create a class that implements the following three `static` methods:

Method	Description
`VerifyLicenseKey()` Parameter: `BSTR bstrKey`	Returns `TRUE` if the passed-in runtime license key is correct
`GetLicenseKey()` Parameters: `DWORD dw, BSTR* pKey`	Returns the runtime license for this object in a `BSTR`
`IsLicenseValid()` No parameters	Returns `TRUE` if the design time license is present and correct

The parameters for these methods are:

- ❏ `bstrKey` is a runtime key
- ❏ `dw` is a reserved parameter and should be ignored
- ❏ `pKey` is used to return a runtime key

You should implement `IsLicenseValid()` to check for a valid design time license. The accepted procedure is for design time licenses to be held under the following key:

```
HKEY_CLASSES_ROOT\Licenses
```

Each license will have a unique UUID and a key under this key. The actual license is the default value of the license key. Your implementation of `IsLicenseValid()` should check for this key and compare the value with what it thinks the value should be. Note that this UUID has no connection with the object's CLSID, and the license string should not have anything that associates it with the object. Indeed this license shouldn't even be a readable string, and to make it useful you should make the key different for every machine where the object is installed.

A trick I use is to encrypt the machine name (or MAC address) so that the key becomes invalid when it is moved to another machine. You can do other things with this license. For example, you could encrypt the installation date so that `IsLicenseValid()` can check if a license period has exceeded, or you could save a usage count to ensure that the object is only used a certain number of times.

> *Professional ATL COM Programming* provides a simple application that will generate an encrypted design time license.

If your object uses runtime licenses it should return the license key from a call to `GetLicenseKey()`. The `VerifyLicenseKey()` should compare the passed key with what it thinks the runtime license should be. Note that the license key is typically a static string. Indeed, since `GetLicenseKey()` will be run on the design time machine and `VerifyLicenseKey()` is called on the runtime machine (which will be different in most cases) you *should not* use machine-specific values in this key.

Implementing Your Own Class Factory

If you want your class factory to implement `IClassFactory` then you can derive from `CComClassFactory` and implement `CreateInstance()` to perform your custom actions. To create a class factory that keeps a count of the instances it has created you can use:

```
class CMyOtherClassFactory : public CComClassFactory
{
public:
    STDMETHOD(CreateInstance)(LPUNKNOWN pUnkOuter, REFIID riid,
                              void** ppvObj)
    {
        HRESULT hr;
        hr = CComClassFactory::CreateInstance(pUnkOuter, riid, ppvObj);
        if (SUCCEEDED(hr))
        {
            m_ulCount++;
            ATLTRACE("Created object number %ld\n", m_ulCount);
        }
        return hr;
    }
private:
    ULONG m_ulCount;
};
```

You declare that the class will be used as a class factory by using the
DECLARE_CLASSFACTORY_EX() macro in the ATL class of the object it creates. The
class above would be declared in your ATL class with:

```
DECLARE_CLASSFACTORY_EX(CMyOtherClassFactory)
```

Now, whenever a new instance of your object is created, the object count number will
be printed to the debug stream. There are some caveats to the use of this class factory.
EXE servers will create just one class factory object, registered in _tWinMain(). DLL
servers create a class factory object when COM calls DllGetClassObject(). COM
actually caches the returned interface pointer so, if your code makes multiple calls to
CoCreateInstanceEx() or CoGetClassObject(), the same class factory object
will be used.

Custom Class Factories

The previous section showed you how to write a class factory that implements the
IClassFactory interface. If your clients will only use CoCreateInstance() or
CoCreateInstanceEx() to create objects, or if you use MTS, then you'll have to
implement this interface. However, if your clients are willing to call
CoGetClassObject() then the class factory object is free to implement any interface
you like. This is useful because IClassFactory::CreateInstance() does not
have a parameter for you to pass initialization data to the new object, so you have to
call an initialization method of your own, or use an interface like
IPersistStreamInit.

Example 1

Imagine that you have a COM object implemented by CPerson and you want to allow
clients to create this object by passing a name. The class factory interface, IPersonCF,
will have a method that the clients can use to pass the name. The class factory will then
create the object and initialize it. For example:

```
class CPersonClassFactory :
    public IPersonCF,
    public CComObjectRootEx<CComGlobalsThreadModel>
{
public:
    BEGIN_COM_MAP(CPersonClassFactory)
        COM_INTERFACE_ENTRY(IPersonCF)
    END_COM_MAP()

    STDMETHOD(CreatePerson)(BSTR bstrName, IPerson** ppObj)
    {
        HRESULT hRes = E_POINTER;
        if (ppObj != NULL)
        {
            *ppObj = NULL;
            CComObject<CPerson>* pObj;
            CComObject<CPerson>::CreateInstance(&pObj);
            pObj->m_bstrName = bstrName;

            hRes = pObj->QueryInterface(ppObj);
            if FAILED(hRes)
                delete [] pObj;
        }
        return hRes;
    }
};
```

Notice that this class has intimate knowledge of CPerson and can initialize it using normal C++ techniques; in this case by accessing the public data member m_bstrName. However, I've not used a constructor to initialize the instance of CPerson. The reason is that the code isn't creating instances of CPerson, it's creating instances of CComObject<CPerson>. CPerson is an abstract class and you use CComObject<> (which derives from its parameter) to provide an implementation of IUnknown to make a concrete class. You can only call the constructor of CComObject<>, which has the responsibility of calling the constructors of its base class. Since this template knows nothing about your class, it can only assume that your class has a *default* constructor, which is invoked implicitly by the compiler.

The CPerson class should use DECLARE_CLASSFACTORY_EX() macro to specify that it uses this class factory.

This example does not implement IClassFactory and so does not derive from CComClassFactory. This is fine for inproc objects but if the object is in an EXE server you should also implement IClassFactory (you can derive from CComClassFactory to do this) because LockServer() is called to ensure that the server is kept alive while the object is being marshaled back to the client.

Since CPerson objects are created with a custom class factory, clients cannot call CoCreateInstanceEx(). Instead, they must get access to the class factory with a call to CoGetClassObject(). (Note that if the objects are likely to be created across apartment boundaries then you should register a proxy-stub DLL for the class factory interface and implement IClassFactory::LockServer().)

The following client code is an example of using this class factory:

```
IPersonCF* pPCF;
hr = CoGetClassObject(CLSID_Person, CLSCTX_INPROC_SERVER, NULL,
                      IID_IPersonCF, static_cast<void**>(&pPCF));
if (SUCCEEDED(hr))
{
    IPerson* pPerson;
    BSTR bstr = SysAllocString(L"Richard");
    hr = pPCF->CreatePerson(bstr, &pPerson);
    SysFreeString(bstr);
    pPCF->Release();
    if (SUCCEEDED(hr))
    {
        pPerson->get_MyName(&bstr);
        _tprintf(_T("My name is %S\n"), bstr);
        SysFreeString(bstr);
        pPerson->Release();
    }
}
```

One final point. If the object is inproc then it's a good idea to make the class factory the same threading model as the object.

Singletons

A singleton object is one that can only ever have one instance. Because of this, when clients call CoCreateInstanceEx() for the object they should get a reference to the *same* instance, rather than references to separate instances. To do this the class factory for the object should create just one instance and implement CreateInstance() so that it passes references to interfaces on this single instance back to the clients. To make your ATL class a singleton you merely have to use the DECLARE_CLASSFACTORY_SINGLETON() macro.

Points to Consider

Before you go ahead with this, you should ask yourself if this is what you really want. The most obvious problem with implementing singleton behavior with a class factory is that it breaks the semantics of CreateInstance(), which should create a new *instance* and not return a reference to an existing instance.

You should also look at the use of the object. Remember that COM is designed to allow location transparency — the client code is the same wherever the object is implemented. However, the behavior of a singleton object is different depending on where it resides:

In-process Objects

If the object is inproc, this means that it is only a singleton as far as the current process is concerned other processes will get their own instance of the object. You could argue that in the inproc case you could get the same behavior by copying an interface pointer for each part of the application that requires access to the object. However, this approach assumes that the interface pointer is global and that all parts of the application have access to it. You will have to take into account when the interface pointer is used in other apartments in the same process. In this situation, a DLL-based singleton is useful to locate the object.

EXE-Implemented Objects

If the object is implemented in an EXE then it is a machine-wide singleton. Whenever other processes on the same machine request an instance, they will get back a reference to the same object. However, other machines may have the same object installed so when clients on those machines request an instance they will get a copy of the object on their machine. To implement a network-wide singleton you have to ensure that when clients on any machine make a request for the object, the same object, from one single machine, will be used.

There are several ways to do this. For example, you can make sure that the object is registered with an AppID and set the RemoteServerName value to have the name of the server machine. Another way is to use the **Class Store** (supposedly central to Windows 2000). This will be part of the active directory services and will allow you to specify that when a request is made for a particular coclass, the request will be made to a specified machine. Thus, when a client makes a request for the coclass, and the local COM can't find the server registered on the local machine, it will pass the request to the Class Store which will then forward the call to the appropriate server.

So, what about singletons implemented in EXEs? Well, the design pattern assumes that multiple clients will try to access the singleton, which would mean that if the server is _ATL_APARTMENT_THREADED (that is, has a single STA) there will be a bottleneck. When one client is accessing the singleton, *no other client will be able to access any of its methods*. It makes sense, therefore to make a singleton EXE server _ATL_FREE_THREADED (that is, have an MTA). This means that many clients can access the singleton's methods concurrently. If you do this, you should ensure that the object uses the free threading model, and that any access to the object's instance data (or data global to the server) is protected from multithreaded access.

Example

So if the *raison d'être* of the singleton is to give access to a shared data item m_ItemVector, then you will have to protect it like this:

```
private:
    std::vector<long> m_ItemVector;
public:
    // make the object a singleton
    DECLARE_CLASSFACTORY_SINGLETON(CMyObject)
    STDMETHOD(PutItem)(long lVal)
    {
        Lock();
        push_back(lVal);
        Unlock();
        return S_OK;
    }
    STDMETHOD(GetItem)(long lIndex, long* pVal)
    {
        Lock();
        if (lIndex > m_ItemVector.size())
            return E_INVALIDARG;
        *pVal = m_ItemVector[lIndex];
        Unlock();
        return S_OK;
    }
```

Non-singleton Objects

With methods such as these, data written by one client will be accessible by any other client that has a reference to the singleton. However, if you go to these lengths why not just create a non-singleton object that accesses a global resource:

```
    // this object is not a singleton
private:
    static std::vector<long> m_ItemVector;
    static CComAutoCriticalSection m_Lock;
public:
    STDMETHOD(GetItem)(long lIndex, long* pVal)
    {
        m_Lock.Lock();
        if (lIndex > m_ItemVector.size())
            return E_INVALIDARG;
        *pVal = m_ItemVector[lIndex];
        m_Lock.Unlock();
        return S_OK;
    }
```

Now each client gets its own object, and through this will get access to the global resource. The advantage of this approach is that the object can have per-client state, which is impossible with a singleton.

SPM

Another way to share data without a singleton is to use MTS, which has a component called the **Shared Property Manager**. In this situation, multiple instances of a component can use the same data by making calls to the SPM. The MTS programming paradigm allows you to assume that there are no synchronization problems (because MTS will handle concurrency issues), thus simplifying the code.

Stateless Objects & Singletons

Another use for a singleton is to provide some global functionality through a stateless object. For example, a 'calculator' object that provides methods that calculate a value based on the parameters it is passed. This is a good case for a singleton because there is nothing to distinguish between individual instances of the object. If the object is implemented as an inproc server then you will waste memory because each instance will have a reference count, a vtable for each interface and other interface specific state. If you make the object a singleton then you'll save this additional memory.

As another example, imagine the case of an object that calls `NetWkstaUserEnum()` to obtain information about all the users logged on to a workstation and then returns this information back to the user in a `SAFEARRAY`. Since this object does not have any state (it is used merely to wrap an existing API), it is a good candidate for a singleton. Indeed, this LanMan function can only be called by accounts that are members of the `Administrators` local group. Consequently, it should be implemented in an EXE, in which case you can ensure that it is run under an appropriate account.

Thread Pooling

Thread pooling is covered in Appendix H, but for completeness I will mention why you should have a special class factory to support it.

ATL thread pooling allows you to create an EXE server than has multiple STA threads. The class factory object lives in the main STA thread (i.e. the first STA thread created), but it delegates the object creation call to a routine running in each STA pool thread. Since the object creation routine is in an STA pool thread it means that the object will live in that particular apartment. ATL allows you to determine how many threads there are in the pool and to design your own algorithm to determine which STA pool thread will be used. It has reasonable defaults for both — you'll get four threads per processor, and a round robin pool selection algorithm.

What is immediately clear is that there must be some mechanism to tell a pool thread to create an object. There are also thread synchronization and marshaling issues. This is why if you want to use thread pooling you must use the thread pooling class factory, which requires the following three steps:

- ❑ Declare `DECLARE_CLASSFACTORY_AUTO_THREAD()` in each ATL class that can be run on an STA pool thread

- ❑ Derive the class for the server `_Module` object from `CComAutoThreadModule<>`

❑ Change the module `Lock()` method to call the same named method in `CComAutoThreadModule<>`

More details about these steps are given in Appendix H.

Aggregation

Aggregation is determined through the Attributes tab of the Object Wizard, which will add a macro to the class. The following table lists the macros that can be used:

Aggregation Macros

Macro	Description
DECLARE_NOT_AGGREGATABLE	The object cannot be aggregated
DECLARE_AGGREGATABLE	The object can be aggregated
DECLARE_ONLY_AGGREGATABLE	The object can only be created as part of an aggregate
DECLARE_POLY_AGGREGATABLE	The object can be aggregated

In fact, the Object Wizard will only add one of the first three macros. The fourth is equivalent to using DECLARE_AGGREGATABLE. Note that both of these macros indicate that the class can be used as the inner object in an aggregate or created in its own right, so clearly the code must be able to handle both situations. DECLARE_AGGREGATABLE does this by creating either a CComObject<> or a CComAggObject<> depending on whether your object is being aggregated, so your code module will contain code for both. The resulting code may be quite large if your object has several interfaces.

DECLARE_POLY_AGGREGATABLE will create a CComPolyObject<> which has code that will work for both the aggregated and non-aggregated cases. Hence, you save code size, but the code isn't optimized for either case.

It's a good idea to use DECLARE_POLY_AGGREGATABLE if your object has many interfaces. This is because you need only one vtable, which reduces the module size if the interface table is large.

CComObject<> and Related Templates

Your ATL class is an abstract class, so you can't create instances on the stack or with the new operator. It's abstract because it derives from IUnknown, but doesn't define the pure virtual functions declared in the interface. To create instances you need to use CComObject<> or one of its related templates. These take your class as a parameter and will derive from it. They implement the IUnknown methods, using code in your class to get access to the interface map to determine how to change the object reference count.

CComObject<>

This is the class you'll see most often. You should create these objects using its `static` member `CreateInstance()`. The class implements `IUnknown` and maintains the object reference count through the data member `m_dwRef`, which is inherited through `CComObjectRootBase` via your class. The implementation of `Release()` ensures that, when the reference count falls to zero, the object is `deleted` hence stack instances of `CComObject<>` can never be created.

When instances are created, the object will increment the module lock count. Conversely, this count is decremented in the destructor, ensuring that the module will remain loaded while an instance of the object exists.

> Note that instances of this class do not support aggregation.

Example

If you have an ATL class implemented in your project and you want to create an instance of it and return an interface pointer, you would use code like this:

```
STDMETHODIMP CMyCreator::GetAnObject(IMyItf** ppItf)
{
   CComObject<CMyObject>* pMyObj;
   CComObject<CMyObject>::CreateInstance(&pMyObj);
   HRESULT hr;
   hr = pMyObj->QueryInterface(ppItf);
   if (FAILED(hr))
      delete pMyObj;
   return hr;
}
```

`CreateInstance()` uses `new` to create the object and then calls `FinalConstruct()`. The reference count is zero, so you *cannot* merely cast to the required interface pointer. You must call `QueryInterface()` which will call `AddRef()` and return the appropriate interface pointer. If this fails, you should delete the object.

If the `CMyObject` class inherits from `CComCoClass<>`, then you can use `CComCoClass<>::CreateInstance()` to create an object instance. This method calls `CreateInstance()` through the `_CreatorClass` class declared with the aggregation macros. This class will be implemented using `CComObject<>` (or one of the similar classes), as indicated in this table:

Macro	Implementor of `CreateInstance()`
DECLARE_NOT_AGGREGATABLE	CComObject<>
DECLARE_AGGREGATABLE	CComObject<> or CComAggObject<>
DECLARE_ONLY_AGGREGATABLE	CComAggObject<>
DECLARE_POLY_AGGREGATABLE	CComPolyObject<>

You can use the CComCoClass<>::CreateInstance() method like this:

```
STDMETHODIMP CMyCreator::GetAnObject(IMyItf** ppItf)
{
    return CComObject::CreateInstance(ppItf);
}
```

CComObjectStack<>

As the name suggests, this template is designed to allow you to create instances of an object on the stack. Because of this there is no CreateInstance() method (it isn't needed because you just declare an instance) and AddRef() and Release() are no-ops (because the lifetime of the object is controlled by the stack frame). QueryInterface() goes one step further; it will assert in debug builds and it will return E_NOINTERFACE for all interface requests. The reason is that this template is designed to make your ATL class concrete so that you can create an instance. If you want to use interface methods you can call them directly.

Note that FinalConstruct() is called in the constructor and FinalRelease() in the destructor so it is created in the same way as a CComObject<> object.

Why would you use this? Put simply, this template enables you to use the functionality that you've put in a class in to your project without the overhead of COM.

CComObjectGlobal<>

What happens if you want to create an object as a global object, or a contained object within another object, and you want to give external access to this object?
In this case the object must implement the reference counting methods of IUnknown because references to the object can be passed by one client to another client. Consequently, the server shouldn't be unloaded while references exist. CComObjectGlobal<> is designed for such use — the reference counting methods increment and decrement the module lock count to keep the module loaded.

You use this object like this:

```
CComObjectGlobal<CMyOtherObject> g_pObj;

STDMETHODIMP CMyCreator::GetAnotherObject(IMyOtherItf** ppItf)
{
    return g_pObj->QueryInterface(ppItf);
}
```

The advantage of this is that any code that has access to the g_pObj variable will be able to use the object. If CMyCreator has code in the same file then those methods can also return an interface pointer to the same global object. Singleton class factories use this class to create a single instance of an object within the class factory object.

CComTearOffObject<> and CComCachedTearOffObject<>

Tear-off interfaces were covered in Appendix A. Essentially, such an interface is implemented by a C++ class, which is separate from the object that implements it. The idea being that the tear-off is created when it's requested rather than when the entire object instance is created. Since the tear-off is not part of your ATL object, it has to have its own implementation of IUnknown. This is so that when the last reference on the tear-off is released, the tear-off object will be destroyed — even if there are still references on the object.

> If the tear-off has its own version of IUnknown then doesn't this violate the COM identity rules? The answer is no, because the implementation of QueryInterface() for the tear-off delegates to the QueryInterface() of the main object and hence any queries for IUnknown will return the interface on the main object.

CComTearOffObject<> will create a new tear-off whenever the interface is queried. CComCachedTearOffObject<> will cache a pointer to the tear-off object so that it can be used on future queries.

You do not use these two templates as they're used in the implementation of COM_INTERFACE_ENTRY_TEAR_OFF() and COM_INTERFACE_ENTRY_CACHED_TEAR_OFF(), which are used in the interface map.

CComAggObject<> and CComPolyObject<>

These two templates are used to implement IUnknown on aggregated objects. The former just handles the case where the object is aggregated, while the latter handles both the aggregated and non-aggregated cases.

CComContainedObject<>

This class is used by ATL to contain inner objects in the aggregation and tear-off classes. In general, you will not want to use it yourself. The template has these properties:

- ❑ AddRef() and Release() are delegated to the outer object
- ❑ QueryInterface() first calls QueryInterface() on the outer object before querying the contained object

CComObjectCached<>

This is used internally by ATL in its implementations of class factories. You can use it to cache objects for your own object's use. However, don't be tempted to give external access to such an object because, if you do, you will have to ensure that the caching object has a lifetime longer than the cached object. For example, *do not* do this:

```
HRESULT FinalConstruct()
    {
        return m_contained.FinalConstruct();
    }

// IOuter
public:
    STDMETHOD(GetInner)(IInner** ppObj)
    {
        // don't do this!
        return m_contained.QueryInterface(IID_IInner, (void**)ppObj);
    }
pubblic:
    CComObjectCached<CInner> m_contained;
};
```

Here, the cached object is a data member, so when the outer object is destroyed the cached object will be destroyed as well, even if there are references on it. One solution could be for the cached object to have a reference on the outer object, but the template is not designed this way. The only work around is to make sure that the outer object is static or global, as is the case with class factory objects.

CComObjectNoLock<>

This template is effectively the same as CComObject<> except that it doesn't affect the module's lock count. Because of this, objects created using this template shouldn't be exposed externally unless you can guarantee that they will be released before all locks on the module are released. It is used by class factory objects.

ATL Threading

Introduction

Win32 is multithreaded. You shouldn't ignore the benefits and pitfalls that are associated with this. The first point to make is that using more than one thread in a server does not necessarily give your application better performance. Indeed, the cost of thread context switches may even *decrease* your server's performance (careful design, though, can reduce this problem). Making your servers multithreaded means that the *availability* of objects improves, which improves their response.

ATL has been designed from the bottom up with threading in mind, so that you have all the facilities at hand to ensure that your object is thread safe.

Module Threading Model

When you create a project (whether DLL or EXE), AppWizard will define the symbol _ATL_APARTMENT_THREADED in stdafx.h. This sets the default threading model for the server. It doesn't specify the threading model of the objects that you add to the server (the Object Wizard does that).

This symbol means that the default threading model of the server is Apartment. Consequently, (if you make no other changes) EXE servers will have a single thread to service requests on both class factories and object calls. DLL objects are created in the apartment type specified by their own ThreadingModel registry entries, specified through the Object Wizard.

For both DLLs and EXEs, the default threading model symbol specifies the threading model that is used by default for certain ATL classes that implement separate objects. This includes the classes used for tear-off interfaces and enumerators. The symbol also determines how synchronization is applied.

The CComModule class is used to implement module-wide methods, one of which is a server lock count (a lock that is used to prevent the server from being unloaded while it is still serving objects). The ATL AppWizard derives a class from this in stdafx.h and implements it in the global object _Module. Since _Module is not affected by the threading model of the objects implemented in the server there must be some indication somewhere of the threading it will use and hence how it can change its instance members. If a single threaded model is used, the _Module can be sure that there will be no other threads accessing its instance data while it is trying to change it, so no synchronization needs to be applied. If the server threading model allows multiple threads to run, one thread could attempt to read the instance data of _Module while another is changing it, so synchronization must be applied.

Be wary here, _ATL_APARTMENT_THREADED does not mean that EXE servers will only ever have one thread. The server can be apartment-threaded and have multiple threads (it just means that those threads will run in multiple STAs). An example of this is ATL thread pooling, which is explained later.

If you want to use another default threading model, you can define one of the following before you include atlbase.h.

Definable Threading Models

Symbol	Description
_ATL_SINGLE_THREADED	The server will only ever have one thread for EXE servers. — alternatively, all objects in a DLL server have their ThreadingModel registry attribute set to Single.
_ATL_APARTMENT_THREADED	For EXE servers, the class factories will run in a single STA. All locking assumes multiple threads
_ATL_FREE_THREADED	Default threading models and locking assume multiple threads

If you change an EXE server to _ATL_FREE_THREADED then the conditional compilation in _tWinMain() will ensure that the main thread of the server will join the process's MTA with a call to CoInitializeEx(NULL, COINIT_MULTITHREADED).

> **Although an STA thread requires a message pump, an MTA thread does not, so the AppWizard generated message pump in _tWinMain() is unnecessary.** *Professional ATL COM Programming* shows how to replace this with a Win32 event object.

Object Wizard Threading Options

The Object Wizard gives you the option of specifying the threading model of the object. There are four options (see Appendix E):

Threading Model	DLL Servers	EXE Servers
Single	Object will run in the client's main STA apartment	Use for servers that are apartment threaded
Apartment	Object will run in an STA	Use for servers that are apartment threaded
Free	Object will run in the client's MTA	Use for servers that are free threaded
Both	Object will run in either the client's MTA or an STA	Use for servers that are free threaded

The first thing to notice is that for EXE servers it doesn't matter if you use Single or Apartment for _ATL_APARTMENT_THREADED servers or Free or Both for _ATL_FREE_THREADED servers. The setting determines the parameter used for CComObjectRootEx<> (CComSingleThreadModel for the former and CComMultiThreadModel for the latter).

For DLLs, the choice of threading model is more important. It will determine the ThreadingModel that will be used in the registration of the object, indicating to COM the type of apartment that the object can be created in. If you get this choice wrong, COM will still create your object (COM will *never* refuse to create an object because the client apartment and the ThreadingModel are incompatible). COM will create a new apartment (or use a suitable existing apartment) to compensate for this, and will use a proxy object to marshal between the apartments. Whether a proxy object (marshaling) is used depends on the types of apartments, as shown in the table below:

Appartment Thread marshaling

Client Apartment	Object ThreadingModel			
	Single	Apartment	Both	Free
Main STA	Direct	Direct	Direct	Proxy
STA	Proxy	Direct	Direct	Proxy
MTA	Proxy	Proxy	Direct	Direct

❑ The 'Client Apartment' is determined by the parameter passed to CoInitializeEx() — it will be an MTA if this is COINIT_MULTITHREADED, otherwise an STA is used

❑ 'Proxy' indicates that a proxy object is loaded if the ThreadingModel and client apartment types are incompatible; 'Direct' indicates that access between client and object is through a C++ pointer

Synchronization Objects

If your object is used in an MTA then several threads can call its methods. On a multi-processor machine, this means that more than one thread could access your object *at the same time*. On a single processor machine one thread could be preempted before it has completely finished running a method, which can be disastrous if it has only partially written an instance variable. This is because if another thread then reads this value it will get an invalid result. To prevent such situations you should protect your code with synchronization code. ATL provides two classes for you to do this:

CComCriticalSection and CComAutoCriticalSection

Both have a Lock() and an Unlock() method which you should use to bracket code that is thread sensitive. The difference between the two classes is that CComCriticalSection requires that you call its Init() method when you first create it, and its Term() method before it is destroyed. CComAutoCriticalSection calls these in its constructor and destructor. You will find that ATL usually uses the latter.

Example – Using ATL Criticals

Your ATL class will have its own critical section object declared by the CComObjectRootEx<> base class, exposed through the inherited methods Lock() and Unlock(). However, there are some things that you should be aware of. The first is that if you use this to protect data in two methods, as shown below, it will lock out all other threads from *both* methods while another thread is executing one:

```
STDMETHOD(PutA)(long lVal)
{
    Lock();
    m_A = lVal;
    Unlock();
}

STDMETHOD(PutB)(long lVal)
{
    Lock();
    m_B = lVal;
    Unlock();
}
```

If one thread calls PutA() and is preempted by another thread before it has completed the operation, it will 'own' the critical section object. When the second thread calls PutB() it will block because it cannot get ownership of the critical section. If this is not what you want, you can use separate critical section objects to protect each method:

```
STDMETHOD(PutA)(long lVal)
{
    AutoCriticalSection cs;
    cs.Lock();
    m_A = lVal;
    cs.Unlock();
}

STDMETHOD(PutB)(long lVal)
{
    AutoCriticalSection cs;
    cs.Lock();
    m_B = lVal;
    cs.Unlock();
}
```

The local cs objects above are critical section objects. AutoCriticalSection is a typedef name referencing CComAutoCriticalSection. The other thing that you need to be aware of is that if your object uses a global resource then access to that resource should be protected with a critical section object for all server types. The reason is that even Apartment model servers can have more than one thread, so more than one thread can have access to the resource.

It is prudent to protect all thread sensitive code with critical section objects, even if the ATL class has been originally specified as Single or Apartment. The reason is that the ATL class's critical section object is implemented according to the threading model, so objects that are marked to run in an STA will have no-ops for Lock() and Unlock(). Changing the object from single threaded to multithreaded (which is a simple operation, as explained next) will activate the locking code and make the code thread safe. In a similar fashion, the AutoCriticalSection and CriticalSection classes have no-ops for single threaded environments and use critical sections for multithreaded environments, as determined by the default threading symbol.

Changing Object Threading

There are two places where you need to make changes:

❑ The parameter to CComObjectRootEx<>

❑ The ThreadingModel in the RGS of the object for DLL servers

For Single and Apartment, the parameter to CComObjectRootEx<> should be CComSingleThreadModel. For Free and Both, it should be CComMultiThreadModel. This is relevant to both EXE and DLL servers. The ThreadingModel can be Single, Apartment, Free or Both.

Defensive code while threading

The following are guidelines for protecting code:

❑ Data that is never written to is safe for unsynchronized multithreaded access

❑ All access to global data should be made using a global critical section object

❑ If an object is Free or Both, you should protect access to instance data because a client may copy the interface pointer and use it from more than one thread, which will result in multiple RPC threads accessing the object

Take special care about creating objects in an object method and returning an interface pointer, in particular with objects like enumerators that have access to data in your class or global data. These sub-objects must be designed to synchronize access to the resource (see Appendix F).

Thread Pooling

ATL allows you to define a pool of STA threads on which your objects will be created. Thread pooling is only available in EXE servers, because in general DLL servers should not create threads (see the next section). Why would you want a pool of threads? If your object will aggregate Apartment model objects then it must run in an STA because you cannot aggregate across apartments. The problem with this is that a server that defines the _ATL_APARTMENT_THREADED symbol has one thread servicing all the class factories and the objects that they create — not a particularly scaleable solution.

A better solution would be for a server to create a pool of STA threads and then use these to create the objects. An object will run on the STA thread that created it, so by implementing a load balancing algorithm you can distribute the objects across the threads in the pool in an attempt to reduce bottlenecks. This solution also allows an object to have *thread affinity*, meaning that it must run on a specific thread. Generally, it is not a good idea to design an object to have thread affinity, but if it is unavoidable, then a thread pool will allow you to have a more scaleable solution. (Objects in an MTA cannot have thread affinity, because RPC allocates threads for the server and may use a different thread to create the object than it uses to call the object's methods.)

Creating a Thread Pool

ATL allows you to create a thread pool using the CComAutoThreadModule<> template. Here are the steps:

❑ Define the _ATL_FREE_THREADED symbol

❑ Derive your CComModule class from CComAutoThreadModule<>

❑ Declare DECLARE_CLASSFACTORY_AUTO_THREAD() in each ATL class that can be run on an STA pool thread

❑ Change the module Unlock() method to call the same named method in CComAutoThreadModule<>

The first step is quite important because it means that the class factories will be run in an MTA, so RPC will maintain a pool of MTA threads to service calls to create objects. (RPC dynamically alters the number of threads in its pool in an attempt to maximize the availability of the class factory objects.) The second step is needed because CComAutoThreadModule<> coordinates the thread communication between the class factory thread and the STA pool thread that will be used to create (and run) the object.

The actual class factory object comes in two parts. The first part has the code that is registered with COM and runs on the RPC managed thread (if you make the server free-threaded). The second part actually creates the object on the STA pool thread, so you need to indicate that the object will be created in this way with the _AUTO_THREAD macro.

After you have carried out the final step, your code should look like this:

```
LONG CExeModule::Unlock()
{
    LONG l = CComAutoThreadModule<>::Unlock();
    if (l == 0)
    {
        bActivity = true;
        SetEvent(hEventShutdown);
    }
    return l;
}
```

This is important because you have to make sure that the server is not shut down while there are still objects running on the STA pool threads. This code counts how many objects are on the STA threads.

Note that you can choose to have some class factories in the server that don't create objects on the STA pool threads. If this is the case, make sure that DECLARE_CLASSFACTORY_AUTO_THREAD() is not declared in the object's class.

Changing the Behavior of the STA Thread Pool

You can adjust the way the STA thread pool works, for example, changing the number of threads in the pool. By default, ATL will create four threads for every processor present in the system. If you want to use a different number you can specify this in the call to _Module.Init() in _tWinMain(). The number of threads is the last parameter, which ATL omits and hence uses the default value.

ATL uses a round robin algorithm to determine which STA pool thread will be used to create the object. This algorithm is present in the class that is passed as a parameter to CComAutoThreadModule<>. By default, CComSimpleThreadAllocator is used. If you decide to change the algorithm, you should create a class with the following method:

```
int GetThread(CComApartment* pApt, int nThreads);
```

ATL will create a CComApartment object for every STA thread in the pool and then pass an array of these objects and the size of the array to GetThread(). Your algorithm should use this information to make a choice about which thread should be used and pass back its index as the method return value.

Miscellaneous Threading Issues

Before winding up this appendix, it's worth pointing out a few of the sore spots.

Marshaling

An interface pointer is only valid in one apartment. If the apartment is an MTA then there will be several threads that can use the interface pointer. If the apartment is an STA then there will only be one thread that can use the interface pointer. To use the interface in another apartment the interface pointer will have to be marshaled. There are three main ways to do this:

- ❑ CoMarshalInterThreadInterfaceInStream() and AtlMarshalPtrInProc()
- ❑ Global Interface Table
- ❑ Method parameters

CoMarshalInterThreadInterfaceInStream() uses CoMarshalInterface() to marshal the interface pointer into a stream object *once*. The receiving apartment uses CoGetInterfaceAndReleaseStream() to unmarshal the interface and release the stream. ATL has a similar method called AtlMarshalPtrInProc() but this will marshal the interface in such a way that it can be unmarshaled many times with calls to AtlUnmarshalPtr() (the stream can be released with a call to AtlFreeMarshalStream().

The global interface table is a system-supplied object that can hold many marshaled interface pointers, which can be unmarshaled many times. More information about how to use this is given in *Professional ATL COM Programming*.

The final marshaling method is often overlooked. Once you have a marshaled interface pointer to an object in another apartment, any parameters of methods on that interface which are interface pointers will be marshaled.

COM supplies an object that you can aggregate into your object to make it apartment-neutral. This object is called the **Free Threaded Marshaler** (see Appendix E). You can use the FTM when you have an object that is thread safe. It allows interface pointers to be marshaled to other apartments in the same process without using a proxy. However, there are pitfalls, particularly if the object holds interface pointers, so heed the warnings given in Appendix E!

Connection Points and Worker Threads

When you create a connection to a connection point on an object, you're passing an interface pointer to that object. This interface may be marshaled to the connection point if the connectable object is in another apartment. One common task that you may need to do is generate events through a connection point on a worker thread. This is perfectly possible, but you have to ensure that one of two things happen: either the worker thread should be in the same apartment as the thread that accepted the client sink interface or, if that's not possible, the sink interface pointer should be marshaled.

The first is easier to implement, since it only involves making sure that the connectable object and the worker thread both join the process's MTA. The second one is more difficult because it involves changing how IConnectionPoint::Advise() marshals the sink interface pointer into the **GIT** (Global Interface Table)or a stream for later use.

> I have seen a hack where
> CoMarshalInterThreadInterfaceInStream() is called in the target
> apartment and is immediately followed by a call to
> CoGetInterfaceAndReleaseStream(). I've tested this myself and
> have found that this appears to work on Windows NT 4 with service
> pack 4. However, it does not follow the accepted convention for
> marshaling the interface pointer, and you cannot guarantee that it will
> work with other operating systems.

Thread Counting

The final point I want to make here concerns creating threads in DLL servers. Your server does not unload itself. Instead, when asked by COM, it indicates whether it can be unloaded. When you create a new thread in a DLL server, you must ensure that if the thread uses an interface pointer to an object implemented by the server then the object will remain alive as long as the thread does. If the thread doesn't use objects in the server it will still need to ensure that the DLL is not unloaded while the thread lives — it could do this by incrementing the module's lock count.

OLE DB Consumer Classes and Macros

Introduction

The ATL OLE DB consumer classes wrap up all the code that you need to access an OLE DB data source. As explained in Chapter 5, you need two parts: a user record class which has storage for query parameters and result, as well as binding information; and a command class that encapsulates the accessor and rowset code.

User Record

The user record class essentially needs two things: storage for parameters and query results along with maps to give binding information for them. The storage can be any of the types declared in the DBTYPEENUM enumeration (in `oledb.h`):

DBTYPEENUM types

Enumeration	Description
DBTYPE_EMPTY	No value
DBTYPE_NULL	NULL value
DBTYPE_I2	short
DBTYPE_I4	long
DBTYPE_R4	float
DBTYPE_R8	double
DBTYPE_CY	LARGE_INTEGER. The data is stored with four digits to the right of the decimal point, and hence scaled by 10,000
DBTYPE_DATE	Automation DATE type

Enumeration	Description
DBTYPE_BSTR	Automation BSTR
DBTYPE_IDISPATCH	IDispatch pointer
DBTYPE_ERROR	32-bit SCODE
DBTYPE_BOOL	VARIANT_BOOL
DBTYPE_VARIANT	VARIANT
DBTYPE_IUNKNOWN	IUnknown pointer
DBTYPE_DECIMAL	Automation DECIMAL type
DBTYPE_UI1	BYTE
DBTYPE_ARRAY	Combined with another type to indicate a pointer to a SAFEARRAY of that type
DBTYPE_BYREF	Combined with another type to indicate a pointer
DBTYPE_I1	signed char
DBTYPE_UI2	unsigned short
DBTYPE_UI4	unsigned long
DBTYPE_I8	LARGE_INTEGER
DBTYPE_UI8	ULARGE_INTEGER
DBTYPE_GUID	GUID
DBTYPE_VECTOR	Combined with another type to indicate a vector of that type
DBTYPE_RESERVED	Reserved for future use
DBTYPE_BYTES	An array of bytes
DBTYPE_STR	ANSI string
DBTYPE_WSTR	UNICODE string
DBTYPE_NUMERIC	Number type, which you can use to specify the scale and precision
DBTYPE_UDT	User defined type
DBTYPE_DBDATE	Structure containing year, month and day
DBTYPE_DBTIME	Structure containing hours, minutes and seconds
DBTYPE_DBTIMESTAMP	Structure containing year, month, day, hours, minutes and seconds

The data type that you should use is defined by the data source. You can get this information using `IColumnsInfo::GetColumnInfo()`. The Object Wizard OLE DB consumer type will make the necessary calls to obtain this information for you.

If you want to use bookmarks you should declare a data member of the type `CBookMark<>` in the user record. The parameter is the size of the bookmark buffer, or you can use a value of 0 (the default for the parameter) if you want the bookmark to dynamically allocate the buffer at runtime.

Parameter Map

Parameter maps declare the binding information used to indicate which data member in the user record is used. Parameter maps are declared in the user record with the following macros:

```
BEGIN_PARAM_MAP(CMyUserRecord)
    // map entries
END_PARAM_MAP()
```

The entries in the map can be one of the following macros:

Parameter Map macros

Macro	Description
`BEGIN_PARAM_MAP(x)`	Indicates the start of the map
`END_PARAM_MAP()`	Indicates the end of the map
`SET_PARAM_TYPE(type)`	Specifies the type of the parameter described next in the map

The parameters are:

❑   x is the user record class

❑   `type` specifies whether the parameter is an input or output parameter, as given in the following table

Parameter Type	Description
`DBPARAMIO_INPUT`	An input parameter
`DBPARAMIO_OUTPUT`	An output parameter
`DBPARAMIO_NOTPARAM`	The accessor is not used for a parameter

`SET_PARAM_TYPE()` refers to the parameter that follows it in the map, and remains in effect until you call it with a different value. If your map doesn't use this macro then all the parameters will be input parameters.

Input parameters are used when you need to pass a parameter to a query or to a stored procedure; output parameters return values from a stored procedure. You specify the parameters using the COLUMN_ENTRY macros given in the next section. For example:

```
LONG m_Data;

BEGIN_PARAM_MAP(CMyUserRecord)
    COLUMN_ENTRY(1, m_Data)
END_PARAM_MAP()
```

The COLUMN_ENTRY() associates a 1-based parameter position with the user record data member that will be used.

Accessor Map

Accessor maps are declared using the following macros:

Accessor Map macros

Macro	Description
BEGIN_COLUMN_MAP(x)	Declares an accessor map that has a single accessor
END_COLUMN_MAP()	Ends the accessor map
BEGIN_ACCESSOR_MAP(x, num)	Declares an accessor map with more than one accessor
END_ACCESSOR_MAP()	Ends the accessor map

The parameters are:

- ❑ x is the name of the user record class

- ❑ num is the number of accessors in the map

If you have a single accessor then you can use a COLUMN map (that is, the user record defines just one way to return columns from a record set). A column map is declared like this:

```
BEGIN_COLUMN_MAP(CMyUserRecord)
    // column map entries
END_COLUMN_MAP()
```

If you have more than one accessor then you should use an ACCESSOR map specifying how many accessors there are, and declaring each of them.

```
BEGIN_ACCESSOR_MAP(CMyUserRecord, 2)
    // declare 2 accessors here
END_ACCESSOR_MAP()
```

Each accessor in an accessor map must be declared within the map using these macros:

Macro	Description
BEGIN_ACCESSOR(num, bAuto)	Starts the description of an accessor
END_ACCESSOR()	Ends the description of an accessor

❑ num is the (zero-based) index of the accessor

❑ bAuto specifies whether the accessor is an auto-accessor

Each accessor gives the binding information to the data members in the user record. One of the accessors can be an auto accessor, which means that it will be used in GetData() (to fill the user record members) if no accessor is explicitly mentioned.

```
BEGIN_ACCESSOR_MAP(CMyUserRecord, 2)
    BEGIN_ACCESSOR(0, true)    // auto accessor
        // accessor members
    END_ACCESSOR()
    BEGIN_ACCESSOR(1, false)  // not an auto accessor
        // accessor members
    END_ACCESSOR()
END_ACCESSOR_MAP()
```

The items in COLUMN, ACCESSOR and PARAM maps are declared using these macros:

Macro	Description
COLUMN_ENTRY Parameters: nOrdinal, data	Specifies the data member that will be bound to a column —the macro determines the column type
COLUMN_ENTRY_TYPE Parameters: nOrdinal, wType, data	In addition to the above, this allows you to specify the type of the column
COLUMN_ENTRY_TYPE_SIZE Parameters: nOrdinal, wType, nLength, data	In addition to the above this allows you to specify the size of the column in bytes
COLUMN_ENTRY_LENGTH Parameters: nOrdinal, data, length	Allows you to specify the size of a column
COLUMN_ENTRY_STATUS Parameters: nOrdinal, data, status	Allows you to specify a member variable to take the status of a column as well as provide the column binding
COLUMN_ENTRY_LENGTH_STATUS Parameters: nOrdinal, data, length, status	Allows you to specify the column size and status variable.
COLUMN_ENTRY_PS Parameters: nOrdinal, nPrecision, nScale, data	For DBTYPE_NUMERIC this allows you to give the precision of the data.

Macro	Description
COLUMN_ENTRY_PS_LENGTH **Parameters:** nOrdinal, nPrecision, nScale, data, length	For DBTYPE_NUMERIC this allows you to give the precision of the data and the size
COLUMN_ENTRY_PS_STATUS **Parameters:** nOrdinal, nPrecision, nScale, data, status	For DBTYPE_NUMERIC this allows you to give the precision of the data and a status variable.
COLUMN_ENTRY_PS_LENGTH_STATUS **Parameters:** nOrdinal, nPrecision, nScale, data, length, status	For DBTYPE_NUMERIC this allows you to give the precision of the data, the size and status variable.
COLUMN_ENTRY_EX **Parameters:** nOrdinal, wType, nLength, nPrecision, nScale, data, length, status	Generic macro used to declare a column.
BLOB_ENTRY **Parameters:** nOrdinal, IID, flags, data	Defines a **Binary Large Object** (binary data)
BLOB_ENTRY_STATUS **Parameters:** nOrdinal, IID, flags, data, status	Defines a Binary Large Object with a column status variable.
BOOKMARK_ENTRY **Parameter:** variable	Specifies which data member will be used to hold the bookmark.

The parameters are:

- nOrdinal is the column number
- data is the data member in the user record
- wType is the data type
- nLength is the data size in bytes
- nPrecision is the precision to use if the data type is DBTYPE_NUMERIC
- nScale is the scale to use if the data type is DBTYPE_NUMERIC
- length is the variable bound to the column length
- status is the variable bound to the column status
- IID is the ID of the interface used to retrieve the BLOB
- flags is the storage-mode flags defined by OLE structured storage
- variable is the CBookmark<> user record data member

For example:

```
LONG m_ID;
TCHAR m_Desc[51];

BEGIN_COLUMN_MAP(CMyUserRecord)
    COLUMN_ENTRY(1, m_ID)
    COLUMN_ENTRY(2, m_Desc)
END_COLUMN_MAP()
```

The queries that use this user record will return two values: the first is a LONG and the second is a string with up to 50 characters.

Accessors

When you perform a query with one or more parameters, the command text will have placeholders (the SQL providers use the ? sign) and the actual parameters will be in the user record in members specified by the PARAM map. Once the query has been performed, the columns for each row in the resultant rowset are placed in the user record members, as specified by the COLUMN map or one of the accessors in the ACCESSOR map. The accessor classes have the functionality required to bind members in the user record to columns in a row and parameters in a query.

When you create a consumer class with Object Wizard it will use CAccessor<> as the accessor class. This is fine for commands that have parameters or return values. However, if your command has neither parameters nor return results then you can use CNoAccessor as the accessor class. This class does not have any base classes and its methods do nothing because there is no accessor.

Although CNoAccessor is the default for the first parameter of CCommand<>, you cannot merely omit the parameter of this template. The reason is that the default for the second parameter (the rowset class) of CCommand<> is CRowset, but the base class of CCommand<> (CAccessorRowset<>) sets the accessor of the rowset through a call to SetAccessor(). SetAccessor() is inherited through the rowset class, which by default is CRowset, and is passed the this pointer of the accessor class. Unfortunately CRowset::SetAccessor() has a CAccessorBase* parameter and, since CNoAccessor does not derive from this class, the cast will fail and your code won't compile.

The solution is simple; if you don't use an accessor then your command class must specify both the CNoAccessor and CNoRowset parameters:

Example – Coding without Accessors

```
CProducts db;
db.OpenDataSource();

// don't try CCommand<> insert;
CCommand<CNoAccessor, CNoRowset> insert;
CDBPropSet propset(DBPROPSET_ROWSET);
propset.AddProperty(DBPROP_IRowsetChange, true);
propset.AddProperty(DBPROP_UPDATABILITY, DBPROPVAL_UP_INSERT);
insert.Open(db.m_session, _T("INSERT INTO Products ")
        _T("VALUES(10, \'Vest\', 24.4)"), &propset);
```

The Object Wizard uses CAccessor<> because the user record has information about the structure of the database. If you don't know the database structure you can use one of the other accessor types, CDynamicAccessor<>, CDynamicParameterAccessor<> or CManualAccessor<>, and use these to determine the columns and their types at runtime.

Rowsets

Data is set and retrieved through a rowset object. ATL encapsulates rowset behavior with the various rowset classes. If a command doesn't use a rowset then you can use the CNoRowset class, as shown in the previous section.

By default CCommand<> will use CRowset as a base class. This is adequate for most rowsets, but be aware that it will obtain a single row at a time. If you are iterating through all the rows in a rowset it can be more efficient to read more than one row at a time and cache the results for when a user next calls MoveNext(). To do this you can use CBulkRowset as the rowset parameter for CCommand<>. This class derives from CRowset, so you use it in the same way. Note that, by default, it will get 10 rows but if you want to change this then you can call SetRows() and pass the new number.

CArrayRowset<>

The CArrayRowset<> class allows you to access a rowset as if it were an array. It takes the user record and a base rowset class (by default CRowset is used) as parameters. It is derived from the rowset class and CVirtualBuffer<> (see Appendix F for more details about this class) with the user record as a parameter. CVirtualBuffer<> will create an array of its type parameter by allocating a specified number of items using the Win32 VirtualAlloc(). The parameter of the constructor of CArrayRowset<> specifies how many items are created; the default value is 100,000. This means that the class is designed to use with huge record sets.

Example

```
// numRows determined elsewhere
CCommand<CAccessor<CProdAccessor>, CArrayRowset<CProdAccessor> > comm;
comm.Open(db.m_session);
int x=0;
while (x < numRows)
{
    cout << comm[x].m_ProductID << ", "
         << comm[x].m_Description << endl;
    x++;
}
```

Note that I count how many records have been read and ensure that this number is no greater than the number of records in the rowset. The reason is that there's a bug in CArrayRowset<>. If an item is accessed which is beyond the buffer allocated by the CVirtualBuffer<> class then an exception is thrown. The exception is handled in an exception filter implemented by CVirtualBuffer<> (called Except()) by allocating a new buffer. The exception filter returns EXCEPTION_CONTINUE_EXECUTION, which forces the statement that caused the exception to be re-executed. (You would expect this because if the exception *was* caused by accessing beyond the end of an array, you would want access to be repeated once the array had been extended).

However, if you read past the end of the rowset CArrayRowset<> the code purposely accesses memory address 0x00000000 to generate an exception. I assume that the intention of this is to propagate the exception out of CArrayRowset<>::operator[]() so that the user code can catch the exception and make no more attempts to read rows. The problem with this bug is that CArrayRowset<>::operator[]() itself catches the exception and handles it with an __except() clause that uses the CVirtualBuffer<> exception filter. This results in the code accessing 0x00000000 again, which throws an exception and thus you get an everlasting loop.

The only way to avoid this bug is to make sure that you don't read past the end of the rowset.

> CVirtualBuffer<> **is a new addition to ATL 3.0 and it clearly hasn't 'matured' yet. See Appendix F for descriptions of other problems with the exception handling of this class.**

Command – CCommand<>

Commands are declared using the CCommand<> template. The first parameter is the accessor class (which is typically CAccessor) and the second is the rowset class to be used (by default CRowset). However, as I mentioned above, you can use the other ATL accessor or rowset classes, or none at all (by specifying CNoAccessor *and* CNoRowset).

CCommand<> encapsulates the accessor and rowset by deriving from its parameters through the CAccessorRowset<> class. The actual command is passed through a parameter of Open(), or can be specified in the user record class using the DEFINE_COMMAND() macro.

By default, CCommand<> has CNoMultipleResults as its third parameter. This specifies that the command will only return a single rowset. If the command calls a stored procedure that returns more than one rowset, you should use CMultipleResults for this third parameter. Then you can call GetNextResult() to get a subsequent rowset.

OLE DB Errors

ATL provides a method called AtlTraceErrorRecords() that can be used to get more information when one of the ATL consumer classes fails. If an error is generated then an OLE DB provider will create an extended error object (see Chapter 4) that implements the IErrorRecords interface in addition to the IErrorInfo interface that you expect. This allows the provider to add more than one error record to the error object. If you want to, you can obtain the number of error records by calling IErrorRecords::GetRecordCount(), and then get an individual error record by passing its index to IErrorRecords::GetErrorInfo().

`AtlTraceErrorRecords()` will obtain the OLE DB generated error object and from this obtain each of the error records and print their descriptions to the output stream.

Example – Error Trace

For illustration, in the code below, `bozo` is not a valid table:

```
CCommand<CAccessor<CProductsAccessor> > comm;
HRESULT hr = comm.Open(db.m_session, "SELECT * FROM bozo");
if (FAILED(hr))
    AtlTraceErrorRecords(hr);
```

This output will be generated:

```
ATL: OLE DB Error Record dump for hr = 0x80040e37
ATL: Row #:    0 Source: "Microsoft JET Database Engine" Description:
  "The Microsoft Jet database engine cannot find the input table or query
  'bozo'.  Make sure it exists and that its name is spelled correctly."
  Help File: "(null)" Help Context: 5003011
  GUID: {0C733A63-2A1C-11CE-ADE5-00AA0044773D}
ATL: OLE DB Error Record dump end
```

In this case, there is only one error record.

Extended Error Objects

Extended error objects are useful in two respects. Firstly, a single method call may fail because one or more of the methods it calls fail. You could have a situation where a method several layers deep in the call stack fails but the `HRESULT` (or the error object) returned could be changed by one of the methods earlier in the stack, thus masking the actual cause of the error. Extended error objects allow methods in the call stack to add their own information to the error object rather than replacing the information of other methods.

The other area where extended error objects improve on error objects is that they don't hold the full error description string, the help file or the help context. Instead, extended error objects hold an error ID and parameters relevant to the error. This means that the information that is contained in an extended error object is as small as possible and that the full information is only returned when the client requests it.

When a client calls `IErrorRecords::GetErrorInfo()` to get a specified error record, it will be returned an `IErrorInfo` pointer on an error object. When the client attempts to get information from this error object (for example, by calling `IErrorInfo::GetDescription()`), the error object will call an intermediate object called a **lookup service**. This object implements `IErrorLookup` and the error record error object will call its methods to get information about the error, based on the error ID.

For example, when the client calls `IErrorInfo::GetDescription()` the error object will call `IErrorLookup::GetErrorDescription()`, passing the error ID and the parameters of the error. This method can format a human-readable description string based on the ID and parameters (as well as returning a source string). If the client does not call `GetDescription()` then this formatting doesn't occur and so there's a corresponding gain in processing and in the amount of data transmitted to the client.

Although extended error objects are described as part of OLE DB, they are clearly useful in other parts of COM. At the moment the only place you will find them mentioned in ATL is in `AtlTraceErrorRecords()`.

Windows and Controls

ATL Windows Classes

ATL has several classes that allow you to manipulate windows, implement windows
with message maps and implement dialogs. This section describes the non-hosting
classes, and the next section describes the classes used to host ActiveX controls.

CWindow

CWindow is used to wrap the HWND of a window. You can initialize it by calling one of
the overloaded Create() methods, passing the window class name as the first
parameter. This calls the Win32 CreateWindowEx(), so it actually creates the
window. In addition, the wrapped HWND data member (m_hWnd), is public so you can
initialize it directly. Alternatively, you can initialize it with a parameter to the
constructor, the assignment operator, or by passing the HWND by calling the Attach()
method.

You can access the wrapped HWND though the operator HWND() conversion
operator, which means that you can use an instance of CWindow as a HWND parameter
of a function. You can also use the Detach() method to extract the HWND and set the
data member to NULL. If you want to explicitly destroy a window you can call
DestroyWindow() (or EndDialog() for modal dialogs).

The methods of this class are shown in the following tables.

This first set of methods operate by sending an appropriate Windows Message. The
Platform SDK has details about the parameters and return values.

CWindow methods

Method	Message	Description
SetFont	WM_SETFONT	Sets the font used to draw text
GetFont	WM_GETFONT	Gets the HFONT of the window's font
Print	WM_PRINT	The window should print itself to the specified DC
PrintClient	WM_PRINTCLIENT	The window should print its client area to the specified DC
SetRedraw	WM_SETREDRAW	Sets the window's redraw flag
SetIcon	WM_SETICON	Associates a new large or small icon with the window
GetIcon	WM_GETICON	Gets the HICON to the window's large or small icon
SetHotKey	WM_SETHOTKEY	Associates a hot key with the window
GetHotKey	WM_GETHOTKEY	Gets the virtual key code of the hot key
GotoDlgCtrl	WM_NEXTDLGCTL	Sets the focus to a specified control (by its control ID)
NextDlgCtrl	WM_NEXTDLGCTL	Sets focus to the next control in the tab order
PrevDlgCtrl	WM_NEXTDLGCTL	Sets focus to the previous control in the tab order

The following methods are thin wrappers around the equivalent Win32 API functions. They have the same parameters and return value as the Win32 equivalent, but use the wrapped HWND:

Methods as thin wrappers around Win32 API Functions	
ArrangeIconicWindows	InvalidateRect
BeginPaint	InvalidateRgn
BringWindowToTop	IsChild
ChangeClipboardChain	IsDialogMessage
CheckDlgButton	IsDlgButtonChecked
CheckRadioButton	IsIconic

Methods as thin wrappers around Win32 API Functions	
ChildWindowFromPoint	IsWindow
ChildWindowFromPointEx	IsWindowEnabled
ClientToScreen	IsWindowUnicode
CreateCaret	IsWindowVisible
CreateGrayCaret	IsZoomed
CreateSolidCaret	KillTimer
DeferWindowPos	LockWindowUpdate
DlgDirList	MapWindowPoints
DlgDirListComboBox	MessageBox
DlgDirSelect	MoveWindow
DlgDirSelectComboBox	OpenClipboard
DragAcceptFiles	PostMessage
DrawMenuBar	RedrawWindow
EnableScrollBar	ReleaseDC
EnableWindow	ScreenToClient
EndPaint	ScrollWindow
FlashWindow	ScrollWindowEx
GetClientRect	SendDlgItemMessage
GetDC	SendMessage
GetDCEx	SendNotifyMessage
GetDlgCtrlID	SetActiveWindow
GetDlgItem	SetCapture
GetDlgItemInt	SetClipboardViewer
GetDlgItemText	SetDlgItemInt
GetLastActivePopup	SetDlgItemText
GetMenu	SetFocus
GetNextDlgGroupItem	SetMenu
GetNextDlgTabItem	SetParent

Methods as thin wrappers around Win32 API Functions	
GetParent	SetScrollInfo
GetScrollInfo	SetScrollPos
GetScrollPos	SetScrollRange
GetScrollRange	SetTimer
GetSystemMenu	SetWindowContextHelpId
GetTopWindow	SetWindowLong
GetUpdateRect	SetWindowPlacement
GetUpdateRgn	SetWindowPos
GetWindow	SetWindowRgn
GetWindowContextHelpId	SetWindowText
GetWindowDC	SetWindowWord
GetWindowLong	ShowCaret
GetWindowPlacement	ShowOwnedPopups
GetWindowRect	ShowScrollBar
GetWindowRgn	ShowWindow
GetWindowText	ShowWindowAsync
GetWindowTextLength	UpdateWindow
GetWindowWord	ValidateRect
HideCaret	ValidateRgn
HiliteMenuItem	WinHelp
Invalidate	

The following are not simple wrapped methods:

Method	Description
GetStyle	Gets all the styles of a window.
GetExStyle	Gets all the extended styles of a window.
ModifyStyle	Modifies the style of the window. The first parameter specifies the styles to remove, the second parameter the styles to add. The final parameter is a flag used to show or hide the window.

Method	Description
ModifyStyleEx	Modifies the extended style of the window; uses the same parameters as ModifyStyle.
SetDlgCtrlID	Sets the control ID of a window that is a child control on a dialog.
GetDlgControl	Gets the IUnknown of an ActiveX child control on a dialog (only applicable for dialogs based on CAxDialogImpl<>).
IsParentDialog	Determines whether a window's parent is a dialog.
GetTopLevelParent	Gets the topmost window in this window's family tree.
GetTopLevelWindow	Gets the topmost owner window.
ResizeClient	Resizes the window so that its client window is the specified size.
GetWindowThreadID	Returns the thread ID of the thread for the current window.
GetWindowProcessID	Returns the process ID of the process for the current window.
GetDescendantWindow	Recursively gets the child window with the specified ID.
SendMessageToDescendants	Sends the message to all descendant windows if the final parameter is true, or to just its immediate child windows.
CenterWindow	Centers the window with respect to a specified window, or its owner window.

CWindowImpl<>

This class is used to implement a window procedure and handle messages sent to a window or to child windows. There are three ways to handle messages:

❑ Access an existing window and replace its window procedure with yours — a mechanism called subclassing

❑ Register a new window class, take an existing window class and replace its window procedure with your own — superclassing

❑ Register a new window class and write it yourself

When subclassing or superclassing, ATL ensures that the replaced window procedure is cached. This allows you to decide whether a message is handled by your code (using a method mentioned in the message map), by the original procedure or by both. To call the original window procedure the message handler can set bHandled to false (it is set to true by default).

As mentioned in Chapter 6, CWindowImplBase<> implements the window procedure through the message map. However, to register a new window class requires more information. To provide this information you should use one of the DECLARE_WND_CLASS macros. CWindowImpl<> uses DECLARE_WND_CLASS(NULL), which passes NULL for the class name — a NULL class name means ATL will synthesize one for you. Consequently, if you derive from CWindowImpl<> or from one of the control classes, you will inherit the effect of this macro. This means that the default values for the cursor, the background brush and the window class style will be used. If you want to use different values then you can use one of the other window class macros:

Window Class Macros

Macro	Parameters	Description
DECLARE_WND_CLASS	WndClassName	Background color is COLOR_WINDOW, the cursor is IDC_ARROW, there is no icon or menu and the class style is: CS_HREDRAW | CS_VREDRAW | CS_DBLCLKS
DECLARE_WND_CLASS_EX	WndClassName, style, bkgnd	Allows you to specify the style and background brush, the cursor is IDC_ARROW, there is no icon or menu
DECLARE_WND_SUPERCLASS	WndClassName, OrigWndClassName	Allows you to specify the name of a registered window class that you want to superclass

The parameters are:

❑ WndClassName is the name used for the new window class — use NULL if you want ATL to generate one for you

❑ OrigWndClassName is the name of a registered window class that will be superclassed

❑   `style` is the style registered for the class

❑   `bkgnd` is the background color

Note that none of these macros lets you change the menu or icon that's used by the window class. This is because the macros are designed to be used for windows that are used for controls. However, it's relatively easy to produce an equivalent because all these macros do is declare a `static` method with the following prototype:

```
static CWndClassInfo& GetWndClassInfo()
```

The method should declare a `static` instance of `CWndClassInfo` with the necessary initialized values and add a reference to it. This class is `typedef`ed to `_ATL_WNDCLASSINFOA` or `_ATL_WNDCLASSINFOW` depending on whether you have an ANSI or Unicode build.

The window class is used when the window is created by calling `CWindowImpl<>::Create()`. This is called when a windowed control is created. In addition this method uses the **window traits** of the class.

Windows Traits

A window traits class has the styles and extended styles considered 'default' for the window. You set the traits using the `CWinTraits<>` template. This has two parameters: style and extended style. These constants are accessed using the `static` members `GetWndStyle()` and `GetWndExStyle()`, both of which take a single parameter. If this parameter is zero the window trait is returned, otherwise the parameter is returned. This behavior is used because the traits are defaults, and so should be used only if the user has not specified a style.

The `CWinTraitsOR<>` class can be used can be used to bitwise OR specified traits with the traits of another traits class. This template has three parameters: the style, extended style and name of a class whose traits are to be used.

Like `CWinTraits<>` this template implements `GetWndStyle()` and `GetWndExStyle()`. However, these work in a slightly different way. If the parameter is zero then the combined traits of the class and the template parameter traits class are returned. If the parameter is non-zero these values and the parameter are bitwise ORed and returned, hence the name of the class.

ATL defines some preconfigured traits classes, given in the following table. The default for most ATL windowing classes is `CControlWinTraits`.

ATL Windows Traits

Class	Description
CControlWinTraits	Styles applicable for child windows
CFrameWinTraits	Styles applicable for MDI frame windows
CMDIChildWinTraits	Styles applicable for MDI child windows
CNullTraits	Zero for both style and extended style

The presence of the CFrameWinTraits and CMDIChildWinTraits is an indication that even if there is no explicit support in ATL 3.0 for writing Win32 applications with ATL, the intention is clearly there, and could possibly be supported in the future.

CContainedWindow<>

As the name suggests, this class is used for child windows. Its purpose is to forward messages received by child windows to the message map in their parent. To distinguish between messages sent to a child window and those sent to its parent and siblings this class takes an alternative message map ID as a constructor parameter (see Appendix A).

When you use this class you have the choice of either superclassing or subclassing, as will be explained in the next section.

Subclassing and Superclassing

There are two ways to superclass another window class:

❑ Add control based on from the Miscellaneous tab of the full and lite controls in the Object Wizard. You can then select one of the Win32 or Common Controls from the dropdown list box, or you can type the name of another class. Object Wizard will ensure that a CContainedWindow<> is added to your control class, initialized in the constructor, and that the contained window is created and superclassed in the WM_CREATE handler.

❑ Derive a class from CWindowImpl<> and use the DECLARE_WND_SUPERCLASS() macro that I described in the last section.

Similarly, there are two ways to subclass a window:

❑ The window should already exist, and you should have a valid HWND for it. Then you can create a class derived from CWindowImpl<> that has a message map containing all the messages that you want to handle. You should then create an instance of this class and subclass the window by passing the HWND to the inherited CWindowImpl<>::SubclassWindow(). When you're finished you can unsubclass the window by calling UnsubclassWindow(). Don't worry if you forget to do this because when the window is destroyed the window procedure will do this for you.

❏ Have a `CContainedWindow<>` member in your class. Use the constructor to initialize it and specify the message map ID that it uses so that its messages are routed through to an alternative message map (see Appendix A for details of how to declare this). You can then subclass an existing window by passing its `HWND` to `CContainedWindow<>::SubclassWindow()`, as before. When you have finished you can call `UnsubclassWindow()` to unsubclass the window.

CDialogImpl<>

This class implements a dialog that contains Win32 but *not* ActiveX controls. The dialog can be modal (by calling `DoModal()` to create it and `EndDialog()` to destroy it), or modeless (by calling `Create()` to create it and `DestroyWindow()` to destroy it). The dialog class derived must have a member called `IDD` that is the ID of the dialog template resource that describes the dialog. If you want to create the dialog resource at runtime you will have to write your own version of `DoModal()` or `Create()`.

To use this class you should implement a message map to initialize the child controls (in a `WM_INITDIALOG` handler), handle notification messages from the child controls and then read the child control's values in the `IDOK` button click handler.

CSimpleDialog<>

This class derives from `CDialogImpl<>` and has a simple message map that handles `WM_INITDIALOG` and clicks on the OK and Cancel buttons (but not the `WM_CLOSE` message). This is suitable for dialogs that have controls that need no initialization and have no values that you want to read. The template has two parameters:

❏ The resource ID of the dialog template

❏ A `BOOL` value that specifies whether the dialog should be centered with respect to its parent window.

The parent is either the current active window, or the window whose HWND is passed as a parameter to `DoModal()`.

Example

```
// IDD_ABOUT is a template resource
// hWnd is some existing window
CSimpleDialog<IDD_ABOUT, TRUE> dlg;
if (IDOK == dlg.DoModal(hWnd))
    ATLTRACE("Clicked on the OK button\n");
else
{
    ATLTRACE("Clicked on the cancel button, \n");
    ATLTRACE("or closed the window some other way\n");
}
```

Hosting Classes

ActiveX controls are windows controls in addition to being COM objects. This means that they can have a visual representation. It's useful to be able to host ActiveX controls on one of your windows, but the bond between an ActiveX control and its container is *intimate*. The container must support certain client site interfaces and must respond to the control in a prescribed way. This is the purpose of the ATL hosting classes: they provide the necessary container code to host an ActiveX control. ·

CAxDialogImpl<>

This extends CDialogImpl<> to allow it to host ActiveX controls. It also needs a dialog described by a resource template, the ID of which must be in a class member called IDD. This template can contain ActiveX controls, which require initialization data — a series of bytes that will be passed to the control's IPersistStream::Load(). The dialog editor in Visual C++ will ensure that the dialog template has this initialization data as a resource.

You can create modeless or modal dialogs, but you must supply a dialog template as a resource. If you want to create a template at runtime you have to write your own version of Create() and DoModal().

CAxWindow<> and CAxHostWindow

CAxWindow<> is used by HTML controls to create the hosting window for the IE 4 web browser control. It is used to create an instance of CAxHostWindow to host an ActiveX control (usually the IE 4 web browser control with a URL, or the MSHTML control with the raw HTML passed as the URL).

CAxFrameWindow and CAxUIWindow

The hosting (CAxHostWindow) object may be used to host controls that will use the IOleInPlaceSite interface, in which case it needs an implementation of this. This is the purpose of the ATL classes CAxFrameWindow and CAxUIWindow. The former implements IOleInPlaceFrame and the latter IOleInPlaceUIWindow.

When the control calls `IOleInPlaceSite::GetWindowContext()` on the host to get access to the container's top level frame window (so that a control can add menu items and translate key strokes) and get information about the container's border space, `CAxHostWindow` creates instances and returns interface pointers to `CAxFrameWindow` and `CAxUIWindow`.

The implementation of these two classes is minimal. The reason is that they're designed to be used with the HTML control Object Wizard type. They will host the Web Browser control without any menus and with the Web Browser expanded to fill the entire window of the control (hence no border). Because of this the `IOleInPlaceFrame` and `IOleInPlaceUIWindow` interface methods should be present, but do nothing.

Controls

You can use the Object Wizard to create control classes. These are derived from `CComControl<>` and provide a basic implementation of many of the interfaces that a control should support, as well as appropriate `Impl` classes (see later).

CComControl<>

You can alter the way that a control behaves by setting some of the `BOOL` data members of `CComControl<>`. These members are summarised in the following table:

CComControl<> Boolean Data Members

Data Member	Description
`m_bAutoSize`	When set, this indicates that the size of the control cannot change
`m_bDrawFromNatural`	Indicates that `GetData()` should return the actual size of the control
`m_bDrawGetDataInHimetric`	Indicates that the control should use `HIMETRIC` units rather than pixels
`m_bInPlaceActive`	Indicates that the control is inplace active (see comments below)
`m_bInPlaceSiteEx`	Indicates that the control supports OCX96 features
`m_bNegotiatedWnd`	Indicates whether the negotiation with the container regarding the windowed or windowless state of the control has been performed

Data Member	Description
m_bRecomposeOnResize	Indicates whether the control should recompose when it resizes
m_bRequiresSave	Indicates whether the control's state has changed since it was last saved
m_bResizeNatural	The control wants its natural size resized when the container changes the control's size
m_bUIActive	The control is UI active (see comments below)
m_bUsingWindowRgn	The control uses the container-supplied window region (ATL 3.0 does not use this)
m_bWasOnceWindowless	Indicates that the control has been windowless (but may or may not be so now)
m_bWindowOnly	Indicates that the control *must* be windowed
m_bWndLess	Indicates that the control is windowless

Inplace Active means that a control can respond to mouse clicks and control its own rendering, but does not have any other user interface elements. A control that has toolbars, menus and keyboard accelerators is **UI Active**. Containers can only have one UI active control.

When m_bInPlaceSiteEx is TRUE the container supports IOleInPlaceSiteEx (which is the case if it supports the derivative interface IOleInPlaceSiteWindowless). This means that the control can take part in the extended activation and deactivation notifications that this interface supports.

Drawing Controls

The OnDrawAdvanced() and OnDraw() methods are passed an initialized instance of the ATL_DRAWINFO structure that stores information about the drawing context.

ATL_DRAWINFO Structure Members

The members of this structure are:

Member	Description
UINT cbSize	Size of the structure
DWORD dwDrawAspect	Aspect of the device context (one of DVASPECT enum)
LONG lindex	The portion of the item that should be drawn — dependent on the value passed in dwDrawAspect
DVTARGETDEVICE* ptd	If the device context is not that of the default device then this gives additional information about the device
HDC hicTargetDev	If ptd is not NULL then this device context can be used to test the capabilities of the device
HDC hdcDraw	The actual device context which you should draw to
LPCRECTL prcBounds	The bounds of the rectangle in which you should draw
LPCRECTL prcWBounds	If the device context is a metafile then this will contain the bounding rectangle
BOOL bOptimize	Indicates whether the device context has been normalized
BOOL bZoomed	Indicates if ZoomNum and ZoomDen have valid values
BOOL bRectInHimetric	Indicates if the units used are HIMETRIC
SIZEL ZoomNum, ZoomDen	Give the ratio of the bounding rectangle to the natural size of the control

If bOptimize is TRUE, then the units are pixels and the origin is in the top left hand corner. ATL provides methods AtlHiMetricToPixel() and AtlPixelToHiMetric() to convert between HIMETRIC and pixels.

Metafile Rendering

Metafiles are essentially a mechanism for recording GDI functions and their parameters so that they can later be 'played' in an actual device's context. Metafiles can be created using one set of scaled units, and played using another. This makes them useful for the representation of a control in a compound document because the representation can be resized without the control being asked to redraw itself.

However, the problem with metafiles is that most, but not all, GDI functions can be used. Here's the useable list:

AnimatePalette	PolyPolygon
Arc	RealizePalette
BitBlt	Rectangle
Chord	ResizePalette
CreateBrushIndirect	RestoreDC
CreateDIBPatternBrush	RoundRectSaveDC
CreateFontIndirect	ScaleViewportExt
CreatePalette	ScaleWindowExt
CreatePatternBrush	SelectClipRgn
CreatePenIndirect	SelectObject
CreateRegion	SelectPalette
DeleteObject	SetBkColor
Ellipse	SetBkMode
Escape	SetDIBitsToDevice
ExcludeClipRect	SetMapMode
ExtFloodFill	SetMapperFlags
ExtTextOut	SetPalEntries
FillRegion	SetPixel
FloodFill	SetPolyFillMode
FrameRegion	SetROP2
IntersectClipRect	SetStretchBltMode
InvertRegion	SetTextAlign
LineTo	SetTextCharExtra
MoveTo	SetTextColor
OffsetClipRgn	SetTextJustification
OffsetViewportOrg	SetViewportExt
OffsetWindowOrg	SetViewportOrg

PaintRegion	SetWindowExt
PatBlt	SetWindowOrg
Pie	StretchBlt
Polygon	StretchDIBits
PolyLine	TextOut

Stock Properties

Normally if you want to add support for stock properties to a control, you should do so when you first create the control class with the Object Wizard. However, if you decide to add support for a stock property at a later stage then the process is relatively easy. Here are the steps:

- ❑ Derive the control class from CStockPropImpl<>
- ❑ Remove the IDispatchImpl<> base class for the interface that has the stock properties
- ❑ Add [propget] and [propput] methods to the IDL for the interface (you will have to add the id() attribute by hand because of the inadequacies of the Add Property wizard)
- ❑ Add an appropriate data member to your class
- ❑ Add the property to the property map

When you derive from CStockPropImpl<> you need to mention the dual interface that has the properties. CStockPropImpl<> will provide an implementation for the IDispatch methods of this interface so you'll have to remove any IDispatchImpl<> that may exist. For example:

```
// public IDispatchImpl<IMyCtrl, &IID_IMyCtrl,
//                                        &LIBID_CONTROLSLib>
public CStockPropImpl<CMyCtrl, IMyCtrl, &IID_IMyCtrl,
                                        &LIBID_CONTROLSLib>
```

These data members have the general form: stock property name prefixed with m_ and a Hungarian notation prefix. See the table below.

Stock Property Data Members

Data Member	Type
m_pMouseIcon	CComPtr<IPictureDisp>
m_pPicture	CComPtr<IPictureDisp>
m_pFont	CComPtr<IFontDisp>
m_clrBackColor	OLE_COLOR
m_clrBorderColor	OLE_COLOR
m_clrFillColor	OLE_COLOR
m_clrForeColor	OLE_COLOR
m_bstrText	BSTR
m_bstrCaption	BSTR
m_bValid	BOOL
m_bTabStop	BOOL
m_bBorderVisible	BOOL
m_bEnabled	BOOL
m_nBackStyle	LONG
m_nBorderStyle	LONG
m_nBorderWidth	LONG
m_nDrawMode	LONG
m_nDrawStyle	LONG
m_nDrawWidth	LONG
m_nFillStyle	LONG
m_nMousePointer	LONG
m_nReadyState	LONG
m_nAppearance	SHORT

The colors are of the type OLE_COLOR, which is a 32-bit value. You will be familiar with the COLORREF type, which is a 32-bit value but only uses the bottom 24-bits to hold the RGB value. You can convert a COLORREF to an OLE_COLOR by copying these three bytes, but ensure that the top 8 bits are zero because OLE_COLOR uses this byte to hold palette information. To convert an OLE_COLOR to a COLORREF you can use the COM API function OleTranslateColor().

The `Picture` and `MouseIcon` properties are of the type `IPictureDisp` and the `Font` property is of the type `IFontDisp`. These are interfaces on the *standard picture object* and the *standard font object*. Instances of these objects are created by the system when you call `OleCreatePictureIndirect()` or `OleCreateFontIndirect()`.

Example

If you have a control that supports the `Font` property then you will have an `m_pFont` data member. This can be initialized in `FinalConstruct()` with:

```
HRESULT FinalConstruct()
{
    FONTDESC fontdesc = {sizeof(FONTDESC), L"Courier New",
                         FONTSIZE(10), FW_NORMAL, ANSI_CHARSET,
                         FALSE, FALSE, FALSE};
    return OleCreateFontIndirect(&fontdesc, __uuidof(m_pFont),
                                             (void**)&m_pFont);
}
```

You can use it like this:

```
HRESULT OnDraw(ATL_DRAWINFO& di)
{
    RECT& rc = *(RECT*)di.prcBounds;
    SetTextAlign(di.hdcDraw, TA_CENTER|TA_BASELINE);
    HFONT hFont, hOldFont;
    CComQIPtr<IFont> pFont(m_pFont);
    pFont->get_hFont(&hFont);
    hOldFont = (HFONT)SelectObject(di.hdcDraw, hFont);
    LPCTSTR pszText = _T("My Control");
    TextOut(di.hdcDraw, (rc.left + rc.right) / 2,
            (rc.top + rc.bottom) / 2,
            pszText, lstrlen(pszText));
    SelectObject(di.hdcDraw, hOldFont);
    return S_OK;
}
```

`CComQIPtr<>` is used to perform a `QueryInterface()` on the `IFontDisp` smart pointer. You can then get an `IFont` interface pointer in order to get hold of the `HFONT` through the `hFont` property. The Object Wizard will add the `Font` property to the property map and specify a property page:

```
BEGIN_PROP_MAP(CMyCtrl)
    PROP_DATA_ENTRY("_cx", m_sizeExtent.cx, VT_UI4)
    PROP_DATA_ENTRY("_cy", m_sizeExtent.cy, VT_UI4)
    PROP_ENTRY("Font", DISPID_FONT, CLSID_StockFontPage)
END_PROP_MAP()
```

This means that the selected font will be persisted and that the control can be initialized from a persisted state. It also means that a control container can display the standard font property page. However, to use this your control must derive from `ISpecifyPropertyPagesImpl<>`, as is the case for all full controls.

Control Interfaces

When you create a control using the Object Wizard you will get support for most of the common interfaces that you need, but not all interfaces are required. This section lists the interfaces and their use so that you can remove support if you wish.

Lite Controls

The interfaces provided on a lite control are the minimum that you need for a control,
so you can't remove any of these.

Interface	Description
IDispatch	Support for scripting clients
IViewObjectEx, IViewObject2, IViewObject	The object has a visual content when not inplace active
IOleInPlaceObject, IOleInPlaceActiveObject	The control has a user interface that can be inplace activated
IOleInPlaceObjectWindowless	Allows the control to use a container-supplied window rather than creating its own
IOleControl	Control support mnemonics, ambient properties and certain events
IOleObject	The control uses this to communicate with the container
IPersistStreamInit	Initialises and persists the control's state to/from a stream

Full Controls

In addition to the mandatory interfaces implemented on a lite control, full controls
have support for the interfaces in the following table. Since these interfaces are
optional, you can remove any of them from a full control.

Interface	Description
ISpecifyPropertyPages	The object Supports property pages
IQuickActivate	Speeds up the initial handshaking between control and container
IPersistStorage	Initialises and persists the control's state using a storage object
IDataObject	Support for data transfer and notification of changes in the control's state, as well as rendering of the control
IProvideClassInfo2	Gives access to a control's type information and the IID of the control's default outgoing interface

Other Implemented Interfaces

In addition, ATL implements several other control interfaces, which are summarized in the following table. Since these are all Impl classes you get the support by deriving your class from these classes and adding an appropriate entry to the interface map. Note that some of these only provide minimal implementations and others are broken (details given below the table).

ATL Template	Description
IPersistPropertyBagImpl	This interface is used to persist properties individually, by their name rather than in a stream, it is used by IE to initialize a control with the <PARAM> tag.
IPerPropertyBrowsingImpl	This interface is used by property browsers (for example the property tool box in VB) to get display strings for properties
IPropertyNotifySinkCP	'Proxy' class used to generate events for bound properties; to use this you need to add the interface to the connection point map, *not* the interface map.
IObjectSafetyImpl	Used to indicate whether the control is safe for scripting or initializing. This is determined by template parameters.
CBindStatusCallback	Used to handle a notification object for asynchronous downloads
IRunnableObjectImpl	Used by controls to indicate that the control is in a running state
IPointerInactiveImpl	Allows the control to interact with the mouse when it is inactive
IOleLinkImpl	Used by objects that support linking to a document

The last two members of the table have stub implementations for the methods. They are designed for you to derive from the Impl class and then override the methods as needed.

The implementation of IPersistPropertyBag is fine for properties that are COM properties on the control, or which are integer data members. For any other class data members you need to implement your own version of this class.

IPerPropertyBrowsingImpl<> is badly flawed. The MapPropertyToPage() method should return the CLSID of a property page for a property based on its CLSID. If the property does not have a property page it should return E_INVALIDARG. The implementation of this method uses the property map, but in the absence of a specified property page it will return CLSID_NULL rather than E_INVALIDARG. To fix this you should implement your own version of this method.

You derive from template CBindStatusCallback<> when you want to support asynchronous downloads. This class does not implement an interface on your control *per se*, it is used to implement a separate notification object whose IBindStatusCallback is passed during a asynchronous moniker binding. To get notifications you must implement a function with the prototype:

```
void func(CBindStatusCallback<T>* pbsc, BYTE* pBytes, DWORD dwSize);
```

You then create an instance of this object by calling the static member Download() and pass a pointer to your callback function.

Wrapper Classes in AtlControls.h

The following are the Win32 and common control wrapper classes implemented in AtlControls.h. Each class has an override of GetWndClassName() that returns the control's window class name, which is used by Create() when it creates an instance of the control. These classes also have an operator=() and a constructor that takes a HWND parameter so you can initialize the class instance with the HWND of an existing control.

AtlControls.h — Win32 & Common Control Wrapper Classes

Class	Win32 class name	Description
CStatic	STATIC	Win32 labels
CButton	BUTTON	Command buttons
CListBox	LISTBOX	List box
CDragListBox	LISTBOX	List box with support for dragging items
CComboBox	COMBOBOX	Combo box
CEdit	EDIT	Text box
CScrollBar	SCROLLBAR	Scrollbar
CRichEditCtrl	RICHEDIT	Rich edit control
CListViewCtrl	SysListView32	List view, like the right hand pane of Windows explorer

Class	Win32 class name	Description
CTreeViewCtrl	SysTreeView32	Tree view, like the left hand pane of Windows explorer
CTreeViewCtrlEx	SysTreeView32	Uses CTreeItem rather than the raw HTREEITEM
CHeaderCtrl	SysHeader32	Headers with resizable columns
CToolBarCtrl	ToolbarWindow32	Tool bar positioned below a menu
CStatusBarCtrl	msctls_statusbar32	Status bar positioned at the bottom of a window
CTabCtrl	SysTabControl32	Tabs, like those used in a tabbed dialog
CToolTipCtrl	tooltips_class32	Tool tip
CTrackBarCtrl	msctls_trackbar32	A slider control used to set a value
CUpDownCtrl	msctls_updown32	A control used to increment and decrement values
CProgressBarCtrl	msctls_progress32	Visual progress indication
CHotKeyCtrl	msctls_hotkey32	Used to specify that a key combination will perform some action
CAnimateCtrl	SysAnimate32	Control used to play an AVI
CReBarCtrl	ReBarWindow32	The fancy toolbars used by IE 4
CComboBoxEx	ComboBoxEx32	A combo box that can have images for the items
CDateTimePickerCtrl	SysDateTimePick32	An edit box-like control through which you can pick a date or time

Class	Win32 class name	Description
CMonthCalendarCtrl	SysMonthCal32	Control that shows a month's dates
CIPAddressCtrl	SysIPAddress32	An edit box-like control with 4 fields separated by dots
CPagerCtrl	SysPager	A control that allows you to 'scroll' another window

These classes are pretty straightforward to use. When you call one of their methods they take the parameters you pass and send the appropriate message to the wrapped control. In addition, AtlControls.h defines several utility classes:

AtlControl.h – Utility Classes

Class	Description
CImageList	Wraps a HIMAGELIST for use with listviews and tree views
CTreeItem	Wraps a HTREEITEM, used with CTreeViewCtrlEx
CToolInfo	Wraps a TOOLINFO, used with CToolTipCtrl
CDragListNotifyImpl	Class used to handle notifications from a drag list box
CFlatScrollBar	Changes a window to use flat control bars
CCustomDraw	Class used to add custom draw support

If you want to send messages to a Win32 TreeView control you can use the CTreeViewCtrl class. When you access items in the tree view you will be returned a HTREEITEM. The CTreeItem class wraps a HTREEITEM so you can either initialise a CTreeItem object or use CTreeViewCtrlEx, which has the same methods as CTreeViewCtrl (except that it uses CTreeItem).

Smart Pointers and Other Wrapper Classes

Type Safe Pointer Access

One nasty little bug that may creep into your code concerns the pointers you pass to
`QueryInterface()`. To understand this bug you have to take a look at the
parameters of this method. It is designed to be generic, so the `[out]` pointer it obtains
is passed to the object (or COM) as a `void**` rather than a typed pointer. Because of
this you cast away the type of a pointer when you call `QueryInterface()`.

```
HRESULT QueryInterface([in] REFIID riid,
          [out, iid_is(riid)] void **ppvObject);
```

So that the method knows which interface you actually want you pass its IID as the
first parameter. This has an added bonus: `QueryInterface()` uses the IDL attribute
`iid_is()` on the `void**` pointer to tell the marshaling layer that although the
parameter is passed as a `void**` it is actually an interface pointer of a particular type.
The marshaling layer can then take steps to make sure that the pointer is marshaled
correctly.

The bug that can creep in here (and with other functions like `CoCreateInstance()`
that use `iid_is()`) is that you could put the address of one interface pointer type as
the second parameter, but use the IID of another interface in the first. The method will
return with an interface pointer, and COM will happily marshal the wrong interface
type. You will only find this out when you call the interface methods: the vtable that
you get will be completely wrong and the code will die horribly. For example:

```
IDog* pDog;
ptr->QueryInterface(IID_Cat,
                 reinterpret_cast<void**>(&pDog));
pDog->Woof(); // bang!
```

The MIDL that is supplied with VC 6.0 does some interesting things in the header file it generates from your IDL. The first thing that it does is define your interface using `MIDL_INTERFACE()`. This macro will use the `__declspec(uuid())` modifier on the interface to associate the IID of the interface with the `struct` used for interface pointers in C++. The effect of this is that whenever you need the IID of an interface pointer all you need to do is use `__uuidof()`:

```
IDog* pDog;
ptr->QueryInterface(__uuidof(IDog),
                reinterpret_cast<void**>(&pDog));
pDog->Woof(); // woof!
```

It can get a bit tedious to type this so the VC 6.0 header files add an extra C++ method to `struct IUnknown`:

```
template <class Q>
HRESULT STDMETHODCALLTYPE QueryInterface(Q** pp)
{
    return QueryInterface(__uuidof(Q), (void**)pp);
}
```

Has this changed `IUnknown`? No it hasn't, `IUnknown` is defined by the vtable and this method is not `virtual` (its not even pure), so it has no effect on the vtable. All it means that whenever you have an `IUnknown` pointer you can call it in a type safe manner:

```
IItfOne* pOne = GetOneFromSomewhere();
IItfTwo* pTwo;
pOne->QueryInterface(&Two);
```

In addition to this, MIDL will read your IDL and for each `coclass` it will define a class with the name of the `coclass` and apply `__declspec(uuid())` to it. This means that you will be able to obtain CLSIDs from the MIDL generated header files, removing the need to add the `_i.c` files to your project.

This means that you can write code like:

```
IEvents* pEvents;
CoCreateInstance(__uuidof(Events), NULL,
    CLSCTX_SERVER, __uuidof(IEvents),
    reinterpret_cast<void**>(&pEvents));
```

Smart Pointers

Objects can have cached state. This state may include interface pointers to other objects, such as database connections or memory intensive objects (like a huge array of bytes). Such an object should not hold these resources for long and certainly should release them when the object is destroyed. If you have an interface pointer you must *always* release it when you have finished with it. If you forget to release the interface pointer to an object that holds large resources (and therefore fail to release these resources) catastrophic effects can potentially arise.

This is one of the big problems with using COM. Although you can code defensively with mechanisms like tear-off interfaces (where resources can be delay loaded when the interface is queried and, for inproc objects, the resources can be released when the interface - rather than the object - is released), it still relies on interface pointers being correctly released.

If the client is VBScript, VBA or Java then there are no problems, because the execution environments of those tools will ensure that interface pointers are correctly handled. The problems come when you write COM client code that has the responsibility of releasing interface pointers, which includes ATL code.

The rules are that when you copy an interface pointer then you should call AddRef() and, when the copy is no longer needed, Release(). When you obtain an interface pointer as an [out] pointer from a method call, that pointer has been copied and it is no longer needed, so you must call Release() on it.

The trouble is that there may be several paths of execution in your code, making it difficult to remember when to release an interface pointer. The solution is to use a smart pointer. This is a class that encapsulates an interface pointer and gives access to the pointer's methods through an operator->(). The smart pointer class can also implement a copy constructor and an assignment operator to ensure that when it is copied the correct reference counting is carried out. It can also implement a destructor to ensure that, when the smart pointer object goes out of scope, the interface is released.

CComPtr<>

ATL provides smart pointer support with the CComPtr<> template. The parameter to this template is the COM interface that will be wrapped by the smart pointer, so you get a new class typed to the interface. You can initialize instances of a smart pointer class by passing an interface pointer to the constructor or by using the assignment operator. These will call AddRef() through the cached interface pointer. For example, if you have a method that returns a IUnknown pointer called GetAPointer():

```
// IUnknown* GetAPointer();
CComPtr<IUnknown> spUnk;
spUnk = GetAPointer();
// or use :
// CComPtr<> spUnk(GetAPointer());
```

The class also has an operator&() so that you can use smart pointer objects where an interface [out] pointer is returned. In this case, AddRef() (correctly) is not called. For example:

```
CComPtr<IMyItf> spItf;
::CoCreateInstance(__uuidof(MyObj), NULL,
    CLSCTX_SERVER,__uuidof(spItf),
    reinterpret_cast<void**>(&spItf));
```

In addition, the class has two overloaded methods called CoCreateInstance(). These are used to create an object with the CLSID (or ProgID) that you pass as a parameter, it avoids the possible problem of calling CoCreateInstance() in a type unsafe way (ie passing an IID other than the type of the pointer to receive the interface pointer) When the smart pointer goes out of scope, and the encapsulated pointer is not NULL, then Release() is called in the destructor to release the interface.

Note that in the text above the smart pointer makes the calls to AddRef() and Release() on the managed pointer. Indeed, CComPtr<> can only maintain a single reference count on the interface pointer. If your code attempts to call AddRef() or Release() through the operator->() it will fail to compile.

However, `CComPtr<>` does have a `Release()` method, which you can use to release the interface so that, if needed, you can release pointers as soon as possible, before waiting for the pointer to go out of scope.

The COM specification says that the identity of a COM object is maintained by its `IUnknown` interface. Hence two interfaces are on the same object if the `IUnknown` interfaces obtained by calling `QueryInterface()` on each of them is the same. `CComPtr<>` allows you to do this check with the `IsEqualObject()` method, which will return `true` if the interface pointer you pass as a parameter is on the same object as the interface in the smart pointer.

In addition, this classes also defines `CopyTo()`, which will copy the interface pointer into another variable (and correctly `AddRef()` the interface). If you want to get hold of the interface without calling `AddRef()` then you can call `Detach()`, which will return the interface pointer and remove it from the smart pointer; similarly there is an `Attach()` method.

`CComPtr<>` also has a type safe `QueryInterface()` that is passed a single parameter, the interface pointer. It will obtain the IID using `__uuidof()` to pass the correct parameters to the interface's `QueryInterface()` (as discussed in the first section of this Appendix).

There are two more methods of interest, both of which are used to set up communications between objects. `SetSite()` is valid if the encapsulated interface is on an object that implements `IObjectWithSite`. This interface also has a method called `SetSite()`, which you can use to pass the `IUnknown` pointer of another object. Once this method is called, your object has an interface pointer on the other object, and can therefore communicate with it.

The other method is `Advise()`, which is used when the wrapped interface is a sink interface that is used to attach to a connection point on another object. Basically, this method is called with the `IUnknown` interface of the connectable object, the IID of the outgoing interface of the object you want to connect to, and a pointer to the `DWORD` that will hold the cookie that represents the connection.

> Unfortunately, this method doesn't take advantage of the fact that the IID of the outgoing interface is the same as the IID of the sink interface wrapped in the smart pointer. It is therefore possible to call this method in a type-unsafe way. You can get round this with the following
>
> ```
> class:template <class T>
> class CSafeComPtr : public CComPtr<T>
> {
> public:
>     HRESULT Advise(IUnknown* pUnk, LPDWORD pdw)
>     {
>         return AtlAdvise(p, pUnk, __uuidof(T), pdw);
>     }
> };
> ```

CComQIPtr<>

This template is used when you want to make implicit conversions from one interface type to another. The template has two parameters, one is the interface and the other is the IID of the interface. However, the default value of this last parameter uses __uuidof(), so as long as you use interface header files generated by the Visual C++ 6 MIDL, you can omit the last parameter.

The assignment operator and the constructors will ensure that if you are attempting to initialize the smart pointer with an interface of another type QueryInterface() is called to make the conversion. However, to do this there must be an overloaded constructor and an overloaded assignment operator that take an IUnknown* parameter. This would mean that you could not create a smart pointer to hold an IUnknown pointer. To get round this problem, ATL provides a specialization of CComQIPtr<> for IUnknown.

You can use this class as shown below:

```
HRESULT Test(IItfOne* pItf)
{
   CComQIPtr<IItfTwo> spItf;
   spItf = pItf;        // calls QueryInterface()
   if (!spItf)          // the call was not successful
      return E_NOINTERFACE;
   spItf->CallSomeMethod();
   return S_OK;
}                       // interface is released
```

This implicit call to QueryInterface() is useful since it makes the assignment operator 'cast' a COM interface pointer of one type to another. You will find the following declared in atlbase.h:

```
#define com_cast CComQIPtr
```

So that you can use this like dynamic_cast<>:

```
HRESULT Test(IItfOne* pItf)
{
   CComPtr<IItfTwo> spItf;
   spItf = com_cast<IItfTwo>(pItf);
```

Using Smart Pointers in Other Projects

Smart pointers are certainly useful, and they help to make sure that your ATL code does not leak interface pointers. What about non-ATL projects? Well, you can include atlbase.h in your project to get CComPtr<>. Your project can be a MFC, Win32 or even a console application, there are no problems with including this file.

Another alternative is to use the Visual C++ smart pointer template _com_ptr_t<>. You can either use this template directly, or you can use the classes generated by #import.

> *Professional ATL COM Programming* has a thorough comparison of CComPtr<> and _com_ptr_t as well as comparisons between the other wrapper classes (CComBSTR and _bstr_t, and CComVariant and _variant_t)

CComBSTR

BSTRs are Automation's version of a string. They are special because the string buffer is preceded in memory with the size of the string. This is used by the marshaler when the BSTR is passed across apartment boundaries, so that the correct number of bytes is transmitted and a buffer large enough to contain the BSTR is created in the importing apartment. For this to work, you must allocate the BSTR using a COM provided memory allocator so that the marshaler can also access the memory. When you have finished with the BSTR, you should inform COM to free the memory it created, in order to prevent a resource leak.

The information about its length that each BSTR has can be used to determine the number of characters in the BSTR rather than using a method like wcslen(). This means that a BSTR can hold binary data, and thus have embedded NULL characters. If a BSTR holds strings then the characters will always be UNICODE. Consequently, you can cast a BSTR to an LPCWSTR. (Notice the const: you should not treat the BSTR as a UNICODE string for writing.)

ATL provides a class to wrap a BSTR to make sure that the correct allocation and freeing rules are adhered to. Aside from the default and copy constructor, CComBSTR provides constructors (and assignment operators) for wide character ANSI strings. You can also create a CComBSTR with an uninitialized string of a specified size (if you want to create a BSTR to use for binary data) or initialize it from a UUID. For example:

```
// contains "{00000000-0000-0000-C000-000000000046}"
CComBSTR iid(__uuidof(IUnknown));
```

The class defines some assignment operators, and there are four overloaded versions of the Append() method (as well as the operator+=() defined for const CComBSTR&) that allow you to add data to existing BSTRs. Note that if you want to add two BSTRs together, you must use AppendBSTR() rather than Append(). The reason for this is that the former will use SysStringLen() to get the length of the string to append. The latter method will treat the BSTR as a LPOLESTR, so the length of the BSTR will be calculated only up to the first NULL, so you won't be able to use binary data.

CComBSTR does not perform reference counting on its data members, so access to the encapsulated BSTR is as direct as is possible for a wrapper class: there is an operator BSTR() and an operator&() to give direct access to the data member. This means that you can use a CComBSTR in all situations where you would use a BSTR. However, there are no conversion operators to an ANSI string so you have to use one of ATL's conversion macros. Also, the encapsulated BSTR is not reference counted, so if you want to use a BSTR value throughout your project it may be necessary to make the CComBSTR global, or make a copy to another CComBSTR.

The destructor for the class ensures that the BSTR is freed when the object goes out of scope or is deleted, thus preventing resource leaks. You can also attach a BSTR to an existing CComBSTR object, and if you need to free the BSTR before the CComBSTR is destroyed, you can get access to it using the Detach() method. The Copy() and CopyTo() methods allow you to make a copy of the BSTR. Using both of these will copy binary data containing embedded NULLs.

There are also methods called `ToLower()` and `ToUpper()` that convert the `BSTR` to lower case or upper case letters, which will only work on the characters up to the first `NULL`. `LoadString()` will initialize the `BSTR` with an application string resource.

To allow you to use `CComBSTR`s with STL containers the class has overloaded operators `operator<()` and `operator==()`, but if you want to use a `set<>` or a `list<>` you must use an adapter class (as explained later). Do bear in mind that `operator<()` (and the equality operator) use `wcscmp()` to compare strings, thereby assuming that there are no embedded `NULL`s.

Finally, the class has two methods called `ReadFromStream()` and `WriteToStream()`. These allow you to pass an `IStream*` pointer to the `CComBSTR` object, which will initialize itself from the stream, or write itself to the stream. These two methods are used by the ATL persistence classes to make property map entries persistent.

CComVariant

A `VARIANT` is essentially a discriminated union that can hold one of many data types. This is used in particular by scripting clients that do not have data types. `VARIANT`s must be initialized before they are used and they must be cleared when they are no longer needed (because they may hold a `BSTR` or an interface pointer).

ATL's `CComVariant` class derives from `tagVARIANT` and thus it has all the data members of the `VARIANT` type. There are constructors for `BSTR` and for `char` and wide character strings — these ensure that the contained `BSTR` will be a UNICODE string. However, they all use `SysAllocString()`, so embedded `NULL`s are not supported. In addition, there are constructors and assignment operators that can be used to initialize the `CComVariant` with the various types that you can use in a `VARIANT`.

The class defines an equality operator to compare its data with a `VARIANT`, but note that although you *initialize* a `CComVariant` from a `BSTR` as a string (that is, up to the first `NULL`), the *comparison* is made on the entire `BSTR`. If you want a `CComVariant` to hold a `BSTR` that contains binary data, you should initialize it directly, through its inherited `bstrVal` data member.

There are no conversion operators in `CComVariant` to access the `VARIANT` data, so you have to access the `union` directly. However, like `CComBSTR`, this class has methods to read the `VARIANT` from (and write it to) a stream.

Adapter Classes

The STL `list<>` and `set<>` containers need to obtain the address of the items that are being inserted. The smart pointer classes and `CComBSTR` have an overloaded `operator&()` which will return the address of the encapsulated interface pointer or `BSTR`. This is clearly not what the STL container requires: it wants the address of the smart pointer or `CComBSTR` C++ object.

The solution is to use the adapter class, CAdapt, which is used to wrap the CComPtr<> or CComBSTR and provides constructors and operators so that automatic conversions are made between the adapted class and the class it is adapting.

So, if you wanted a set<> of CComPtr<IMyInterface>s, you should use:

```
std::set<CAdapt<CComPtr<IMyInterface> > > container;
```

Debugging Support

Introduction

ATL 3.0 provides support for producing trace messages, asserting that conditions are correct, tracking interface reference counts and indicating when leaks occur. In this appendix, I will briefly outline how this works and how you can use it.

Assertions

In debug builds, ATL defines the macro `ATLASSERT()` using the C runtime library `_ASSERTE()` macro. The parameter of the macro is an expression that will be tested to see if it is `TRUE`. However, you should be wary about calling functions that will have side effects on the object because the expression will not be evaluated in release builds. If the expression is `FALSE`, then a dialog will be shown giving you the option of aborting the process or ignoring the assertion. A third option called **Retry** will stop the program in the debugger at the point where the assertion occurred (starting a new instance of the debugger if necessary). Assertions are used to ensure that invariant conditions are met, but remember that they're only effective in debug builds.

Trace Messages

Trace messages are useful for determining which methods are called and tracing how class data members are changed. To do this, ATL provides a macro called `ATLTRACE()`. This macro can be used in a similar way to `printf()` in that it has a format string and a variable list of parameters. The actual implementation uses `OutputDebugString()` with a buffer of 512 characters, so you must ensure that the trace message is less than this size, otherwise memory will be corrupted.

`ATLTRACE()` is defined as having no action in release builds, but note that in debug builds it can affect performance. The reason is that `OutputDebugString()` writes the buffer to a shared section, and uses Win32 kernel objects to synchronize access to it. If you're running other processes that use `OutputDebugString()` (for example another debugging session) then there will inevitably be times when `ATLTRACE()` is waiting to access the shared section.

In debug builds, all messages passed to ATLTRACE() will be sent to the debug stream. ATL defines another macro, ATLTRACE2(), that can be used to restrict the number of messages shown. This macro has two additional parameters: a category and a level. You can thus specify that only messages of a particular category, or of particular importance levels, are shown.

Message Categories

The categories are defined in enum atlTraceFlags:

Symbol	Value
atlTraceUser	0x00000001
atlTraceUser2	0x00000002
atlTraceUser3	0x00000004
atlTraceUser4	0x00000008
atlTraceGeneral	0x00000020
atlTraceCOM	0x00000040
atlTraceQI	0x00000080
atlTraceRegistrar	0x00000100
atlTraceRefcount	0x00000200
atlTraceWindowing	0x00000400
atlTraceControls	0x00000800
atlTraceHosting	0x00001000
atlTraceDBClient	0x00002000
atlTraceDBProvider	0x00004000
atlTraceSnapin	0x00008000
atlTraceNotImpl	0x00010000

The first four can be used to define your own categories. To specify which categories will be shown in the debug stream you need to OR the categories in the symbol ATL_TRACE_CATEGORY, which, by default, has all categories. To change this you should define it in stdafx.h before atlbase.h is included (or as a preprocessor define in the project settings). For example:

```
// windowing and control trace
#define ATL_TRACE_CATEGORY 0x00000b00
#include <atlbase.h>
```

The level is defined such that the higher the level the less important the message (the most important message has a value of 0). To use this you should set the importance level using the ATL_TRACE_LEVEL symbol (again in stdafx.h before you include atlbase.h or as a preprocessor define) and the default value is 0.

You can use ATLTRACE2() like this:

```
ATLTRACE2(AtlTraceControls, 1,
          "Size is %ld\n", m_size);
```

This uses the AtlTraceControls category and an importance level of 1.

Interface Debugging

ATL maintains the interface reference counts with the object-wide m_dwRef (inherited from CComObjectRootBase). Thus if a client holds several interfaces on the same object and leaks a reference on one of them, you have no idea which one it is. Indeed if the object with the leaked interface reference holds references to interfaces on other objects, those interfaces will not be released. Hence, you may discover many leaks in your server with no idea of whether the leaks are related or from where they originated.

ATL helps here with interface debugging. To use this facility you should define the _ATL_DEBUG_INTERFACES symbol in stdafx.h before including atlbase.h. This has a dramatic effect on all of the COM classes implemented in your server. The first thing that it does is add a thunk — a small piece of code (implemented by _QIThunk) that sits between your object's vtable and the pointer passed back to the client. The thunk must imitate your interface's vtable so that it can intercept calls to AddRef(), Release() and QueryInterface(). Because ATL has no knowledge of how many methods your interface has, it makes the thunk's vtable large enough to be used with all possible interfaces. It has 1024 virtual methods, which is the maximum number of methods possible in an interface on NT. Interfaces hardly ever need more than 5 or 6 methods, so you'll never exceed this limit.

When an interface is obtained (for instance, through a call to a class factory or a call to QueryInterface()) the thunk is returned. CComModule maintains a list of all the thunks that have been created. If the request is for IUnknown, it will check the array to see if it has already been requested (and return that, to preserve identity), otherwise it will create a new thunk. The thunk implements AddRef() and Release() to change its own reference count before passing the call on to the actual interface's methods. Consequently, the thunk's reference count *and* the object's reference count will be changed. When the *thunk* reference count changes to zero, the thunk is removed from the thunk array and deleted because it knows that the interface is no longer being used through that pointer.

When the server unloads, it will call a method called DumpLeakedThunks() that will look in the thunk array. If there are any members, it indicates that they are leaked interfaces. This method calls a method called Dump(), implemented on each thunk, to dump information about the interface to the debug stream.

> **All this code will severely affect your object's performance. However, _ATL_DEBUG_INTERFACES is not related to _DEBUG so you can have a release build with this symbol defined. Make sure that you check stdafx.h carefully when you compile a release build.**

Reference Counts

When `AddRef()` or `Release()` is called, the change and the new interface reference count will be printed to the debug stream. For example:

```
1> CComClassFactory - IUnknown
1> CComClassFactory - IClassFactory
1> CTest - IUnknown
0< CComClassFactory - IClassFactory
```

The first two lines are for the class factory object that is used to create the object. This is an inproc object, so COM has called `DllGetClassObject()`. `IUnknown` is obtained first and then `IClassFactory`. At this point, each of these interfaces have a reference count of 1, making a total reference count on the object of two. After that, the object implemented by `CTest` has its `IUnknown` reference count incremented. Finally, a class factory's `IClassFactory` interface is released so its reference count is decremented to zero.

There is one problem here. How do you know that the messages from the class factory object are from one object, or from three objects? You don't know. The only way to change this is to edit `atlbase.h` and use the `IUnknown` pointer of the interface that the thunk is intercepting:

```
//this is defined inline in the _QIThunk class
ULONG InternalAddRef()
{
    if (bBreak)
        DebugBreak();
    ATLASSERT(m_dwRef >= 0);
    long l = InterlockedIncrement(&m_dwRef);
    ATLTRACE(_T("%d> %08x "), m_dwRef, pUnk);
    AtlDumpIID(iid, lpszClassName, S_OK);
    if (l > m_dwMaxRef)
        m_dwMaxRef = l;
    return l;
}

inline ULONG _QIThunk::Release()
{
    if (bBreak)
        DebugBreak();
    ATLASSERT(m_dwRef > 0);
    ULONG l = InterlockedDecrement(&m_dwRef);
    ATLTRACE(_T("%d< %08x "), m_dwRef, pUnk);
    AtlDumpIID(iid, lpszClassName, S_OK);
    pUnk->Release();
    if (l == 0 && !bNonAddRefThunk)
        _pModule->DeleteThunk(this);
    return l;
}
```

You will then get output like this:

```
1> 01401ac4 CComClassFactory - IUnknown
1> 01401ac4 CComClassFactory - IClassFactory
1> 0076f404 CTest - IUnknown
0< 01401ac4 CComClassFactory - IClassFactory
```

Now you can tell that the three references to a class factory object refer to the *same* class factory object.

Interface Leaks

If you watch the Output window, you'll be able to see, *eventually*, that an interface has leaked. The problem is that you will see so many changes to interface reference counts that it's difficult to see immediately which have leaked.

As I mentioned earlier, when a server closes down it checks to see if there are any outstanding thunks and, if so, information is dumped to the output stream. Here is some sample output:

```
INTERFACE LEAK: RefCount = 2, MaxRefCount = 5,
  {Allocation = 4} CTest - ITest
```

This indicates that the ITest interface that is implemented on the object implemented by the CTest class has leaked. The values provide the following information: there are two unreleased reference counts, the maximum number of reference counts at any one time was 5, and this was the fourth thunk to be created.

How do you use this information? CComModule maintains the count of the number of thunks created. When the thunk count reaches the value stored in its m_nIndexBreakAt data member, the program will stop in the debugger. This allows you to start debugging when the leaked interface is first returned to the client.

So, to break when the offending ITest is returned, you can put this code in the DllMain() or WinMain() of the server:

```
#ifdef _ATL_DEBUG_INTERFACES
    Module.m_nIndexBreakAt = 4;
#endif // _ATL_DEBUG_INTERFACES
```

The thunk also has the Boolean _QIThunk::bBreak that you can use to specify whether the program should break in its reference counting methods. It's set to TRUE when the thunk is created only if m_nIndexBreakAt is the current thunk number. Thus whenever AddRef() or Release() is called on this thunk, the debugger will break. However, since bBreak is a public member of _QIThunk, you can change its value, as you can get hold of a thunk. For example:

```
#ifdef _ATL_DEBUG_INTERFACES
    _Module.m_paThunks->operator[](3)->bBreak = true;
#endif // _ATL_DEBUG_INTERFACES
```

This means that when AddRef() or Release() is called on the third thunk, it will break.

Final Warning

ATL 3.0 provides many new facilities to debug your objects and to determine if an interface has leaked. However, _ATL_DEBUG_INTERFACES and the COM_INTERFACE_ENTRY_BREAK() macro (introduced in Appendix A) can be used in release builds but this will seriously affect the performance of your object. It may also cause breakpoints to be hit and hence kick off the system debugger. My advice is to bracket them with #ifdef _DEBUG and to check your code carefully before doing a release build.

String Conversions

Unicode and ANSI

Windows 9x natively uses the **ANSI** character set — single bytes (and occasionally multiple bytes) for string characters. Windows NT natively uses **Unicode**, which is two bytes per character. COM uses Unicode.

Advantages of Unicode

The advantage of Unicode (sometimes known as **wide chars**) is that there are 65536 possible characters (compare this to the 256 in the ANSI code page). There are so many characters that all character sets of every language used in the world are included, and there is still space for an extended WingDings symbol set! The bottom 256 characters map to the ANSI character set so that they're viewable in the debugger as ANSI characters interspersed with zeros. So this code:

```
wchar_t wcsStr[8];
char szStr[8];
wcscpy(wcsStr, L"Richard");
strcpy(szStr, "Richard");
```

will produce this memory layout:

```
0012FF18   52 69 63 68 61 72 64 00   Richard.
0012FF20   52 00 69 00 63 00 68 00   R.i.c.h.
0012FF28   61 00 72 00 64 00 00 00   a.r.d...
```

As you can see, the C runtime comes in two flavors: the wide char version (with *most* of the methods prefixed with wcs that take wchar_t* pointers) and the standard version (where the methods are usually prefixed with str and take char* pointers).

Debugging

If you do a lot of debugging with both ANSI and Unicode then it's useful to select Display Unicode strings on the Debug tab of the Tools I Options dialog. This will ensure that the debugger will show wchar_t pointers as strings in the watch window rather than treating them as short arrays.

COM API

All of the COM APIs that take strings will expect an LPOLESTR. On 32 bit systems this is defined as a wide chars pointer. COM is designed to be extendable and flexible and consequently, if you want to have string pointers as parameters to your methods, you *must* make them of type LPOLESTR. If you use single byte characters you're asking for trouble. One problem that will immediately bite you is that MIDL assumes that a char is an unsigned char, whereas C++ assumes that it is signed. You can get round this problem, but the best advice is to avoid it entirely. In any case, one day all Windows operating systems will be Unicode, so it's best to get into the habit early!

Which Character Set to Use

Windows NT and Windows CE

If you're targeting NT, you should make sure that your code compiles as a Unicode build (in other words, it defines the UNICODE symbol for the Win32 API and _UNICODE for the C runtime). If you don't do this then the code will still run because NT has ANSI versions of the Win32 API (they have an A suffix) that merely convert ANSI to Unicode and then call the Unicode versions (which have a W suffix). Obviously this produces a performance hit. If you're targeting Windows CE (CE 2.0 can use inproc servers) then you *must* use Unicode because CE only supports Unicode.

If the build is Unicode, then your strings should be contained in WCHAR arrays, pointed to by LPWSTR pointers and initialized with literal strings qualified with an L.

Windows 9x

Windows 9x does not have Unicode versions of the Win32 API so you must compile the project for an ANSI build. Strings should be held in CHAR arrays pointed to by LPSTR pointers. This means that if you want to use the COM API you will have to convert from ANSI to Unicode.

Both Unicode and ANSI Environments

If you're targeting both environments, then you need to ensure that the correct functions are called, and the correct string types are used, depending on whether you are compiling a Unicode or ANSI build. In fact, the SDK header files will do this for you and will make its choice of function based on whether the UNICODE symbol is defined or not. You just call the required Win32 function *without* the W or A suffix, and the preprocessor will use the _UNICODE symbol to determine if the W or A version should be called.

C Runtime Implications

Similarly, if you use the C runtime then you need to call the appropriate _tcs function as declared in tchar.h. These are essentially the C runtime functions with the str prefix replaced with _tcs (for example, use _tcslen() instead of strlen()). The preprocessor will use the _UNICODE symbol to determine whether the ANSI version or the Unicode version (with a wcs prefix) will be called.

String Literals and Conversion Macros

If you have literal strings in your code, you should use the _T() or _TEXT() macros (defined in tchar.h) around the string which preprocess either to nothing (for ANSI) or L (for Unicode). However, this does not take into account strings that are created at runtime. Since COM *always* uses Unicode you will need to convert the string at runtime if you have an ANSI build.

To take this into account, you can use the ATL conversion macros whenever you pass a string pointer to a method. These macros are declared in atlconv.h, which will be included for you in atlbase.h.

```
A2BSTR()    OLE2A()     T2A()       W2A()
A2COLE()    OLE2BSTR()  T2BSTR()    W2BSTR()
A2CT()      OLE2CA()    T2CA()      W2CA()
A2CW()      OLE2CT()    T2COLE()    W2COLE()
A2OLE()     OLE2CW()    T2CW()      W2CT()
A2T()       OLE2T()     T2OLE()     W2OLE()
A2W()       OLE2W()     T2W()       W2T()
```

Here, A refers to ANSI (LPSTR), W is UNICODE (LPWSTR), OLE is an LPOLESTR, T is an LPTSTR and BSTR is (believe it or not!) a BSTR. These macros allocate data on the stack before making their conversion. To initialize the variables that are used in the macros, you must declare the USES_CONVERSION macro before you call a conversion macro. If you get compiler errors to the effect that variable _lpa or _lpw cannot be found, it means that you haven't called this macro.

As an example, imagine that you call a function that returns a BSTR and you want to compare it with a literal string. You should use code like this:

```
USES_CONVERSION;
BSTR bstrName = GetName();
if (_tcscmp(W2CT(bstrName), _T("Richard")) == 0)
    _tprintf(_T("Hello Richard"));
SysFreeString(bstrName);
```

This uses the _tprintf() and _tcscmp() defines, which will be preprocessed to printf() and strcmp() or wprintf() and wcscmp() according to whether _UNICODE is defined. The literal strings are bracketed by _T() so, for example, _T("Richard") will be preprocessed to "Richard" for ANSI builds and L"Richard" for Unicode builds. Thus, the bstrName will be converted to either a LPCSTR or a LPCWSTR respectively.

Support and Errata

One of the most irritating things about any programming book can be when you find that the bit of code you've just spent an hour typing in simply doesn't work. You check it a hundred times to see if you've set it up correctly and then you notice the spelling mistake in the variable name on the book page. Of course, you can blame the authors for not taking enough care and testing the code, the editors for not doing their job properly, or the proofreaders for not being eagle-eyed enough, but this doesn't get around the fact that mistakes do happen.

We try hard to ensure no mistakes sneak out into the real world, but we can't promise that this book is 100% error free. What we can do is offer the next best thing by providing you with immediate support and feedback from experts who have worked on the book and try to ensure that future editions eliminate these gremlins. The following section will take you step by step through the process of posting errata to our web site to get that help. The sections that follow, therefore, are:

- ❑ Finding a list of existing errata on the web site
- ❑ Adding your own errata to the existing list
- ❑ What happens to your errata once you've posted it (why doesn't it appear immediately?)

There is also a section covering how to e-mail a question for technical support. This comprises:

- ❑ What your e-mail should include
- ❑ What happens to your e-mail once it has been received by us

Finding Errata on the Web Site

Before you send in a query, you might be able to save time by finding the answer to your problem on our web site: http:\\www.wrox.com.

Each book we publish has its own page and its own errata sheet. You can get to any book's page by clicking on support from the left hand side navigation bar.

From this page you can locate any book's errata page on our site. Select your book from the pop-up menu and click on it.

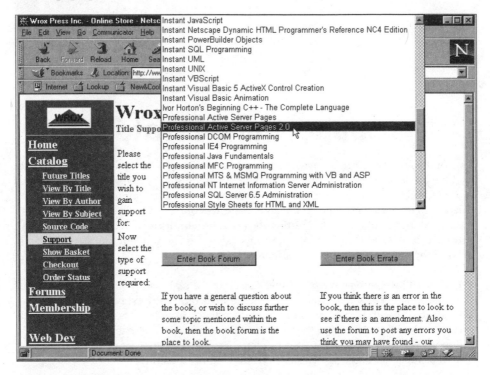

Then click on Enter Book Errata. This will take you to the errata page for the book. Select the criteria by which you want to view the errata, and click the apply criteria button. This will provide you with links to specific errata. For an initial search, you are advised to view the errata by page numbers. If you have looked for an error previously, then you may wish to limit your search using dates. We update these pages daily to ensure that you have the latest information on bugs and errors.

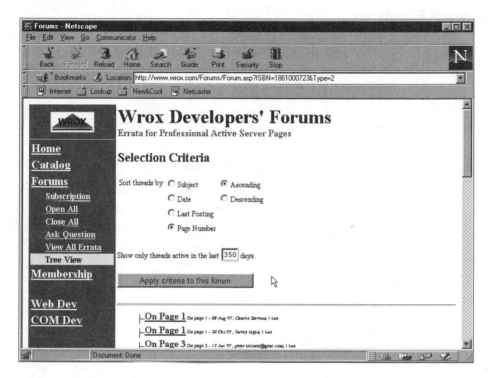

Adding Errata to the Sheet Yourself

It's always possible that you may find your error is not listed, in which case you can enter details of the fault yourself. It might be anything from a spelling mistake to a faulty piece of code in the book. Sometimes you'll find useful hints that aren't really errors in the listing. By entering errata, you may save another reader hours of frustration and, of course, you will be helping us provide even higher quality information. We're very grateful for this sort of advice and feedback. You can enter errata using the 'ask a question' of our editors link at the bottom of the errata page or the Ask Question option on the left hand navigation bar. Click on either link and you will get a form on which to post your message.

Fill in the subject box, and then type your message in the space provided on the form. Once you have done this, click on the Post Now button at the bottom of the page. The message will be forwarded to our editors. They'll then test your submission and check that the error exists, and that the suggestions you make are valid. Then your submission, together with a solution, is posted on the site for public consumption. Obviously this stage of the process can take a day or two, but we will endeavor to get a fix up sooner than that.

E-mail Support

If you wish to directly query a problem in the book with an expert who knows the book in detail then e-mail support@wrox.com, with the title of the book and the last four numbers of the ISBN in the subject field of the e-mail. A typical e-mail should include the following things:

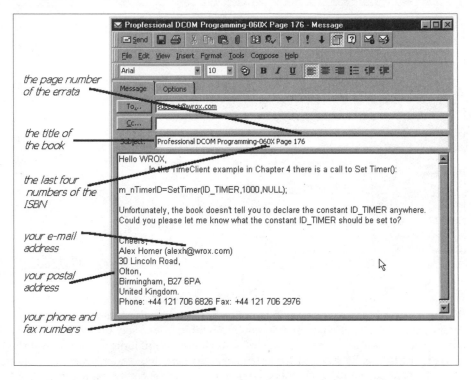

the page number of the errata

the title of the book

the last four numbers of the ISBN

your e-mail address

your postal address

your phone and fax numbers

We won't send you junk mail. We need the details to save your time and ours. If we need to replace a disk or CD, we'll be able to get it to you straight away. When you send an e-mail, it will go through the following chain of support:

Customer Support

Your message is delivered to one of our customer support staff who are the first people to read it. They have files on most frequently asked questions and will answer anything general immediately. They answer general questions about the book and the web site.

Editorial

Deeper queries are forwarded to the technical editor responsible for that book. They have experience with the programming language or particular product and are able to answer detailed technical questions on the subject. Once an issue has been resolved, the editor can post the errata to the web site.

The Authors

Finally, in the unlikely event that the editor can't answer your problem, s/he will forward the request to the author. We try to protect the author from any distractions from writing. However, we are quite happy to forward specific requests to them. All Wrox authors help with the support on their books. They'll mail the customer and the editor with their response, and again all readers should benefit.

What we can't answer

Obviously, with an ever-growing range of books and an ever-changing technology base, there is an increasing volume of data requiring support. While we endeavor to answer all questions about the book, we can't answer bugs in your own programs that you've adapted from our code. So, while you might have loved the Events Calendar example in Professional COM Applications with ATL, don't expect too much sympathy if you cripple your company with an adaptation you customized from Chapter 10. But do tell us if you're especially pleased with the routine you developed with our help.

How to tell us exactly what you think

We understand that errors can destroy the enjoyment of a book and can cause many wasted and frustrated hours, so we seek to minimize the distress that they can cause.

You might just wish to tell us how much you liked or loathed the book in question. Or you might have ideas about how this whole process could be improved. In which case you should e-mail feedback@wrox.com. You'll always find a sympathetic ear, no matter what the problem is. Above all you should remember that we do care about what you have to say and we will do our utmost to act upon it.

Index A Methods

Symbols

A

B

C

D

T

U

V

W

Index B General

B

Professional ATL COM Programming

Authors: Dr. Richard Grimes

ISBN: 1861001401

Price: $59.99 C$89.95 £55.99

For experienced Visual C++ programmers with knowledgee of COM and ATL. The coverage throughout, is for ATL version 3.0 and as such is essential reading for getting the most out of your COM servers.

Author, Richard Grimes - famous for his definitive text on DCOM, has applied his specialist knowledge of ATL usage 'in the field' to give you *the* book on ATL architecture and usage. If you've ever looked at Wizard-generated ATL code and wondered what's behind it. If you've ever wondered how it works, why it's implemented in that way and the options for customising and extending it – then the answer is in these pages. You will learn all about the plumbing behind ATL via example code that will be useful in your own projects. You should read this if you wish to: debug, get the right factory, thread, marshal, use Windows classes, use connection points, sink events, build composite control and

Professional NT Services

Author: Kevin Miller

ISBN: 1861001304

Price: $59.99 C$89.95 £55.49

Professional NT Services teaches developers how to design and implement good NT services using all the features and tools supplied for the purpose by Microsoft Visual C++. The author develops a set of generic classes to facilitate service development, and introduces the concept of *usage patterns* — a way of categorizing the roles that services can fulfil in the overall architecture of a system. The book also gives developers a firm grounding in the security and configuration issues that must be taken into account when developing a service.

To date, the treatment of NT services has been sketchy and widely scattered. This book is aimed at bringing the range of relevant material together in an organized way. Its target readership is C/C++ Windows programmers with experience of programming under Win32 and basic knowledge of multithreaded and COM programming. At an architectural level, the book's development of usage patterns will be invaluable to client-server developers who want to include services as part of a multi-tiered system.

Instant UML

Authors: Pierre-Alain Muller
ISBN: 1861000871

Price: $34.95   C$48.95   £32.49

UML is the Unified Modeling Language.
Modeling languages have come into vogue with the
rise of object-oriented development, as they provide a
means of communicating and recording every stage
of the project. The results of the analysis and
design phases are captured using the formal syntax
of the modeling language, producing a clear model
of the system to be implemented.

Instant UML offers not only a complete description of the notation
and proper use of UML, but also an introduction to the theory of object-oriented
programming, and the way to approach object-oriented application development. This is
UML in context, not a list of the syntax without rhyme or reason. This book is relevant
to programmers of C++, VB, Java and other OO-capable languages; users of Visual
Modeler (which comes with the Enterprise Edition of Microsoft's Visual Studio) and
novice users of Rational Rose or similar UML-compliant tools.

Professional COM Applications with ATL

Authors: Sing Li and Panos Econompoulos

ISBN: 1861001703

Price: $49.99   C$69.95   £45.99

This book examines how and why you should use COM, ActiveX controls and DNA Business
Objects, and how these components are linked together to form robust, flexible and
scalable applications.
A key part of the book is the extended case study in which we produce a distributed
events calendar that fits Microsoft's Distributed interNet Applications (DNA) model. This
three-tier application uses flexible browser-based controls for the client user interface,
business objects on both client and server to process the required information efficiently
and Universal Data Access to perform the queries and updates. It depends on the support
for component-based development now available for Windows NT server.

The additions and changes to this book make it both significant and relevant to readers
of the first edition: Professional ActiveX/COM Control Programming.

'Ever thought about writing a book'

Have you ever thought to yourself "I could do better than that"? Well, here's your chance to prove it! Wrox Press are continually looking for new authors and contributors and it doesn't matter if you've never been published before. We're interested in your programming skillset and how to relate your leading edge knowledge to others.

Interested?

Contact John Franklin
johnf@wrox.com